The Rugby World in the Professional Era

Twenty years of professionalism has seen rugby union undergo dramatic trans-formations, from changes to everyday training cultures to the growth of the Rugby World Cup into one of the largest global sporting events. *The Rugby World in the Professional Era* is the first book to examine the effect that profes-sionalism has had across a number of different aspects of the game and the wider socio-cultural significance of these changes through case studies from across the globe.

Drawing on contributions from scholars from across the rugby-playing world, the book explores the role of rugby's professionalisation through a number of social-scientific lenses, including:

- labour migration
- race and indigenous populations
- the globalisation of the game
- mega-event management
- male sexualities
- media representations of rugby – from broadcasting matches to rugby in museums and on stage and screen.

Offering insights into under-researched areas of the sport, such as the growth of rugby sevens into an Olympic sport, and providing the most up-to-date recent history of the sport available, *The Rugby World in the Professional Era* is essen-tial reading for anyone with an academic interest in rugby, and any student or scholar with interests in sports history, sports sociology, sport management or the economics of professional sport.

John Nauright is Chair and Professor of the Department of Kinesiology, Health Promotion and Recreation at the University of North Texas, USA. He is the author of *Rugby and the South African Nation* and *Long Run to Freedom: Sport, Cultures and Identities in South Africa*. He is also editor of *Making Men: Rugby and Masculine Identity* and *Making the Rugby World: Race, Gender, Commerce*. He was consultant and talking head for the BBC Wales series *The Union Game*, a global history of rugby union.

Tony Collins is Professor of Sports History and former Director of the International Centre for Sports History and Culture at De Montfort University in Leicester, UK. He is the author of *The Oval World: A Global History of Rugby*; *A Social History of English Rugby Union*; *Rugby's Great Split: Class, Culture and the Origins of Rugby League Football*; *Rugby League in Twentieth Century Britain*; and *Sport in Capitalist Society*.

Routledge Research in Sport, Culture and Society

60 **Sport and Alcohol**
An ethical perspective
Carwyn R. Jones

61 **Designing the Olympics**
Representation, Participation,
Contestation
Jilly Traganou

62 **Families, Young People,
Physical Activity and Health**
Critical Perspectives
*Edited by Symeon Dagkas and
Lisette Burrows*

63 **Women and Sport in Latin
America**
*Edited by Rosa López de D'Amico,
Tansin Benn and Gertrud Pfister*

64 **Success and Failure of Countries
at the Olympic Games**
Danyel Reiche

65 **Sexual Abuse in Youth Sport**
A sociocultural analysis
Michael J. Hartill

66 **Football, Culture and Power**
*Edited by David J. Leonard,
Kimberly B. George and
Wade Davis*

67 **Human–animal Relationships in
Equestrian Sport and Leisure**
Katherine Dashper

68 **Embodying Brazil**
An ethnography of diasporic
capoeira
*Sara Delamont, Neil Stephens and
Claudio Campos*

69 **Sport, Medicine and Health**
The medicalization of sport?
Dominic Malcolm

70 **The International Olympic
Committee, Law, and
Accountability**
Ryan Gauthier

71 **A Genealogy of Male Body
Building**
From classical to freaky
Dimitris Liokaftos

72 **Sport and Discrimination**
*Edited by Daniel Kilvington and
John Price*

73 **Seeking the Senses in Physical
Culture**
Sensual scholarship in action
Edited by Andrew C. Sparkes

74 **The Role of the Professional
Football Manager**
Seamus Kelly

75 **The Rugby World in the
Professional Era**
*Edited by John Nauright and
Tony Collins*

The Rugby World in the Professional Era

**Edited by
John Nauright and
Tony Collins**

Routledge
Taylor & Francis Group

LONDON AND NEW YORK

First published 2017 by Routledge

2 Park Square, Milton Park, Abingdon, Oxon OX14 4RN
605 Third Avenue, New York, NY 10017

Routledge is an imprint of the Taylor & Francis Group, an informa business

First issued in paperback 2021

British Library Cataloguing in Publication Data
A catalogue record for this book is available from the British Library

Library of Congress Cataloging in Publication Data
Names: Nauright, John, 1962– author. | Collins, Tony, 1961– author.
Title: The Rugby World in the Professional Era / Edited by John Nauright
and Tony Collins.
Description: Abingdon, Oxon ; New York, N.Y. : Routledge, 2017. |
Series: Routledge Research in Sport, Culture and Society ; 75 | Includes
bibliographical references and index.
Identifiers: LCCN 2016039047 (print) | LCCN 2016058293 (ebook) |
ISBN 9781138665446 (hardback) | ISBN 9781315619873 (ebook) |
ISBN 9781315619873 (eBook)
Subjects: LCSH: Rugby Union football–History. | Rugby Union football–
Cross-cultural studies. | Rugby Union football–Social aspects. | Rugby
football–History. | Rugby football–Cross-cultural studies. | Rugby
football–Social aspects. | Professionalism in sports. | World Cup (Rugby
football)–History.
Classification: LCC GV946.2 R87 2017 (print) | LCC GV946.2 (ebook) |
DDC 796.333–dc23
LC record available at https://lccn.loc.gov/2016039047

ISBN: 978-1-138-66544-6 (hbk)
ISBN: 978-0-367-35949-2 (pbk)

Typeset in Times New Roman
by Wearset Ltd, Boldon, Tyne and Wear

MIX
Paper from
responsible sources
FSC
www.fsc.org FSC™ C013985

Printed in the United Kingdom
by Henry Ling Limited

Contents

Introduction: the rugby world in the professional era   1
TONY COLLINS AND JOHN NAURIGHT

PART I
Professional rugby on and off the field   7

1   Professional rugby and Irish society 1995–2015   9
    LIAM O'CALLAGHAN

2   Cows in the heartland: New Zealand rugby and rural
    change in the professional era   25
    GREG RYAN

3   The world comes to one country: migration, cultures and
    professional rugby in France   38
    PHILIP DINE

4   Cultural diversity in action: developing and engaging
    effective responses within rugby union in Australia   52
    JIOJI RAVULO

5   Rugby union and Māori culture in Aotearoa/New Zealand
    1995–2015   62
    FARAH RANGIKOEPA PALMER

6   The impact of the professional era on Pacific Islands rugby   78
    ROBERT DEWEY

7   The globalisation of rugby sevens: from novelty to the
    Olympic Games   93
    JEREMY STEWART AND MARC KEECH

 8 The Rugby World Cup as a global mega-event   108
    KAMILLA SWART

PART II
Rugby cultures and representation in the professional era   119

 9 Making men in the twenty-first century: metrosexuality and
    bromance in contemporary rugby   121
    ADAM WHITE AND ERIC ANDERSON

10 The road from Wigan Pier: professional rugby and the
    changing dynamics between Wales and England   132
    JOHN HARRIS

11 'When jerseys speak': contested heritage and South African
    rugby   147
    MARIZANNE GRUNDLINGH

12 Performativity, identities and rugby from field to stage in
    the new South Africa   161
    CARLA LEVER

13 Dressed for success: historicizing Nelson Mandela's
    involvement in the 1995 Rugby World Cup   175
    ALBERT GRUNDLINGH

    Index   185

Introduction

The rugby world in the professional era

Tony Collins and John Nauright

'Where stands rugby today?' After twenty years of professionalism, rugby union in 2015 would be almost unrecognizable not merely to its founding fathers but also to many of those who played the game for most of the twentieth century. Fully professional, highly commercialized and increasingly tailored to meet the entertainment demands of a worldwide television audience, the sport has travelled considerable distance since the days when it prided itself on its amateur distinctiveness and proclaimed that it was a game for those who played rather than those who watched. The game's journey since the 1990s is arguably the most dramatic transformation of any sport since soccer adopted professionalism and the league system in the 1880s and opened the way for its transformation into a truly global sport.

In September 2015 over 100 delegates assembled at the University of Brighton at the 'World in Union: Rugby, Past, Present and Future' conference to discuss the progress and problems of the game since the momentous decision to legalize professionalism was made in 1995. The conference was held in conjunction with the 2015 Rugby World Cup that was taking place in England, and Brighton itself was one of the host cities. It marked the twentieth anniversary of the third Rugby World Cup (RWC), held in, and won by, South Africa, a historic occasion not just for rugby but for the entire South African nation as it moved slowly away from its apartheid past, symbolized in the most striking way by Nelson Mandela's wearing the Springbok jersey at the World Cup final itself.

The Rugby World in the Professional Era expands upon many of the papers from that conference and marks another stage in the developing historiography of rugby. The book can in many ways be seen as the third volume in a series that began in 1996 with the publication of *Making Men: Rugby and Masculine Identity*, edited by John Nauright and Timothy Chandler. With the exception of Eric Dunning and Ken Sheard's 1979 sociological study *Barbarians, Gentlemen and Players*, *Making Men* was the first serious attempt to look at the history of rugby in a scholarly historical context. The two editors followed it up in 1999 with *Making the Rugby World: Race, Gender, Commerce*, which, as well as extending the historical and geographic scope of the studies, also enabled some of the chapters to make an initial balance sheet of the first years of professionalism and the emergence of rugby as a serious commercial enterprise.

These two books not only marked the new era that was opening in the history of rugby but also within the historiography of the sport. Gareth Williams' collection on Welsh rugby, *1905 And All That*, came out in 1991, and was followed by Greg Ryan's *Forerunners of the All Blacks* (1993); Albert Grundlingh, Andre Odendaal and Burridge Spies' *Beyond the Tryline: Rugby and South African Society* (1995); Tony Collins' *Rugby's Great Split* (1998); John Nauright and David Black's *Rugby and the South African Nation* (1998); and Philip Dine's *French Rugby Football* (2001).

The new century saw works by Collins on English rugby league (2006) and rugby union (2009); Ryan's iconoclastic analysis of the 1905 All Blacks, *The Contest for Rugby Supremacy* (2005) and his edited collections *Tackling Rugby Myths* (2005) and *The Changing Face of Rugby* (2009); Mary Bushby and Thomas Hickie's 2007 *Rugby History: The Remaking of the Class Game*; Liam O'Callaghan's 2011 *Rugby in Munster*; and Albert Grundlingh's *Potent Pastimes: Sport and Leisure Practices in Modern Afrikaner History* (2013). These were merely the most prominent books that have been published over the past three decades, to say nothing of the dozens of journal articles and book chapters that have also appeared.

The Rugby World in the Professional Era is therefore not merely the third in the series that began with *Making Men* but is also a major contribution to the growing literature of the sport. Each of its chapters extends and deepens the debates about many of the themes and issues that have been central to rugby historiography.

Perhaps not surprisingly given rugby's origins and strength in what were once known as the 'white dominions' of the British Empire, race remains at the heart of many of the debates about the game. Farah Palmer's chapter on the 'Maorization' of New Zealand rugby explores the tensions that lurk under the surface of the game as social and demographic changes in society challenge traditional assumptions about the nature of rugby. The issue of race and integration is also dealt with at the practical level by Jioji Ravulo, who uses his experience of working to raise awareness of the issues facing Pacific-born and Pacific-heritage players in Australian rugby union. As in New Zealand, demographic changes in Australia (and New Zealand) over the past thirty or so years have significantly changed the composition of the sport.

The biggest change in a society within the rugby world has of course been the transition from apartheid in South Africa, and Marizanne Grundlingh's chapter explores the ways in which the state-of-the-art Springbok Experience museum in Cape Town has grappled with the conflict-ridden history of South African rugby and sought ways to bring the black and mixed-race histories of rugby into the mainstream historical narrative. Carla Lever also explores how the wounds of the apartheid years have not healed and the way in which the process of memory and forgetting in rugby has been expressed in the Afrikaans play *Balbesit*.

The issue of race is not confined to the countries of the former British Empire. As Philip Dine points out in his chapter on France, demographic changes and migration flows over the past twenty years are also impacting on the traditional image of French rugby. When the multicultural French soccer team won the FIFA World Cup in 1998, the African and Arab backgrounds of many of their players were contrasted with the much more monocultural French rugby union side. But this has begun to change, and in 2015 France's RWC squad was markedly more reflective of modern French society than in previous years.

Each of these chapters underlines the fact that the past is never gone from rugby. Indeed, William Faulkner's famous comment that the 'past is never dead, it's not even past' could apply equally well to the sport as it does to Faulkner's gothic American South. John Harris's chapter on Welsh rugby union's relationship to rugby league and the north of England explores how the legacy of Welsh union players 'going North' continued to impact on the Welsh game in the 2000s. Jeremy Stewart and Marc Keech's exploration of the rise of the seven-a-side game charts the development of the 'short-form' game from its origins in northern England to its emergence as an Olympic sport, underlining the interplay between this very early form of the game and its reshaping as a a twenty-first century commercial vehicle.

The power of the past to shape the appreciation of the present is highlighted in Greg Ryan's unpacking of the relationship between the mythology of pastoral nostalgia in New Zealand and the very real and deep-going economic changes that continue to undermine rugby union in New Zealand's rural areas. Ryan uses the analytical tools of the historian to deconstruct the mythologizing power of sporting nostalgia and its yearning for a past that did not exist. In contrast, Liam O'Callaghan uses those same tools to interrogate the blind optimism of the present by examining just how much (and how little) Irish rugby has changed since the introduction of professionalism and the extent to which it will continue to grow. Closely tracking the rise of Irish rugby with that of the 'Celtic Tiger' economy of Ireland, O'Callaghan's nuanced understanding of Irish rugby's route to its period of greatest-ever success highlights the importance to historians of exploring the interconnected issues of continuity and change.

Indeed, these twin themes are at the very heart of *The Rugby World in the Professional Era*. The tension between the weight of tradition and the rapidly changing nature of today's world is the context for the decisions that rugby as a whole – from senior officials to coaches to supporters – takes. Often framed as 'the spirit of the game', the cultural continuity of the sport remains the bedrock of rugby union's collective consciousness. Although rugby now inhabits a world of global television contracts and multi-million dollar sponsorship deals, many of the chapters in this book underscore the historical issues that rugby is still unable to resolve.

Nowhere is this more clear than in Robert Dewey's survey of rugby union in the Pacific Islands. Ever since Fiji's historic victory over the Australian Wallabies in 1952, the Pacific Islands have been viewed as rugby's emerging powerhouse, yet as the chapter makes clear, Fiji, Samoa and Tonga are no nearer being able to compete at the elite 'Tier 1' level today. Despite the huge amounts of money that have poured into the international game since professionalism, the Pacific Islands still suffer from lack of funding, a dismissive attitude from the rugby authorities and the depredations of player drain, both to professional clubs and to Tier 1 national sides. Indeed, it could be argued that their plight has worsened under the professional regime.

The reasons for this are complex and go significantly beyond the oft-repeated claim that the relatively small population of the islands makes them an unattractive commercial proposition for television broadcasters. The history of colonialism and the unequal relationship between the Pacific Islands and Australia and New Zealand, together with stereotyped narratives about Polynesian bodies, have played a large role in inhibiting and stifling the development of Pacific rugby, once again demonstrating how much rugby's underlying attitudes remain unchanged despite the apparent transformation of the sport over the last two decades.

At the other end of the spectrum, Kamilla Swart's chapter on the Rugby World Cup as a 'mega-event' marks the fullest extent of the changes that have taken place in the game over the past thirty years. The very idea that a rugby match could be a commercial 'event' would have been anathema to previous generations who believed that rugby was a game for its players, yet such has been the pace of change in the sport that it is now axiomatic that rugby must take its place in the global entertainment industry.

In some ways this rapid pace of change has been reflected in rugby scholarship. Until the last decades of the twentieth century, rugby history was largely the preserve of journalists and antiquarians. Today it is an increasingly varied and sophisticated field for historical and sociological enquiry – and most importantly it has kept its focus on the ways in which the exploration of rugby can inform debate on broader historical and societal questions. Although working on smaller scale, historians of rugby have tended to avoid the pitfalls of soccer scholarship, which has to some extent moved away from seeking to understand what the sport can tell us about the nature and development of society to inhabit a largely solipsistic world isolated from mainstream historical thought.

In contrast, as this collection makes clear, rugby scholarship is at its best when it interrogates the history of the game to understand historical and contemporary change in society. Questions of Imperial ideology, the effects of racial oppression in South Africa, the complex history of Ireland, the impact of neoliberalism on New Zealand and many other questions can fruitfully be viewed through the lens of rugby.

What does the future hold for rugby scholarship? As the chapters in this book demonstrate, the field continues to expand, both in the scope of its research topics and the sophistication of its analysis. Yet it remains stubbornly monolingual. Although Philip Dine and Marizanne Grundlingh in this collection have explored literature in French and Afrikaans, the majority of rugby scholarship is based on Anglophone sources. This is regrettable because there exists a large scholarship in French on the history and sociology of French rugby, not to mention a huge amount of literature in Afrikaans on the history of South African rugby. To take one example, research into the relationship between French rugby and its local communities – such as Sébastien Darbon's *Rugby mode de vie:*

Ethnographie d'un club, Saint-Vincent-de-Tyrosse and *Du rugby dans une ville de foot* – is so far unmatched in the Anglophone world.

Such local 'micro-history' studies serve to remind us that while there is a significant amount of work that has been carried out that allows us to understand how rugby has developed at the national and institutional levels, there has been little exploration in the English-speaking world of the sport at local level. Greg Ryan's chapter in this book provides a framework for understanding the impact of national trends on local rugby, but there is yet to appear a significant work on rugby at the club level such as those of Darbon in France.

Thinking about rugby outside of linguistic limitations will also allow us to apply a broader comparative perspective to our understanding of the development and dynamics of rugby. This should not merely apply to rugby across various countries but also extend to comparing rugby with other sports. Too often historians of sport accept contemporary definitions of particular sports as a way of inadvertently ignoring the parallels and similarities between them. It is enough to be reminded that throughout the nineteenth century (and well into the twentieth in some regions) 'football' referred to all types of the game and not just soccer. It is impossible to consider the emergence of professionalism in sport in Victorian England without looking at the parallel developments in rugby and soccer at that time. The organization of clubs, community support and commercial pressures have borne down on clubs in rugby union, rugby league, soccer, cricket and many other sports in equal measure, and without a comparative perspective only a small and possibly unrepresentative part of the bigger picture can be painted.

Nowhere is this more striking than when examining questions of gender. There is still a considerable amount of research to be done uncovering the early history of women's rugby. Just as important is the need to explore the way that rugby reflected gender relations through its definition as a self-consciously masculine sport – indeed, for many men involved in the game, its exclusion of women was one of its most attractive features. But this can only be done effectively in comparison with other sports. For example, the rise of women's soccer in the First World War is not unconnected with the fact that in rugby-playing areas women were discouraged from playing rugby because it was seen as a male preserve. To develop a full understanding of the role of rugby in reflecting and influencing gender relationships and ideas about sexuality (which, of course, was one of the intentions behind the publication of rugby's foundational novel *Tom Brown's School Days*), we need to consider rugby as part of a much broader sporting and societal culture.

By the time the next Rugby World Cup takes place in Japan in 2019 we can be confident in anticipating that scholars will be grappling with multilingual sources, exploring local micro-histories and using comparative methodologies. The pace of change is quickening not only in the sport itself but also in the scholarship of the game. Rugby and its scholars have come a long way in the last twenty years, but it is a journey that is only just beginning.

Part I

Professional rugby on and off the field

1 Professional rugby and Irish society 1995–2015

Liam O'Callaghan

Harold Wilson's famous observation that 'a week is a long time in politics' has been appropriated by sports commentators to the point of tedium. Yet as a cliché it had a particular resonance with Irish rugby in October 2015. On the morning of Ireland's Rugby World Cup pool match with France on 11 October, Eamon Sweeney wrote in the *Sunday Independent* that rugby 'is not just the biggest show in town, it is on the verge of becoming the biggest show there's ever been in town'.[1] This comment was made in the context of the impressive television audience that witnessed an earlier pool match against Italy, a fact that prompted Sweeney to observe that

> right now Irish rugby is probably at an all-time high in terms of public affection. After two Six Nations titles in a row and a decade of the most extraordinary heroics from Munster and Leinster, this affection has reached critical mass. Rugby is on the verge of [an] explosion in popularity at grassroots level.[2]

Though Ireland would defeat France, a comprehensive loss against Argentina the following Sunday led to a decisive shift in the media tone. The principal naysayer was another journalist, Ewan McKenna. For McKenna, irked at what he perceived as the overly sympathetic treatment that rugby received in the media, the supposed popularity of the game was little more than hype:

> I think it goes back to people in key positions in newspapers, television stations and whatever else. People at a boardroom level often tend to come from private rugby playing schools and I think they set the agenda.... I think that's why it [rugby] gets so much coverage. I think it's overblown as to how popular it is.... I remember working in the *Sunday Tribune* before it went bust a few years ago, and we could never hold our first edition for a big soccer match, yet the managing director, who was a rugby fan, would always make sure that we'd pay extra money and hold it if there was a rugby match on. And that's kind of the elephant in the room. A lot of the people who work in the media know that. They've seen it ...[3]

Notwithstanding the usual journalistic concession to exuberance and exaggeration on both parts, the contrasting views of Sweeney and McKenna, two of Ireland's most respected sports commentators, highlight a difficulty in arriving at a conclusion as to the success or otherwise of Irish rugby in the professional era. While there can be little doubt that rugby at the provincial and international levels, in the context of social and economic progress, garnered an unprecedented public profile for itself, the extent to which it meaningfully expanded beyond its middle-class, fee-paying school roots remained in question.

On the surface, however, professionalism has been good for Irish rugby in purely sporting terms. Between 2004 and 2015, the international team's winning of four Triple Crowns, a Grand Slam (only the team's second) and three championships represents Ireland's most condensed period of success ever. The domestic professional game also flourished. Three of the four provincial teams won the premier European competition, with Munster winning two titles and Leinster taking three. Irish representation on British and Irish Lions tours, an imperfect but not completely invalid way of comparing individual players across the four nations, has increased dramatically since the final pre-professional tour of New Zealand in 1993, when prop Nick Popplewell was the sole Irish representative on the test team. Since then two Irishmen and icons of the professional game, Paul O'Connell and Brian O'Driscoll, have captained the Lions and in 2009, there were as many as sixteen Irishmen selected for the tour to South Africa. In 2009, arguably the most successful year in Irish rugby history, former Irish fly half Ollie Campbell was gushing in his praise of how successful the game had become:

> Rugby in Ireland now has a profile that we couldn't have imagined or dreamt of back in 1982 ... rugby now is mushrooming in the whole country at a rate of knots. Every kid has a replica jersey and as often as not now, you will see kids playing with a rugby ball as distinct from a soccer or GAA [Gaelic Athletic Association] ball.... Rugby is cool and sexy in Ireland now.[4]

Rugby success in the 2000s was in keeping with the broader economic context and cultural *zeitgeist*. This was the era of the Celtic Tiger, when economic growth, increased disposable income and living standards were accompanied by accelerated secularisation and changes in cultural attitudes. The following chapter, then, has three aims. First, it will outline the changes in rugby and Irish society that occurred around the professional era separately. Second, it will analyse the extent to which there are any links between the success of professional rugby in Ireland and the broader economic and cultural trends outlined. And finally, this chapter will offer some suggestions as to how matters might evolve from here.

Prospects for Irish rugby at the dawn of professionalism were not promising. In the first instance, the rugby governing bodies were not suited to the necessary cultural change that professionalism would bring with it. The Irish Rugby

Football Union (IRFU) and its four provincial branches in Ulster, Leinster, Munster and Connacht were austere institutions, famously parsimonious and high-handed in their dealings with clubs and players. The extant Munster Branch Committee minutes exhibit an organisation that engaged in constant penny-pinching – in 1975, for example, the honorary secretary was permitted to purchase a 'second-hand' Dictaphone[5] – and one that was sturdily resistant to the broader changes occurring in the game from the 1960s.[6]

Amateurism did not emerge organically in Ireland: it was an ideological import. Its appeal lay in its convenience. It allowed generations of committee-men (commonly called 'alikadoos' in Ireland) to maintain strict control of the game, to uphold its exclusivity, and to preserve the backslapping, stout-swilling atmosphere of the clubhouse. Questioned in 1969 as to whether a perceptible emphasis on the social side of the game was somehow leaving Ireland behind its contemporary competitors, IRFU president Chris Crowley told *Irish Times* rugby writer Edmund van Esbeck that there 'was nothing at all wrong with working up a good thirst', before cautioning that 'the ordinary player, having played a match and enjoyed a few drinks, it still very loyal to his club, and knows his responsibility to it'.[7]

Rugby existed in a comfort zone. Success, while desirable, was not a pressing matter. Also speaking in 1969, former Irish international and Lions coach Ronnie Dawson, by any contemporary standards a rugby progressive, reflected on the status of rugby in Ireland and bemoaned a

> total lack of understanding that rugby is a real live thing. It is ever evolving and if legislators, administrators and players did not keep abreast of the evolution, there was nothing surer than that the game would diminish in stature here … not enough people have a deep enough conviction about what is required, and, in fact there is a necessity for improvement at all.[8]

Dawson referred in particular to the embryonic status of coaching and competition in Irish rugby. It would be fifteen years, however, before moves would be made to introduce a nationwide club competition and even at that, opposition to the idea from a number of clubs delayed the inauguration of the All Ireland League by another five years.[9] Reflecting on the contemporary stasis of club rugby in 1984, van Esbeck ruefully observed that the prevailing structure in Leinster, for instance, meant that players were guaranteed just four competitive games per season and that in 'contrast to the level of competition enjoyed by players from other countries' there were 'far too many meaningless friendly fixtures between clubs from the same province'.[10] The IRFU, characteristically, was a strenuous opponent of the inauguration of the Rugby World Cup, fearing it would be 'another step along the way towards the slippery slope of professionalism'.[11] It was no surprise, therefore, that in the summer of 1995, when professional rugby appeared at the committee tables of the northern hemisphere unions as a sort of existential crisis that they had no choice but to reckon with, the IRFU could still complacently announce that it would:

oppose the payment of players to play the game and payment to others such as coaches, referees, touch-judges and members of committees for taking part in the game because the game is a leisure activity played on a voluntary basis.[12]

Prospects on the field were equally grim. In 1995, the international team had won just four matches across the previous five stagings of the international championship. The club game, while locally competitive, provided but a miniscule commercial base on which to try to establish any form of professionalism. Munster, Connacht, Leinster and Ulster, largely ignored by the rugby public, were strictly representative teams, selected from the clubs. The four teams played off a much-unloved interprovincial championship each year, from which, in theory, the Irish selectors would pick the international squad. This, essentially, was the system that had been in place since the late 1870s. And all of these efforts were supported by an administrative structure and culture that was both strictly amateur and, in places, amateurish.[13]

It was August 1996 before the IRFU attempted to gain some measure of control over the game's new dispensation by setting up a working party to look into the domestic game and how it would function professionally. By then, a steady stream of Ireland's best players had already decamped to the professional game in England. In the final international match of the 1996 Five Nations Championship, ten of the sixteen players used were Irish-based; by the opening international of the following season, an embarrassing defeat at the hands of Samoa, the number of those selected playing in Ireland had fallen to three out of sixteen.[14]

The very existence of the provincial teams, however, lacking in popularity as they may have been, provided a useful structure for the professional club game when the IRFU centralised the award of contracts to professional players from 1997. Each of the provinces was awarded a set number of contracts to the best players in the club system, and the provinces began their transition into club entities to compete in European and, later, Celtic competition. While contracted players continued, for a period, to line out for their clubs, by the early 2000s the four provinces each had a roster of full-time professional players. Moreover, the four teams were remarkably successful in attracting back to Irish rugby players who had joined English clubs initially after the game went open, and in retaining new Irish talent. By the 2003 World Cup, all but three of the thirty-two players who featured for Ireland were registered with Irish clubs and playing professionally with one of the provinces.[15] This, ultimately, was the structure upon which Irish rugby became so successful.

Though the rugby hierarchy and the media were initially hostile towards professionalism, the completely unexpected success of the Munster professional team, beginning with their Heineken Cup final appearance in 2000, heralded the dramatic change in fortunes for Irish rugby already outlined. The extent to which this was unexpected can be observed in the suggestion by rugby journalist Gerry Thornley in 1997 that the IRFU should encourage Irish international players to join London Irish rather than languish in the domestic game at home.[16] Another journalist, Michael Larkin, suggested in 1999 that the formation of a super-club comprising just the clubs of Limerick was the best way forward for professional rugby in Munster.[17] Yet Munster's success led to the invention of a proud Munster rugby tradition that somehow made the success of the 2000s the inevitable outcome of the game's heritage in the province. Professional sports organisations are most adept at making things up about the past in order to create brand heritage.[18]

Over the course of around three seasons, the profile and popularity of the Munster rugby team underwent a bizarre metamorphosis. In September 1997 a home victory against Bourgoin in the Heineken Cup drew a crowd of around 6,000 to Limerick.[19] Just two years later another pool match, on this occasion against Saracens, was a 12,000 sell-out, again in Limerick.[20] By 2000, when Munster played their first ever home quarter-final in the tournament, fans queued overnight to buy tickets, an incident described in one newspaper headline as a 'Ticket Frenzy'.[21] When Munster reached the final of the competition in 2006, an estimated 70,000 fans of the provincial team made the journey to Cardiff for the match.[22] From around 2001 onwards, Munster's home matches were routinely sold out, and the Thomond Park stadium in Limerick was expanded in 2008 to accommodate 26,000 supporters, more than double its previous capacity.

Leinster, whose popularity soared in a fashion similar to that of their neighbours in Munster, played their opening European Cup fixture in 1996 against Italian opposition in what was later described as 'a soft opener, home to Milan … it was all a bit lacklustre and the absence of atmosphere was compounded by the fact that the attendance numbered no more than 500'.[23] As with Munster, the initially tepid reception that the Leinster team received from supporters was supplanted by a level of hype comparable to that experienced by the neighbouring province when success came. Moreover, a Leinster/Munster rivalry was invented to further satiate the provinces' arriviste supporters.[24]

It was probably fortunate for Irish rugby that professionalism coincided with the Celtic Tiger – the unprecedented era of social, economic and cultural change that Ireland underwent from the mid-1990s. A country whose history since independence had been marked by economic stasis, population decline and deference to the Catholic Church now became one of the richest states in Europe, embraced secularism rapidly and divested itself of an irredentist, inward-looking nationalism. Much of the economic progress was facilitated by the liberalisation of the European economy brought about by the European Union (EU), and the structural funds that Ireland received in the 1990s from the EU to improve the country's theretofore primitive infrastructure. In the context of an economy made more open by liberal tax policies, especially for American multinationals, foreign direct investment flowed into Ireland in the late 1980s, and by the early 1990s the Republic was recording impressive year-on-year growth rates. Between 1994 and 2000, for instance, Irish Gross National Product grew at an average of over 8 per cent per annum.[25]

Emigration, for decades a social plague that Ireland could not eradicate, was reversed: the population of Ireland increased by almost one million, or just over 25 per cent, between 1996 and 2011.[26] Net migration trends veered dramatically from the negative to the positive end of the scale, with many so-called 'New Irish' arriving from eastern Europe, Asia and Africa. Between 1961 and 2011, the urban population increased from 46 to 62 per cent, and there was a sharp increase in urbanisation from 1996 onwards, although Dublin's share of the urban population decreased, with property prices in the capital driving people out to the commuter belt. Again from the early 1990s, economic growth rates began to increase, and did so each year until 2007, with increases in GDP often exceeding 10 per cent in given years. Tuition fees were abolished in universities in 1995 and a growing, educated and ambitious population looked to enjoy the fruits of the boom with rampant consumerism. A conspicuous feature of consumer spending was foreign air travel and it was this, as much as anything else, that fuelled the increasing popularity of Irish provincial teams. Dublin Airport recorded passenger number increases throughout the 2000s, reaching a peak of 23 million passengers in 2008.[27]

Economic progress was accompanied by social and political change. Beginning in the 1960s but gathering pace in the 1990s and 2000s, Ireland became a more secular society. The Catholic Church, once an institution of profound social and political influence in Ireland, began to lose its authority in the southern state, a process hastened by a series of child sex abuse scandals slowly drip-fed to an astonished Irish public from the 1990s. In this context, priesthood vocations and mass attendance plummeted. In addition, the Northern Ireland peace process also coincided with this period and contributed to the positivity and outward embrace that became associated with Ireland in the 1990s and 2000s. In sporting terms, this was powerfully symbolised by the Gaelic Athletic Association's removal of rules prohibiting members of the Northern Ireland security forces from joining the association in 2001 and the staging of 'foreign' sports at the GAA headquarters, Croke Park, in 2005.[28] And while some commentators argue, to an extent legitimately, that the post-2008 economic crash exposed the transient, even bogus nature of progress in the 1990s and 2000s, there can be little doubt that Irish identity had become more inclusive and outward looking, divesting itself of much of the irredentism that had characterised it since independence.[29] Rugby, no doubt, prospered in that context. Though the labelling of rugby as an Anglophile game had lost much of its impact since the GAA's removal of its ban on 'foreign' games in the 1970s, the success of the provinces, allied to the more inclusive embrace of Irish identity already outlined, meant that in the era of Irish economic expansion and success on the rugby field, only the most narrow-minded of cranks could have harboured continuing doubts as to the game's cultural purity. Writing in 2009 about the old relationship between rugby and Gaelic games, GAA writer Eugene McGee summarised the situation thus:

> For a century or more there were clear distinctions between the GAA public and the rugby public which ensured that the two sports remained almost

isolationist in the overall picture of Irish sport. This largely emanated from two sources – the secondary schools system with the classification into 'rugby schools' and 'GAA schools' and Rule 27 which banned GAA players from playing rugby (and soccer) or even attending rugby matches. For their own reasons both organisations liked to believe that THEY were the elite ones in Irish sport.[30]

The extent to which a new spirit of sporting ecumenism had replaced the division of sports into distinct cultural camps was best exemplified in 2007 when Croke Park, bastion of Irish sporting nationalism and the scene in November 1920 of the massacring of fourteen civilians by British forces, hosted a rugby international between Ireland and England. Writing in the *Daily Telegraph*, John Inverdale described proceedings as 'one of the most joyous sporting occasions it has ever been my privilege to attend, and when all the revellers woke on Sunday morning … it was time to put the hangover of history to bed and embrace the future'.[31] Though the 'hangover' referred to specifically by Inverdale was Anglo-Irish relations, the long-standing ideological rift between Gaelic games and sports of British origin in Ireland was emphatically bridged. Further proof of the latter surely came in the person of one of the tiny handful of protestors at Croke Park, whose intellectual capacity (or grasp of irony) was exhibited in his brandishing of a sign reading 'No to foreign games' while wearing a Glasgow Celtic soccer shirt.

Establishing a correlation between rugby success and national success (however defined) is quite easy, depending on what measures one chooses: just a series of upward curves that roughly map onto each other chronologically. Yet inferring causation from correlation is a trap best avoided. And identifying the links between the buoyancy of Irish rugby and broader economic and cultural change, apart from the area of national identity politics, is not straightforward.

One means of measuring this is to examine playing numbers. Did all of the change outlined, both in rugby and Irish society, affect playing numbers and did it suddenly present rugby as a threat to other team sports, namely soccer, Gaelic football and hurling? And did this somehow contribute to the success of the 2000s? The prevailing perception in Ireland among commentators seemed to suggest so. In 2009, the *Irish Independent* ran a series of stories investigating how rugby could co-exist with GAA and soccer given the apparently growing popularity of the oval ball game. In introducing the series, the *Independent* reported:

> Rugby in this country is in one of those grooves right now where it can do no wrong and any wrong it does it can casually get away with. The emperor clearly wears no clothes. That's why rugby can name its competitions after drinks brands, douse each other in champagne after Six Nations and punch each other's lights out without much intense scrutiny or screaming headlines of disgust from the media.[32]

The report went on to quote the Kerry Gaelic football icon Mick O'Dwyer, who had remarked that

> The days are gone when Irish rugby was happy to live out a sedate life in fee-paying secondary schools and other small pockets around the country. It was no threat to Gaelic games then, but in the new professional age it is developing rapidly as a global sport.... Rugby has another appeal too in that it suits the Irish psyche. [It's] a hard, manly game. Bear in mind that rugby has been a professional game for little over a decade, yet it has made enormous strides.[33]

Notwithstanding the musings of social commentators, establishing causal links between economic and sporting success requires a subtle examination of the evidence. The headline numbers for rugby were impressive, however. From 2004 onwards, when Irish rugby teams began to succeed on the field, it seems that across all levels nominal numbers of rugby players increased year-on-year until the 2013/2014 season, when IRFU statistics indicate a sharp decline in adult playing numbers while the underage level continued to flourish. In 2005, there were 87,700 players, of whom 15,700 were adult players. By 2006, this was, according to the Union, 'in excess of 90,000'.[34] Again from 2006 into 2007, all metrics increased: adult playing numbers increased from 21,740 to 25,171 and schools players from 23,586 to 26,224, increases of 16 and 11 per cent respectively.[35] Numbers across all levels have continued to increase to the extent that by 2013 the IRFU claimed a record 161,000 players across all levels.[36]

But by around 2010, numbers began to flatline before going into decline. To some extent, this reflected a slight decline overall across Irish sport as the effects of recession and emigration took hold.[37] In 2014/2015, the IRFU recorded just over 13,000 adult males playing rugby, a huge fall from the 26,000 claimed by the union in 2011/2012. It seems unlikely that Irish rugby really lost 50 per cent of its adult playing strength in just three seasons; this statistical fall probably reflects a methodological change, with only active players being included, rather than anyone on a club's books being counted. In any case, there was no obvious proportional change in Irish rugby-playing numbers at adult level across all sports over roughly the period from 2005 to 2015, and between 2011 and 2013 rugby's proportionate share increased modestly.[38] Over this period, rugby's share of Irish people participating in sport has fluctuated between 1 and 1.5 per cent. This leaves it slightly behind hurling – a sport only seriously played in around twelve counties – quite a distance behind Gaelic football and very far behind soccer.[39] In addition, young men and women who played GAA in the summer were four times more likely, in 2013, to play soccer than rugby in the winter, indicating, perhaps, continued social and geographical barriers around rugby.[40] Statistics from the Economic and Social Research Institute in Ireland also indicate that rugby is behind GAA and soccer in retaining players who have played the game at school.[41] Ultimately, economic progress and middle-class expansion is a boon to flexible activities such as running, exercise and cycling. The pressures of professional work patterns are scarcely conducive to the restrictions of team sports' training and match schedules and the voluntarism needed to sustain clubs. The real benefits of increased playing numbers can be seen at underage level, where numbers lining out for clubs more than doubled in the 2006–2015 period, undoubtedly on the strength of the performance of the provincial and international teams. More people than ever were willing to try the game out. Yet retention is the challenge for all team sports going forward. What we can derive from these figures is that economic progress and professionalism did not really put any new players on the Irish team. At best, these processes may have prevented some players who may have progressed to international level from emigrating. But this is imponderable, as is the idea that the current boon in underage rugby will keep the good times going at elite level.

The main ingredient in Irish rugby success, ultimately, and particularly from the early 2000s, was luck. Just at the most opportune moment in terms of broader economic and cultural change, Ireland produced what was arguably its most talented generation of players ever. This was not attributable to any other factor than luck. As Tony Collins has recently commented of Irish rugby in the 2000s: 'It was … an era when the genetic fruit machine played out. The cohort of players who represented Ireland in the late 1990s and 2000s were a golden generation of Irish rugby.'[42]

This explanation seems odd, particularly when one considers the links between success or failure on the rugby field and broader economic vicissitudes, as established in the work of Gareth Williams on Wales and Phil Dine in France.[43] But it is an inescapable fact that due to factors such as socioeconomic status, family tradition and educational institutions attended, players such as Brian O'Driscoll, Paul O'Connell and Ronan O'Gara would most likely have played rugby with or without professionalism and with or without Celtic Tiger era economic expansion. Indeed, if we momentarily leave imported players aside, professional rugby in Ireland remains dominated by what one might consider the traditional routes into the game, namely the group of fee-paying private schools that have competed in the various provincial schools cups since the late nineteenth century. The Irish team that won the Grand Slam in 2009, for instance, featured just one player, John Hayes, who did not attend a rugby-playing school. The 2015 Championship-winning side also featured just one player, Mike Ross, who had not played rugby at school. This observation can be extended to the successful provincial teams. Ten of the twelve Munster-born players who started the province's victorious Heineken Cup final appearance in 2006 were the products of rugby-playing schools, while in the case of Leinster, the equivalent figure in their first victorious European Cup final in 2009 was nine out of eleven. Of these, Blackrock College, arguably the most prestigious of all fee-paying rugby schools in Dublin, contributed Lions test players Luke Fitzgerald and Brian O'Driscoll, and the team captain, Leo Cullen.

The comparative rarity of players graduating from the club system to the international team is underscored by the fact that their presence often draws media comment. Of Mike Ross, *Irish Times* rugby writer Gerry Thornley has commented:

> He's ploughed his own, independent path, and cannot be described as the product of any system. He likes to think his case history could be an example for some young fella who's not getting a look in. He can look at me and see it doesn't have to be schools/academy/province.[44]

Players coming from the club system have been the exception and have often been cherished in the media for their folksy, rural ruggedness. Of John Hayes, Kathy Sheridan (again of the *Irish Times*) has written:

> In John Hayes's world, it's a good day when he can slip away entirely unnoticed. Then he can fold his mighty 6 ft 4 in frame into the Mondeo and trundle on home to the family farm in Cappamore, Co Limerick, to the same fields where he and generations of Hayeses grew up and learned to be judges of cattle.... For Munster supporters in a hard-knock run, there are few more cheering spectacles in a hostile stadium than the unfurling of the massive red banner with the words: 'Go on Bull, 'tis your field.'[45]

John Hayes was presaged in the amateur era by Moss Keane and Mick Galway, two Kerrymen and top-class Gaelic footballers who played international rugby. Players such as these remain a novelty and Irish rugby's class profile at the elite level has yet to significantly change, economic progress and professionalism notwithstanding. They are the exceptions that prove the rule. For all the gibberish spouted by the media about the classlessness of Munster rugby, for instance, the game at the elite level remains steadfastly middle class. Only Keith Earls and Donncha O'Callaghan in recent years could credibly claim that rare accolade of being a working-class Irish rugby international from Munster. And even at that, O'Callaghan was recruited to the rugby-playing Christian Brothers College on a sport scholarship.

Yet, despite the social homogeneity of rugby, commentators came to gush at what they saw as the game's inclusive embrace. In 2015, Eamon Sweeney cautioned against 'the chatter of the odd sociologically-inclined pundit' and affirmed that 'people would really want to give this "middle-class game" stuff a rest. For one thing this faux streetwise nonsense is a relatively new development.'[46] He compounded his error by describing the Irish team thus:

> The squad encompasses the rural Munster grit of Paul O'Connell and Mike Ross and the city boy flair and flash of Simon Zebo and Johnny Sexton. Robbie Henshaw is there to represent the once-condemned rugby province of Connacht and Seán O'Brien flies the flag for the oft-overlooked little county that is Carlow. Jamie Heaslip is the product of the Irish military tradition, Keith Earls of working-class Limerick rugby and, importantly, Iain Henderson and Rory Best represent Northern Ireland and remind us that on

an island where we too often focus on the stuff which divides us rugby has always stood in an unassuming way for a practical, decent form of unity between Irish people on both sides of the border.[47]

That the game, for instance, is almost exclusively urban at senior level in Munster, that Jamie Heaslip attended a rugby-playing school, and that rugby's (albeit commendable) accommodation of northern Protestants and southern Catholics has traditionally been aided by the game not generally having to accommodate the extreme ends of either community, was not allowed to hinder a seductive media soundbite.

At best, economic progress led to on-field success indirectly by facilitating the popularity of the professional provincial teams, giving these and the IRFU, in turn, the financial power to hold on to Irish players. The more apparent links between social change and Irish rugby were in the media, cultural and commercial profile of the game. Progress was certainly made in the numbers of Irish people attending rugby fixtures of all kinds. Between 2007 and 2011, the percentage of Irish adults that attended rugby fixtures more than doubled, increasing from 1.1 to 2.5 per cent. This most certainly suggests the arrival of new fans to the game in the context of Munster, Leinster and Ireland's success.[48] The media profile of the more high-profile players sky-rocketed. In 2009, *Irish Independent* writer Vincent Hogan reported that a PR executive claimed that, and I quote, 'If I want to get a product in the paper tomorrow, the rugby players are my guarantee. I won't go for a pretty model if I have a chance of getting Brian O'Driscoll or Ronan O'Gara.'[49] Ultimately, local success in international competition has proved very seductive to the Irish sporting audience. Andrew Mawhinney, a senior administrator with the Limerick FC soccer club, summed up the relative advantage rugby enjoyed over soccer in terms of domestic prestige and esteem:

> You can watch Heineken Cup and see Irish lads playing for an Irish club competing for their equivalent of the Champions League. The international team has won the equivalent of the European Championship and people can watch them here ... soccer can't compete with those standards.[50]

Television audiences also increased. Much was made in the media of the fact that, at 891,000, the Ireland–France rugby match was, in numerical terms, the most-watched television sport event in Ireland in 2014. This was an increase of almost 400,000 on the audience for the Grand Slam decider against England in 2003. Yet in audience proportion terms, the GAA hurling and football finals were still more popular television events than the 2014 rugby championship clincher.[51] But overall this was successful for rugby, and suggests that people who would not traditionally have watched the game had begun doing so.

Exact quantitative links between the financial status of professional rugby and the Celtic Tiger are difficult to establish, precisely because of their common chronological origin. Though the IRFU's turnover increased sevenfold in the

1997–2013 period (from around €10 million to €70 million), it is impossible to disaggregate income attributable to macroeconomic factors and that which would have been earned anyway due to newly available revenue streams brought about by professionalism.[52] Yet it seems likely that economic buoyancy boosted the coffers of the IRFU and the provinces at least to some extent.

If the quantitative links between rugby and national finance are difficult to establish, then it is a truism that professional rugby seamlessly weaved its way into the Celtic Tiger economic *zeitgeist*. Amateurism, in the context of how business was conducted in the Celtic Tiger era, was rendered anachronistic. In the 1990s, Irish financial institutions took full advantage of deregulation of capital markets and easy access to credit to engage in frantic competition with each other, particularly when it came to property investments.[53] Irish banks, traditionally risk averse and models of probity, were somewhat analogous to the rugby governing bodies in the amateur era. From the mid-1990s, both spheres were forced to revolutionise the manner in which they conducted their business. With the dawn of the professional era and in the context of Ireland's open deregulated economy, the traditional alliance between rugby and banking, one that originated in the nineteenth century, evolved to embrace contemporary corporate culture. With Irish rugby internationally competitive, the revenue streams open to the IRFU through corporate hospitality were fully capitalised upon by financial institutions. In this regard, Ireland resembled the English experience where Thatcher-era financial reforms and their implications for middle-class business attitudes did much to chip away at amateurism in rugby union in the 1980s.[54] Indeed, rugby became something of a symbol of Celtic Tiger era excesses when the economic crisis took hold. A banking Inquiry, established in 2014 by the Irish government in order to assess the role of banks in the financial crisis, heard several witnesses testify that pre-rugby international hospitality meetings were important in solidifying the lethal alliance between banks and property lenders during the boom years. Rugby as a useful motif for the economic crash was best exemplified, perhaps, by the economist Morgan Kelly's now famous and pithy comment that the banking crisis was caused by the ineptitude of a few 'faintly dim former rugby players'.[55]

In another, quite intangible, sense, rugby also benefited from shifting identities that emerged in the Celtic Tiger era. For the commuter generation, it is conceivable that the new-fangled provincial teams provided a psychological sense of place, ameliorating the dislocation that living in newly constructed housing estates creates. This, however, is a point that cannot be pushed too far without further research. In addition, any cultural barriers to supporting rugby, such as a its perceived Anglophilia, now belonged to a different generation. In this atmosphere, foreign players were easily assimilated and events such as the All Blacks versus Munster fixture in 2008, entirely stage-managed by the teams' sponsors, Adidas, and where both fans and players indulged in an orgy of invented traditions (New Zealand-born Munster players performed the *haka*), were made possible by transient and flexible notions of place and identity in Celtic Tiger Ireland and the maturity, in an Irish rugby context, of the capitalist media-sport nexus.[56]

In October 2015, then, the bright outlook for Irish rugby was swiftly replaced with pessimism and the excessive navel-gazing that often follows a heavy and unexpected defeat. It is almost tempting to treat the rise and fall of Irish rugby as analogous to the fate of the Celtic Tiger. Yet, just as caution is required when ascribing rugby success to economic buoyancy, a similar approach is needed when trends seemingly go into reverse. The economic crisis did have some financial implications. In the teeth of the macroeconomic crisis during the 2010/2011 season, the IRFU scored a financial and public relations own goal by overpricing match tickets, and in 2013 it suffered a €26 million shortfall in ten-year ticket sales, again as demand for an expensive product was rather tepid.[57] Yet the continued success of the provinces, particularly Leinster, throughout the worst of Ireland's economic collapse, and the generally strong demand for international tickets, meant that the IRFU continued to record year-on-year increases in turnover. The future, however, looks uncertain. Defeat to Argentina at Cardiff was followed by a series of bad results for the provinces and concerns about dwindling crowds, particularly in the case of Munster. The crowd for the province's opening fixture in the European Champions Cup against Treviso in November 2015 only half-filled Thomond Park. When a crowd of just 7,200 watched Munster defeat Ulster that month, Munster coach Anthony Foley urged fans to start attending games: 'It's important for Limerick that everyone comes out and supports the game. It's a big stadium that needs filling and it's a great atmosphere.'[58]

Success at provincial level is based on two key metrics: the number of top-class players each province can produce from within the province itself, and progression to the latter stages of domestic and European competition. When Munster won the Heineken Cup in 2008, eleven of the starting fifteen and the entire pack were from the province itself. Bearing in mind that this is a province with a population of just 1.2 million where rugby is the fourth most popular team sport, we can fully appreciate the scale of the achievement. The Leinster starting team in the 2012 final featured eight Dublin-born players and two others, Gordon D'Arcy and Sean O'Brien, who were born elsewhere in the province. There were just three non-Irish players on the team. They squared up against an Ulster fifteen featuring eight players from the province, all the products of the schools rugby system. When one considers that RC Toulonnais won the equivalent tournament in 2015 with only four Frenchmen and just one, Xavier Chiocci, actually from the city of Toulon, there is a clear trend towards international recruitment among Europe's top clubs, and the likelihood of sustained salary inflation. This must be a worry for the IRFU. The idea that Irish provinces can continue to compete using a majority of local players seems doubtful to say the least. Decisive shifts in the political economy of professional rugby appear to have pulled the rug from under the provinces' feet. Clubs such as RC Toulonnais, with their seemingly limitless funds for investment in playing resources, have brought the fragility of the Irish business model into sharp relief, And just as the initial injection of talent provided by the 'golden generation' created a virtuous circle for the provinces, the retirement of that generation and its replacement with players of lesser stature may steepen the downward spiral that came vaguely into view in the autumn of 2015.

Philip Dine has observed that French clubs such as Stade Francais and RC Toulonnais are 'distinctively French examples of a thoroughly pragmatic and media-aware sporting eclecticism and cosmopolitanism'.[59] Eclecticism and cosmopolitanism, while visible in Irish rugby, are strictly circumscribed by the IRFU's control over the provinces' recruitment policies and the emphasis on home-grown talent. All of this rests on a financial knife-edge. For instance, Munster's diminishing success on the field has had serious financial implications, and by 2014 the province was running a yearly deficit.[60] This is due to lost income from non-qualification for European knock-out stages and the fact that a number of recent rugby converts seem to have jumped off the bandwagon. Former Irish international, rugby league convert and Garryowen stalwart Paddy Reid described Munster's 'soft' support thus:

It's like something for the Romans, the Coliseum, just to amuse people. There are people following rugby and if you threw a tennis ball onto the pitch they wouldn't know the difference. They haven't a bull's notion what's going on. I've seen women at matches and they might as well be knitting. And since Munster started winning, 'tis like Puck Fair! You see fellas dressed in scarlet from their heads to their toes. And none of them members of clubs.[61]

Eugene McGee was equally sceptical in 2009:

So, is the GAA really threatened by the growth of rugby in nearly every county in Ireland? The short answer is no. While rugby is the glamour game now, that is largely based on world-class success by Ireland along with Munster and Leinster in the Heineken Cup. But success at that level is transient in all sports and will be replaced by less glamourous results in time.[62]

Munster Rugby's strategic plan for 2014 to 2017 – which has, as targeted outcomes, knock-out qualification in European competition every year and one outright win – seems, in this context, to be a touch optimistic. Yet it is too early to confidently predict anything in a volatile and ever-changing rugby world. It may well be that a lot of the support that the provinces attracted in the good years will dry up – but, without a sustained period of decline in crowd numbers and success on the field, and in the absence of systematic economic research, we cannot fully appreciate what, exactly, drives demand for professional rugby in Ireland.[63] It remains to be seen whether Ireland's luck holds out.

Notes

1 *Sunday Independent*, 11 October 2015.
2 Ibid.
3 www.balls.ie/football/audio-ewan-mackenna-on-why-the-irish-media-is-biased-towards-rugby/313185, accessed 10 August 2015.
4 *Irish Independent*, 29 April 2009.

5 *Munster Branch Committee Minutes*, 13 February 1975.
6 See T Collins, *A Social History of English Rugby Union* (London: Routledge, 2009), 187–93.
7 *Irish Times*, 24 January 1969.
8 *Irish Times*, 22 January 1969.
9 L O'Callaghan, *Rugby in Munster: A Social and Cultural History* (Cork: Cork University Press, 2011).
10 *Irish Times*, 14 March 1984.
11 *Irish Times*, 29 June 1985.
12 B Fanning, *From There to Here: Irish Rugby in the Professional Era* (Dublin: Gill and Macmillan, 2007), 25; for an overview of professionalism, see T Collins, *The Oval World: A Global History of Rugby* (London: Bloomsbury, 2015), part vii.
13 For an insight, see Fanning, *From There to Here*; O'Callaghan, *Rugby in Munster*, Chapter 7.
14 Fanning, *From There to Here*, 47.
15 Ibid., 242–3.
16 *Irish Times*, 28 October 1997.
17 M Larkin, 'What Future for Rugby?' *Old Crescent RFC Season Programme 1998–99*.
18 For the Munster case, see L O'Callaghan, 'The Red Thread of History', *Media History*, 17, 2 (2011), 175–88.
19 *Irish Times*, 22 September 1997.
20 *Irish Times*, 29 December 1999.
21 *Irish Times*, 6 April 2000.
22 *Irish Times*, 19 May 2006.
23 *Irish Independent*, 18 April 2008.
24 O'Callaghan, 'Red Thread', 180–2.
25 Central Bank of Ireland, *Quarterly Bulletin*, Autumn 2004, 92.
26 *Census of Population 2011* (Dublin: Stationery Office, 2011), 9.
27 Dublin Airport Authority Annual Reports 2007, 2008 and 2009.
28 See G Fulton and A Bairner, 'The GAA, Croke Park and Rule 42', *Space and Polity*, 11:1 (2007), 55–74.
29 For a critical view, see G Smyth, 'Irish National Identity after the Celtic Tiger', *Etudios Irlandises*, 7, 132–7; F O'Toole, *Enough is Enough: How to Build a New Republic* (London: Faber and Faber, 2010); see also RF Foster, *Luck and the Irish: A Brief History of Change 1970–2000* (London: Allen Lane, 2007), 64–5.
30 *Irish Independent*, 30 May 2009.
31 *Daily Telegraph*, 28 February 2007.
32 *Irish Independent*, 27 April 2009.
33 Ibid.
34 *IRFU Annual Report 2005–6*, 8.
35 *IRFU Annual Report 2006–7*, 86.
36 *IRFU Annual Report 2013–14*.
37 *Irish Sports Monitor*, 2013, 76.
38 Ibid., 20.
39 See *Irish Sports Monitor*, 2009.
40 *Irish Sports Monitor*, 2013.
41 Economic and Social Research Institute (ESRI, Ireland), *Keeping Them in the Game*, 56.
42 T Collins, *The Oval World*, 174.
43 G Williams, 'From Grand Slam to Grand Slump: Economy, Society and Rugby Football in Wales during the Depression', *Welsh History Review*, 11, 3 (1983), 339–57; P Dine, *French Rugby: A Cultural History* (Oxford: Berg, 2001).
44 *Irish Times*, 1 October 2011.

45 *Irish Times*, 5 December 2009.
46 *Sunday Independent*, 11 October 2015.
47 Ibid.
48 *Irish Sports Monitor*, 2013, 79.
49 *Irish Independent*, 29 April 2009.
50 *Irish Independent*, 28 April 2009.
51 RTE, 'Top 20 Sports Programmes in 2014', https://tvmediasales.rte.ie/top-programmes-2014/, accessed 26 October 2016; *Irish Times*, 17 January 2004.
52 For IRFU finances, see IRFU annual reports 2004–2013.
53 A Bielenberg and R Ryan, *An Economic History of Ireland Since Independence* (London: Routledge, 2013), 156.
54 Collins, *English Rugby Union*, 196.
55 *Irish Times*, 7 May 2011.
56 L O'Callaghan, 'The Pacific Islander in Irish Rugby: From Exotic "Other" to Global Professional Colleague', *International Journal of the History of Sport*, 31, 11 (2014), 1345–58.
57 *Irish Times*, 20 July 2013.
58 *Irish Independent*, 2 November 2011.
59 P Dine, '*Une certaine idée du rugby*: Sport, media and identity in a "glocalised" game', *French Cultural Studies*, 25, 1 (2014), 65.
60 Munster Rugby, 'Munster Rugby AGM Financial Update', www.munsterrugby.ie/news/20714.php#.VmRPir82BRB, accessed 30 November 2015.
61 *Irish Independent*, 23 April 2008.
62 *Irish Independent*, 30 May 2009.
63 For a review of demand for professional sport, see J Borland and R MacDonald, 'Demand for sport', *Oxford Review of Economic Policy*, 19, 4 (2003), 478–502.

2 Cows in the heartland

New Zealand rugby and rural change in the professional era

Greg Ryan

Popular interpretations of the history and international success of New Zealand rugby have been permeated by rural nostalgia – the belief that the strength and values of the game reside in country clubs and the smaller provincial rugby unions and that the most successful All Black teams were dominated by farmers. During the professional era, a belief has persisted that the modern game, with its emphasis on urban-based franchises in transnational competitions, has been particularly disadvantageous for rural rugby, leading to the closure of clubs, the deterioration of competitive structures and the alienation of core support. But it is debatable whether the apparent malaise of rural rugby should be attributed to fault in the governance of the professional game or to broader economic and social forces acting on New Zealand society to produce dramatic rural change over the last half-century. While critique of professional rugby has its place, it is prone both to a selective reading of the past to paint the present in an unfavourable light and to a myopic tendency to divorce rugby from the shifting contexts in which it is played.

To understand the seeming rural–urban divide in contemporary New Zealand rugby we must first examine the longer history of the game and the ways in which it has been interpreted as a, now vulnerable, rural rugby idyll.

It is commonly accepted that rugby expanded rapidly into the countryside following its diffusion to New Zealand around 1870, and that its growth epitomized pioneering endeavour. The stamina and tenacity required to tame the colonial frontier was apparently mirrored on the rugby field by a New Zealand male 'type' noted for strength, determination, versatility and initiative.[1] It followed from this conception of origins that the considerable success of the All Blacks during the twentieth century was derived primarily from players of the rural 'heartland' and its plethora of local clubs governed by small provincial rugby unions.[2] The iconic status of long-serving All Black forward and later administrator Colin Meads, voted the New Zealand rugby player of the twentieth century, is as much about his achievements as a player as his embodiment of the ideal characteristics of a bygone era. His training methods working on his Te Kuiti farm, his personal humility and loyalty to teammates, and his devotion to both his local club and the small King Country Rugby Union seemed to confirm that Meads' exceptionalism was derived not from anything unusual, but from an uncompromising dedication to rugby honed in his rural background.[3]

In recent decades, the values of the rural heartland have been invoked most strongly when the All Blacks, always the embodiment of New Zealand rugby as a whole, are perceived to be in crisis. At the turn of the century, and especially following an unexpected loss to France in the semi-finals of the 1999 Rugby World Cup, explanations for the 'failure' of the All Blacks contained a strong undercurrent of opinion that the traditional values and amateur spirit of rugby as epitomized in the heartland were being undermined by urban-based professionalism. Global commercial imperatives apparently had no place for the community values and social capital of the small country club and its dedicated members who were willing to make the personal and financial sacrifices necessary to maintain rugby. At the end of 2000, Kevyn Male, author of several popular books on rural rugby, condemned 'pampered' and 'prima donna' All Blacks who could learn from the dedication of 'backblocks' players who travelled long distances each week to train and play: 'They have to get back to the people, go back to the grassroots or the game is going to peter into the Superbowl … it's entertaining but just for the top 200 players.'[4] Another correspondent wistfully reflected on the sort of rugby played by former All Black and farmer Gordon Slater.

> Rugby as it used to be played. When farmers like the Slaters slogged their way through a couple of hundred cows before driving an hour or more to training – or even to a major match. With their one pair of boots in a war assets kitbag. No sleek cars from sponsors. No women's magazines exclusives. When parents like theirs – or the neighbours – took over milking so the local heroes could join the team for the big away games. When All Blacks actually played club footie! I've heard the arguments – that those sorts of amateurs wouldn't stand a show against the new pros, that things have changed, moved on, improved. I'm not convinced. The Slater brothers and their mates like the tough men of Northland have shown that some things don't change, that pride and dedication, hard work and a will to win for some old-fashioned reasons still count for something. That sheer guts can sometimes discount chequebook star quality.[5]

There is no better illustration of the faith in rural rugby than the almost euphoric reaction to the renaissance of East Coast, one of New Zealand's smallest provincial unions, during the late 1990s. As the editors of the *Rugby Almanack* put it: 'These small rural communities have been stripped of all other pieces of their infrastructure in the quest for profits, but rugby remains as a single uniting force.' In so far as anything is said of the importation of players from urban clubs to strengthen the East Coast team, it is generally in the context of a desire to return home to their 'roots' and a strong sense of community.[6]

In truth there is little substance for any interpretation of the success of the All Blacks and New Zealand rugby more generally in terms of frontier masculinity or rural dominance. Not only was the game urban in its origins, but its fastest growth and greatest playing strength, in terms of both numbers and results, remained in the four main cities and various larger provincial towns. The game undoubtedly secured a footing in many rural towns and districts, but relatively speaking, and in a precursor to themes pursued later in this chapter, growth was constrained by obstacles such as poor transport and communication networks, small populations and rural transience, long working hours and limited access to the sort of secondary school infrastructure that nurtured sport.[7] Many small towns and country areas simply lacked the population and resources to sustain regular rugby of any standard. Wherever one looks in the various provincial histories of New Zealand rugby – Buller, Poverty Bay, South Canterbury, Waikato and others – the pattern of fluctuation, frustration and rural complaint at urban neglect is the same. It follows that, rather than being dominated by farmers, an All Black team at any time in its history was likely to be significantly more urban, educated and occupationally professional than the average of the population.[8]

The disjuncture between the perceived and actual nature of New Zealand rugby is not unique. The historical significance of rural ideals and idealization in New Zealand is well documented.[9] In a contemporary context, Nick Perry suggests that the survival of the notion of rural New Zealand as a representative national culture may derive from its comparative plausibility. Although New Zealand is one of the most urbanized countries in the world, about 86 per cent in 2015, such urbanization is not linked to large-scale production and manufacturing. Relatively speaking, the economy, and the basis for prosperity, is still dependent on primary production for export earnings. Hence the rural sector maintains a strategic importance despite the statistically dominant urban sector.[10] At the same time, in sharp contrast to many urban settings around the world, New Zealand urbanization is characterized by relatively large spaces and low population density.[11] The virtues of the rural are not therefore an alien concept, and there is also a multitude of contemporary imagery to reinforce this sense of rural plausibility.[12] The various 'Southern Man/Pride of the South' Speights beer advertisements developed during the 1990s, replete with stunning images of a South Island high country inhabited by taciturn shepherds, draw on a cultural tradition associating the rural with simplicity and authenticity and implicitly conveying a distrust of the effete and urban.[13] Further, anyone watching television coverage of the New Zealand provincial rugby competition over many years cannot help but notice the large number of advertisements for farm products such as sheep drench, pasture supplements and rural insurance. At the very least, rural people are perceived to be the most devoted followers of the provincial if not national game. Echoing Raymond Williams' interpretation of the relationship between country and city, it is not surprising that the reaction of many rugby followers to the rapid transition to professionalism in 1995, and its subsequent transformation of competition structures within the national and international game, has been to find solace in hybrid memories of rural rugby supremacy and great performances by All Black teams dominated by the likes of Colin Meads, Ian Kirkpatrick and Richard Loe, farmers all.[14]

The unease of fans with the changes wrought by professional rugby, of which the rural game is but one part, has been simultaneously reinforced and shaped by a strand of popular writing redolent of the wider literature of protest against aspects of modern professional sport. Perhaps most significant here is Nick

Hornby's *Fever Pitch*, which, by means of the author's own obsession with Arsenal Football Club, traced the changing relationship between fan and club amid the increasing commercialization of British football during the 1970s and 1980s.[15] For New Zealand, former All Black captain David Kirk used his 1997 autobiography *Black and Blue* to question whether the game would be stripped of its spontaneity and flair as professionalism appeared to value winning more than excellence. He also doubted whether the grassroots sporting community of his amateur playing days could survive the transformation.[16] Five years later, in *The Judas Game: The Betrayal of New Zealand Rugby*, leading journalist Joseph Romanos depicted the reshaping of New Zealand rugby during the professional era as a 'betrayal' of the game's traditions and especially those of club and provincial rugby: 'The New Zealand Rugby Union has … been very concerned with the game at the top level, where it is most visible, and forgotten about the foundations of New Zealand rugby. And we're about to pay the price.'[17] In 2010 former All Black and commentator Chris Laidlaw weighed in with *Somebody Stole My Game*, a portrayal of rugby lurching inexorably towards crisis because

> the market has got its hands firmly round the game's throat. Markets bring a confusing mixture of wealth and suffering. In rugby those two conditions can be neatly equated with the two dimensions of the game, the professional and the amateur. One is consuming like there's no tomorrow, while the other is sitting outside with a begging bowl.[18]

Here contradictory elements, such as the cyclical sense of crisis that has gripped New Zealand rugby since at least 1905, or the century-long frustration of most writers with a conservative administration that did not adapt to external change, are conveniently set aside to tacitly reinforce a sense that the latest crisis is unique and uniquely destructive. If the likes of Romanos and Laidlaw are not always and explicitly aiming at the state of rural rugby, their work has sustained that part of the critique of professionalism more vigorously than others.

The New Zealand media has also repeatedly drawn on a cadre of former prominent players with strong rural rugby credentials to legitimize the picture of a rural rugby malaise. In August 1995, just as the new southern hemisphere Super Rugby structure was being revealed, former All Blacks captain, coach and farmer Brian Lochore warned of the dangers for the New Zealand Rugby Union (NZRU) in focusing exclusively on the larger unions and top players. 'We have to look after rugby in the small areas. If we don't, we won't have a good base. If we don't look after this breeding area, rugby will die.'[19] In 2003 Colin Meads, having witnessed the progressive decline of his King Country union since the advent of professionalism, described the provincial rugby championship as 'a shambles' and lamented 'The big boys are getting bigger and the smaller ones are getting smaller.' Lochore's successor as All Blacks coach, and another farmer, Alex Wyllie, described the five New Zealand teams in the then Super 12 competition as 'stuffing' New Zealand rugby.[20] Five years later, when his

Glenmark club was forced to merge many of its lower-grade teams with neighbouring Cheviot in order to survive, he raged:

> I just can't understand that something hasn't been done about it by some of
> the so-called heads of the union within the provinces or at the New Zealand
> Rugby Football Union itself. It's bloody disgraceful the way the game's
> being treated. It's all about professional rugby, that's all they care about.[21]

A decade later, Meads was still being quoted on similar themes. 'An All Black could come from Te Kuiti, or Waimate, but they will never play their rugby there. The young ones get scholarships, put into the academy system, get a Super 15 contract, and move to the big cities.'[22]

Such pessimism is perhaps amplified by evidence to suggest that rural sports clubs have contributed to social capital and cohesion in a manner more discernible than their urban counterparts. In settings where small populations limited the sort of social class and sometimes sectarian divisions evident in city clubs, those in the country had a stronger claim to represent a true cross-section of their communities. Without a wide variety of other amenities, the rugby club not only served as a sporting focal point but the premises were also used for a variety of other communal activities ranging from dances to meetings to funerals.[23]

The contrast between urban and rural cultures, rugby and otherwise, was reinforced in 2015 with the release of *The Ground We Won*, a documentary about the small Reporoa club in the Bay of Plenty. Like many rural clubs, it once had four or five teams but was now struggling to field one and was drawing on a wider catchment to do so. Adding to its difficulties, Reporoa was in the midst of a prolonged drought, prompting one reviewer to draw a comparison with John Ford's film of John Steinbeck's *The Grapes of Wrath*:

> The opening shot of telegraph poles, the dust bowl, the suffering of farmers,
> the dignity of human spirit in the face of adversity, the slow death of the
> American/New Zealand Dream. There are common themes that run deep
> throughout both films.

The documentary makers were determined to capture the essence of a club in which the involvement of members was about much more than simply playing sport. As one observed,

> It's a communion. There's no other word for it. What they are doing is transcending the daily grind in their daily lives. Getting outside of themselves
> and being a part of a bigger whole. There's like a style of communication
> that goes on inside that changing shed that doesn't happen outside those
> four walls.

One of the players added, 'The rugby club is a modern day church. We all congregate round it and share our problems and stories and what's happening. It's a communal point, anyway.' But the film also served as a touchstone for critics to lament the deleterious effect of professional rugby on the rural game. One suggested the title could just as easily have been *The Ground We Are Losing*, 'because rural community rugby is relentlessly being driven back over its own line by the forces of commerce' as talented young players were being removed from their communities and put into professional 'boot camp'.[24] Another columnist remarked that 'notwithstanding its unrelenting boozy machoism, I can't help thinking that amateur rugby, Reporoa-style, is morally preferable to the greed and corruption of corporate international sport as exemplified by Sepp Blatter's Fifa'.[25]

Quantifying the decline of rural rugby, either numerically or as a measure against the overall social capital generated by the game, is not easy. As noted earlier, the entire history of New Zealand rugby has witnessed the rise and fall of clubs and the changing of provincial union and sub-union boundaries as populations have shifted with economic fortunes, thus rendering competitions more or less viable. As but one example, during the mid-twentieth century, Kimbolton in the Manawatu had its own sub-union competition with teams from the local township, Rangiwahia, Cheltenham, Apiti and Colyton. Long before the advent of professionalism, only the Oroua club remained.[26] In this regard Paul Thomas's *A Whole New Ball Game* (2003) offers a contrast to the literature of protest mentioned above. He views change since the advent of professionalism as part of a cyclical readjustment in the ever-evolving world of mass spectator sport. Rather than taking rugby away from its origins, change, especially through significantly increased broadcasting, ought to be seen as creating a 'truly national game' and 'a game for all New Zealanders'.[27] Reinforcing this argument, NZRU Deputy-Chairman Steve Tew argued in 2011 that rugby had grown exponentially during the first 15 years of professionalism before plateauing.[28]

Testimony to the adaptive capacity of the NZRU may also be seen in its wholesale restructuring of provincial rugby in 2006, when the three-division structure that had prevailed since 1976 was replaced with two divisions – a 14-team professional first division and a 12-team semi-professional Heartland Championship. The latter includes competition among its top four teams for the Meads Cup and for the Lochore Cup for teams ranked 5 to 8.[29] Moreover, there is no doubt that this competition has injected enthusiasm and community pride into a number of smaller provincial rugby unions that had struggled for opportunities and profile under previous competitive structures. As one journalist captured the resurgence of North Otago rugby and its victory in the Meads Cup final in 2007, shortly after the All Blacks had departed from the Rugby World Cup at the quarter-final stage:

> All it took to consign the World Cup disaster to the rubbish bin was a beautiful North Otago afternoon, a cold can of beer and 15 men making a community proud. This was redemption in the rugby heartland, a glorious reminder that you can travel to the other side of the world in search of the Holy Grail and find it in your own backyard. North Otago is the champion

again, beating Wanganui 25–8. And the freezing workers and farmers, students and salesmen who make up the team did it without rotation or reconditioning. They did it for the jersey, for their brothers in gold, and to see the looks on the faces of the loyal corps of supporters who dared to dream this could be the year.[30]

Since 1988 the NZRU has also selected a Divisional, now Heartland, XV for a series of end-of-season fixtures, and frequently a tour to the Pacific, in an effort to expose the best players from small provincial unions to a higher standard of competition and potential professional opportunities.[31] But the name of the competition and its trophies, and the manner in which it is 'packaged' to the rugby public – with an emphasis tending more towards community than competitiveness – encapsulates popular understanding about the primacy of rural rugby in New Zealand.

Available statistics and analysis from the NZRU tend to highlight success in the upper echelons of the game and give a broad-brush account of overall player numbers rather than club numbers and regional distribution, and tend to mask variations – such as the many clubs that have shrunk or merged some of their teams but not actually disappeared, or those such as Oroua that are sustained by city players journeying out to the country to play. Wrights Bush in Southland had a different fate – going into recess in 1996 because of insufficient playing numbers, but reviving in 2009 when young players returned to the district.[32] Meanwhile the Geraldine Rugby Club responded to the threat to its senior competition status by placing an advertisement in the local newspaper warning: 'If local support is not forthcoming then unfortunately the committee will have to look at more dire options.'[33] For nearby Waimate, the problem was not a lack of players generally, but a specific shortage of prop forwards. As the club President remarked, 'We can cover all other positions except prop. No props, no team.'[34] Meanwhile, the success in the Heartland Championship is somewhat deceptive in that all of the competing provinces rely on loan players from the larger unions to sustain their competitiveness. Indeed, in 2007 the four smallest rugby unions in New Zealand, Buller, East Coast, North Otago and West Coast, sought joint legal advice when the NZRU unilaterally decided to reduce the maximum number of loan players from six to four. The clear implication was that they could not compete without them.[35]

Moving beyond rugby, changing leisure patterns in New Zealand as a whole are accentuated among smaller rural populations, where the 'margins' within which clubs and teams find players are slimmer. Here the arguments of Robert D. Putnam with respect to the decline of community in the United States are equally applicable to New Zealand.[36] First, economic reforms and liberalization of employment practices since the 1980s have produced an increasingly casualized workforce wherein many are obliged to work on Saturday or Sunday and take a weekly holiday at another time.[37] This, combined with increases in both single-parent and two-career families, has greatly undermined the traditional notion of the 'weekend' as a time that can easily be devoted to team sport.

Second, more disposable income and elements of cultural globalization have exposed New Zealand to a much wider range of individual and team sports that erode the numbers playing the traditionally dominant sports such as rugby and cricket. Basketball and football have both had periodic booms, and the latter is now securing a numerical dominance, especially as the New Zealand population profile changes with increasing Asian and other recent migrant components. Meanwhile, there is some evidence of 'white flight' from rugby as the game becomes dominated by more physically mature Maori and Pacific islands-heritage (Pasifika) players from secondary school level onwards.[38] At the same time, there is evidence to suggest that participation and club membership among all sports has declined sharply in favour of sedentary leisure activities such as computer games, films, live music, theatre and television watching. Even in rural areas, the contraction of distance due to better roads and vehicles allows people to travel further for different leisure outlets.[39] As the teenage son of one of the Reporoa players remarked, 'I hate rules. I want to play video games.'[40] Similarly, a stalwart of Dargaville's Ruawai Rugby Club reflecting on changes since the 1970s said, 'There are other opportunities now that we didn't have back then, it's moved from a physical sport to playing PlayStation games on the weekend.'[41]

Although long-term analysis of New Zealand trends has not yet been conducted, it is also likely, as Putnam argues, that generational change has a role to play. As those whom he terms the 'civic generation', whose more cooperative social habits were shaped by the mid-twentieth century experience of war and depression, are gradually replaced by generations of less involved individuals without the same overarching imperative to cooperate, there is an attendant decline in such things as team and club membership. Even in smaller centres, where the spirit of community cooperation has perhaps endured longer, there were difficulties: the junior rugby organization in Taupo, for example, announced in 2001 that it was stretched for personnel to assist with its administration and may well have to go into recess. Only two parent volunteers were running the game at junior level.[42] Likewise the Taranaki RFU was struggling to retain teenagers due to both sporting alternatives and a lack of suitable coaches. Even the use of representative players at coaching clinics was being stifled by a congested professional rugby programme that limited access to top players.[43]

For all who argue that the juggernaut of professional rugby has directly undermined the rural game, there are others closely involved with rugby who recognize that the roots of change are to be found in the dramatic demographic, economic and social transformation of New Zealand society since at least the early 1980s, and especially the restructuring of the rural economy.

During a long period of National government dominance from 1949 to 1984, farmers benefited from a myriad of subsidies and incentives covering areas as diverse as fertilizer, farm chemicals, weed and pest control, mortgage assistance for aspiring farmers, and guaranteed meat, wool and milk prices. By 1984 subsidies had reached $1 billion a year. But with the election of the fourth Labour government and its somewhat unexpected embrace of neoliberal economic philosophies, farmers were quickly subjected to the full range of the free market. Subsidies and other assistance were almost immediately removed, in contrast to the gradual phasing out of protections for urban manufacturing and other sectors – a process that caused bitterness and accentuated the sense of a rural/urban divide. The consequence for small-town New Zealand was job losses, failed businesses, reduced services and depopulation. In turn, this process has created more efficient and productive rural industries based on a smaller number of capital-intensive, higher-yielding farms in which new technologies are readily adopted, thus further reducing the need for labour. Rural exodus was also triggered by an increase in the numbers moving to larger centres for tertiary education and new employment opportunities.[44]

Census details reveal that rural population decline was evident in a number of the traditional bastions of rural rugby in the far north, on the East Coast and in the central North Island, and especially the Waikato and King Country, including Colin Meads' Te Kuiti base.[45] Further, the remaining rural population is disproportionately ageing beyond active sport, and where there is population increase in rural areas it is often via urbanites or migrants relocating for lifestyle reasons. As Oroua player and farmer Scott Wilson explained,

A lot of guys don't have many staff. The guy next door took over another farm and one worker has gone now, that sort of thing is happening almost every day now.... Poms, there are 12 families here now, no rugby players in the village amongst them though.[46]

Tony Lepelaars of the Central Hawke's Bay Rugby and Sports Club added,

The lack of player numbers is a reflection of the state of the economy in the rural areas. The labour force isn't as big as it used to be ... there aren't the same number of shepherds on stations as there were 10 years ago and there aren't the number of apprenticeships down here like there used to be.[47]

For Mary-Anne Roberts, manager of the Fairlie club, the problem was stability.

Like other rural rugby clubs, we are struggling for numbers and it seems to be getting worse. The jobs are not available up country, so we don't have farm work for players. With no industry in Fairlie, we don't have a stable work force so even if we get players it is hard to find them jobs.[48]

All were faced with the reality that declining club membership led to a declining fundraising base at a time when the cost of operating clubs was increasing. But as Brent Anderson, former All Black and NZRU director of community rugby, stressed,

We can't make people live in some of those areas and play rugby. If people are leaving the district then there just aren't the people there to fuel rugby.

It's not that the NZRU doesn't care, the people just aren't there. Things have changed in New Zealand. We have now got 1.5 million people living in Auckland.[49]

Amid the broader rural transformation, the large-scale conversion to dairy farming has had quite specific consequences for rugby. During the 40 years to 2015, the number of dairy cows increased from 2 million to 4.78 million. More noticeably, in the decade from 2004, the number increased by 31 per cent as sheep numbers declined by 25 per cent and beef cattle by 18 per cent. Moreover, herd sizes increased in a move away from small family units to larger capital-intensive farms.[50] With daily milking rosters, dairy farming demanded longer and more structured hours of its workers than sheep or beef farming, and constrained their movements. As Dion Gordon, a dairy farm manager and former Dunsandel club player, explained, 'My blokes might only get one day off on a weekend every third week. Rugby is getting killed.' He also noted that an increasing proportion of the dairy farm workers in the Dunsandel district, as is the case throughout New Zealand, are Filipino or Brazilian, and added, 'Filipinos aren't that big on the rugby.' In due course the Dunsandel club merged with nearby Leeston.[51] Another obstacle to consistent sporting involvement is 'gypsy day' on 1 June every year, when dairy herds are moved for winter grazing and the workers and managers on dairy farms generally move on to another farm or to other work, and their families move with them.[52]

For those who can find some time to play, there is evidence that performances are compromised by work demands. In the mid-1990s, before the dairy boom had gathered its full momentum, former All Black fullback and Taranaki dairy farmer Kieran Crowley observed of his Kaponga club, 'We have enough players but we lack size and anyway we don't normally come right until everyone has dried off their cattle'. In similar vein, Jeff Smellie, a coach at the Hinuera club in the Waikato, conceded that some of his players were prone to 'go right off the boil' early in the season when calving started and they were required to work long hours. In broader terms, Colin Meads added that whereas farmers of his generation had done much of their fitness training while working, technology had reduced the physical demands of farming to the point where players had to find extra time for gym work.[53]

There is no doubt that New Zealand rural rugby has changed over time and perhaps more markedly since the advent of professionalism in 1995. But there is a case to be made that change has been constant throughout the history of New Zealand rugby, that it has almost always been driven by socio-economic and other forces external to the administration of the game, and that, despite much popular mythology to the contrary, change at the rural grassroots of rugby does not make a great deal of difference to its upper echelons and especially the long-standing success of the All Blacks. As for the future, Brent Anderson pragmatically observed in 2008 that

There are examples all over the country where the rugby club is still the centre of social activities in the district. You possibly can't win the battle in some places, but by putting good programmes in place and providing appropriate support, the clubs can continue to fill the role they've filled in their communities in years past.[54]

At the same time, the chief executive of the King Country Rugby Union suggested that the spate of club closures and mergers had probably bottomed out: 'All of the clubs struggle but I can't see any more folding in the short term around here. I think we are at our baseline and it is now about consolidating what we've got.'[55] Indeed, seven years on from these assessments it seems that debates about the future of rural rugby in the professional era are not as widespread or intense as they were during its first decade. There appears to be greater recognition among the rugby community that the administrators of the game are not to blame for all of its ills. But it may also be that the changes that once caused so much angst have now settled down to become the new normal, as rugby has worked its way through another cycle of change and emerged in a more or less recognizable form.

Notes

1 Jock Phillips, *A Man's Country?: The Image of the Pakeha Male: A History* (Auckland: Penguin, 1987), 86–130.
2 See Robin Longhurst & Carly Wilson, 'Heartland Wainuiomata: Rurality to Suburbs, Black Singlets to Naughty Lingerie', in Robin Law, Hugh Campbell & John Dolan, *Masculinities in Aotearoa/New Zealand* (Palmerston North, New Zealand: Dunmore Press, 1999).
3 See for example *Waikato Times*, 13 January 1998; 13 January 2001; *The Evening Post*, 3 December 1999; *The Press*, 15 June 2001; Alex Veysey, *Colin Meads: All Black* (Auckland: Collins, 1974); Paul Verdon, *Tribute: Ranking the Greatest All Blacks of All Time* (Auckland: Cumulus, 2001), 15–22.
4 *Waikato Times*, 16 March 2000. See also Kevyn Male, *Coast to Coast: The Grassroots of New Zealand Rugby* (Auckland: Penguin, 2000); *The Rugby Post: Rugby's Place in Heartland New Zealand* (Auckland: Penguin, 1999).
5 *North Harbour News*, 25 October 2000.
6 Clive Akers & Geoff Miller, eds, *The Sky Television 2000 Rugby Almanack* (Auckland: Hodder Moa Beckett, 2000), 6; See also *Marlborough Express*, 19 September 2001; *The Dominion*, 13 October 2001; *New Zealand Herald*, 1 October 2001; *Evening Standard*, 11 October 2001.
7 Greg Ryan, 'Rural Myth and Urban Actuality: The Anatomy of All Black and New Zealand Rugby 1884–1938', *New Zealand Journal of History*, 35, 1 (2001), 45–69.
8 Ibid.; Greg Ryan, 'The End of an Aura: All Black Rugby and Rural Nostalgia Since 1995', in Greg Ryan, ed., *Tackling Rugby Myths: Rugby and New Zealand Society 1854–2004* (Dunedin: Otago University Press, 2005), 151–72.
9 Tom Brooking, 'Use It or Lose It: Unraveling the Land Debate in Late Nineteenth Century New Zealand', *New Zealand Journal of History*, 30, 2 (1996); Miles Fairburn, 'The Rural Myth and the New Urban Frontier', *New Zealand Journal of History*, 9, 1 (1975), 3–21.
10 Nick Perry, *The Dominion of Signs: Television, Advertising and Other New Zealand Fictions* (Auckland: Auckland University Press, 1994), 41–9.
11 Claudia Bell, *Inventing New Zealand: Everyday Myths of Pakeha Identity* (Auckland: Penguin, 1996), 29–30, 164–74.

12 Kai Jensen, *Whole Men: The Masculine Tradition in New Zealand Literature* (Auckland: Auckland University Press, 1996), 17–21.

13 Hugh Campbell, Robin Law & James Honeyfield, 'What It Means to Be a Man: Hegemonic Masculinity and the Reinvention of Beer', in Law *et al.*, *Masculinities in Aotearoa/New Zealand*, 177–9; Robin Law, 'Masculinity, Place and Beer Promotion in New Zealand: The Southern Man Campaign', *New Zealand Geographer*, 53, 2 (1997), 25; Bell, *Inventing New Zealand*, 40–54; Paul Cloke & Harvey Perkins, 'Pushing the Limits: Place Promotion and Adventure Tourism in the South Island of New Zealand', in Harvey C. Perkins & Grant Cushman, eds, *Time Out: Leisure, Recreation and Tourism in New Zealand and Australia* (Auckland: Longman, 1998), 275–6.

14 Raymond Williams, *The Country and the City* (London: Chatto and Windus, 1973), 45; see also Georgina Boyes, *The Imagined Village: Culture, Ideology and the English Folk Revival* (Manchester: Manchester University Press, 1993), 96–9.

15 Nick Hornby, *Fever Pitch* (London: Victor Gollancz, 1992); see also Simon Kelner, *To Jerusalem and Back* (London: Pan, 1997).

16 David Kirk, *Black & Blue* (Auckland: Hodder Moa Beckett, 1997).

17 Joseph Romanos, *The Judas Game: The Betrayal of New Zealand Rugby* (Wellington: Darius, 2002).

18 Chris Laidlaw, *Somebody Stole My Game* (London: Hachette, 2010).

19 *The Evening Post*, 22 August 1995.

20 *Sunday Star-Times*, 25 May 2003.

21 *New Zealand Herald*, 12 April 2008.

22 *Timaru Herald*, 29 April 2013.

23 This argument is derived from Australian examples. See in particular Lionel Frost, Margaret Lightbody & Abdel Halabi, 'Expanding social inclusion in community sports organizations: evidence from rural Australian football clubs', Discussion Paper 31/13, Department of Economics, Monash University, 2013; L. Frost & A. Halabi, 'The Country Football Club: Measuring Its Success as a Community Institution', in Peter Burke & June Senyard (eds), *Behind the Play: Football in Australia* (Melbourne: Maribyrnong Press, 2008), 73–88.

24 *The Dominion Post*, 20 May 2015. See also *The Press*, 26 April 2015.

25 *Manawatu Standard*, 3 June 2015.

26 *Manawatu Standard*, 5 July 2006.

27 Paul Thomas, *A Whole New Ball Game* (Auckland: Hodder Moa Beckett, 2003), esp. 16, 39, 234–5.

28 *Southland Times*, 29 June 2011.

29 See www.heartlandchampionship.co.nz.

30 *New Zealand Herald*, 23 October 2007.

31 www.allblacks.com/Teams/Heartland.

32 *Southland Times*, 28 June 2015.

33 *Timaru Herald*, www.stuff.co.nz/timaru-herald/sport/71033068/Geraldine-rugby-crisis-talks-over-senior-side, accessed 26 October 2016.

34 *Timaru Herald*, 18 February 1999.

35 *Timaru Herald*, 8 June 2007.

36 R.D. Putnam, *Bowling Alone: The Collapse and Revival of American Community* (New York, Simon & Schuster, 2000), esp. 184–284.

37 Canterbury Cricket Association, *The Report of the Taskforce on Club Cricket*, Christchurch, CCA, 1997, B2.

38 *Sunday Star-Times*, 28 June 2015.

39 Hillary Commission, *Survey on Sport and Physical Activity in New Zealand*, Wellington, Hillary Commission, 1996; *New Zealand Herald*, 12 April 2008.

40 *The Press*, 26 April 2015.

41 *Dargaville News*, 4 November 2009.

42 *Taupo Times*, 30 August 2001.
43 *The Press*, 26 May 2007.
44 Neal Wallace, *When the Farm Gates Opened: The Impact of Rogernomics on Rural New Zealand* (Dunedin: Otago University Press, 2014).
45 *New Zealand Herald*, 6 December 2012; *Waikato Times*, 16 October 2013. See also population details derived from Statistics New Zealand, www.stats.govt.nz/browse_for_stats/population.aspx, accessed 1 December 2015.
46 *Manawatu Standard*, 5 July 2006.
47 *Hawkes Bay Today*, 6 March 2015.
48 *Timaru Herald*, 30 June 2000.
49 *New Zealand Herald*, 12 April 2008.
50 *Dairy Statistics 2012–13*, www.lic.co.nz/user/file/DAIRY%20STATISTICS%20 2012-13-WEB.pdf, accessed 30 November 2015; *Compendium of New Zealand Farm Facts*, 5–9, www.fedfarm.org.nz/files/2012-Compendium-of-New-Zealand-farm-facts.pdf, accessed 26 October 2016.
51 *New Zealand Herald*, 12 April 2008. See also Rupert Tipples & David Lucock, 'Foreign Workers and Dairy Farming', *Primary Industry Management*, 7, 4 (2004); Rupert Tipples & Judith Wilson, 'The Dairy Farming Population and Migrations', *Primary Industry Management*, 8, 1 (2005), 41–5.
52 *Waikato Times*, 31 March 2015.
53 *New Zealand Farmer*, 2 May 1996; *Rural Waikato*, August 1996, p. 4; *Timaru Herald*, 29 April 2013.
54 *New Zealand Herald*, 12 April 2008.
55 Ibid.

3 The world comes to one country

Migration, cultures and professional rugby in France

Philip Dine

Introduction: the 'Black Saturday' of the *XV de France*

If there is one thing that most people in the world of rugby agree on, it is that it has experienced a profound mutation not only at a national level but also on the international stage, and that this is because of its official opening up to professionalism since 1995. The terms used to describe this transformation are in no way an exaggeration of the phenomenon: an upheaval and revolution mark the end of an outdated amateur rugby and herald the arrival of a new era composed of exchanges and relations, both sporting and commercial, largely on a global scale.[1]

It is with this emphasis on 'a profound mutation' that sociologist Sébastien Fleuriel and historian Joris Vincent open their institutional analysis of the advent of professional rugby in France. In the cultural overview that follows, the discussion will similarly highlight significant changes, as well as some notable continuities, with a view to charting the impact of this organizational upheaval on the attitudes and behaviours of players, administrators and supporters. To open this study, we might conveniently characterize French rugby as a sport historically practised in the 'wrong' place, for the 'wrong' reasons and in the 'wrong' way. Its heartland is the rural south and west of the country, rather than the industrial centres of the north and east; that is to say the regions closest to the British Isles, which became instead soccer's organizational hub and spiritual home. French rugby has long had its own way of doing things, reflected in the fact that its most abiding social function has been as a marker of frequently belligerent local and regional identities, instead of the amateurism and clubbable sociability that characterized the game as originally adopted by Parisian Anglophiles in the later nineteenth century. Subsequent investment in the game outside the capital was typically material as well as moral, and almost always parochial in nature, as reflected in the French tolerance for much of the nominally amateur era of both institutionalized violence and illicit payments to players. Crucially, this national distinctiveness has also included an authentically creative approach to the game on the pitch and intense scrutiny of its myriad meanings off it.[2] Such debates have centred most frequently and most vociferously on the selection, coaching and achievements – or, *a fortiori*, the lack of them – of the national side, as was clearly evidenced by reactions to the disappointing French performance at the 2015 Rugby World Cup (RWC). The headline used by *Le Monde*, the national journal of record, for its report on the concluding French involvement in the competition was a case in point: 'Samedi noir pour le XV de France' [A Black Saturday for the French Fifteen].[3]

Hosted by France's nearest rugby-playing neighbour and hereditary enemy, the 2015 tournament in England was thus primarily remarkable for the record-breaking (62–13) defeat inflicted on *Les Bleus* by the eventual winners, New Zealand. Coached by former star winger Philippe Saint-André, the *XV de France* were obliged to meet the All Blacks in the quarter-finals following the team's comprehensive (24–9) defeat at the pool stage by a weakened Irish side. Nevertheless, the coach and his players, as well as many supporters and at least some media commentators, seem to have clung to the hope of an upset to rank alongside the memorable triumphs recorded in the 1999 and 2007 encounters between the two nations. After the event, *Le Monde* reporter Bruno Lesprit reflected on the reasons for what he characterized variously as *une déroute* [a rout], *un naufrage* [a shipwreck] and, most colourfully, *une déculottée* [a trousers-down thrashing]. While Lesprit primarily attached blame to the coach, whose 44 per cent win record made him France's least successful coach of the professional era, he also echoed Saint-André's own regularly reiterated criticism of the structural weaknesses of the French game, summed up by the coach as 'players who play eleven months out of twelve and take part in 40 matches a year'.[4] These charges highlight both the commercial prioritization and the competitive attrition of the two club competitions that dominate French rugby in the professional era, namely the domestic Top 14 tournament and the European Rugby Champions Cup.

In an ironic twist and possible sub-text to *Le Monde*'s 'Black Saturday' headline, the French squad for RWC 2015 was easily the most ethnically diverse to have been assembled. The group combined players from the game's traditional hotbeds in the *Midi* (southern France) with others originating right across the country, as well as in France's ex-imperial hubs in North and sub-Saharan Africa, such as Algiers, Abidjan and Ouagadougou, together with Kinshasa in the former Belgian Congo. The squad also had a strong representation from the southern hemisphere, with both a Fijian and a New Zealander of Samoan heritage, as well as no fewer than three South Africans. The presence of Brussels-born Vincent Debaty added further spice to the mixture, as did that of his fellow props Rabah Slimani and Eddy Ben Arous, who came respectively from the Parisian *banlieue* [disadvantaged suburbs] of Trappes and Sarcelles, which had seen rioting in 2013 and 2014. As journalist Gavin Mortimer commented incisively: 'How times have changed. The two props who played for France in the 1987 World Cup final, Pascal Ondarts and Jean-Pierre Garuet-Lempirou, were men of the deep southwest, born and bred on the edge of the Hautes-Pyrenees.'[5] In contrast, the shared migrant heritage of their Parisian counterparts in 2015, although by no means identical, meant that they represented not only their country but also a distinct sub-national, and actually transnational, community. While France's sporting debt to sub-Saharan Africa, as represented by Eddy Ben

Arous and his Nigerian antecedents, is undoubtedly profound, the focus here will be on the North African connections of Rabah Slimani, whose own Algerian family background is a reminder of the abiding competitive and cultural significance of what was, until 1962, France's most important colony.

The Maghrebi contribution to France's sporting heritage is particularly rich and began in athletics, as exemplified by the triumph in French colours of Algerian-born marathon runners Ahmed El Ouafi at the 1928 (Amsterdam) Olympics and Alain Mimoun at the 1956 (Melbourne) Games. In association football, Moroccan star Larbi Ben Barek played with distinction for France between 1938 and 1954, while leading Algerian players Rachid Mekhloufi and Mustapha Zitouni would play for *Les Bleus* in the later 1950s, before opting in 1958 to join the nationalists' own soccer team as part of the ultimately successful struggle against the colonial presence in their homeland. This political mobilization of sport helps us to understand the complex societal impact, as well as the evident sporting significance, of the so-called *black-blanc-beur* [black-white-Arab] French team that won the 1998 football World Cup, which was also hosted by France. While this historic achievement cannot be reduced to the remarkable persona of Zinedine Zidane, it is undoubtedly epitomized by him. As the team's talismanic playmaker, the Franco-Algerian star encapsulates a long history of successful sporting integration of the country's ethnic minorities that had no obvious equivalent in French rugby prior to the professional era.

French rugby from William Webb Ellis to the Webb Ellis Cup

Although both locally entrenched and socially conservative, rugby in France has always been characterized by migration, of both people and ideas. Almost in spite of itself, this most traditional of games has thus become a privileged site of cultural exchange. So it is that the Fédération Française de Rugby (FFR) honours the passing in 1872 of William Webb Ellis by maintaining his grave in Menton, in the *département* of the Alpes-Maritimes. While this celebrated figure's contribution to rugby's international diffusion may be essentially symbolic, the fact that he should have chosen to spend his final years on the Côte d'Azur retains its affective force as an emblem of the French adoption of this quintessentially English game. As the major exception to the pattern of rugby's diffusion as a cultural artefact of British imperialism, France came relatively late to this form of recreation, as it did to athletic sports as a whole. Nevertheless, rugby was the country's first modern team game, its implantation and widespread diffusion significantly preceding that of association football. Rugby's subsequent remaking in the image of its adoptive nation has necessarily informed the game's continuing transformation in the professional era. Today's media-led revolution in practices and their supporting discourses has seen rugby mobilized as the signifier of a variety of both complementary and competing identities: local, national and, increasingly, transnational. To make sense of the new meanings as well as the institutional changes prompted by the advent of professionalism in 1995, we need briefly to consider the long century of the game's evolution up to that pivotal date.

More specifically, if we wish to understand France today, and particularly changing constructions of French-ness – whether in sports history or in history *tout court* – it is necessary to return to the Third Republic (1870–1940), the determinedly modernizing regime that effectively transformed 'Peasants into Frenchmen', in Eugen Weber's celebrated formulation.[6] Against this political backdrop, we may usefully highlight the coincidence of two events in Paris that shed light on sociocultural factors that continue to influence developments in French rugby. In April 1882, students of the prestigious Right-Bank *lycée* Condorcet played a leading role in the establishment of the Racing Club de France, the country's first indigenous sports association. The following year, Stade Français, the club's great rival in both educational and competitive terms, was founded by students from the equally privileged Left-Bank *lycée* Louis-le-Grand. The specifically national vocation of these first French rugby clubs was underlined by their names, thereby reflecting the political mood of the day. This had been memorably captured by the historian and philosopher Ernest Renan shortly before the foundation of the Racing Club and just across the Boulevard Saint-Michel from the *lycée* Louis-le-Grand. It was thus at the Sorbonne, on 11 March 1882, that Renan famously asked the question 'Qu'est-ce qu'une nation?' [What is a nation?], offering in response a vision of France as a model state that did not rely on shared origins for its cohesion, but rather on the constantly renewed willingness of its citizens – in his celebrated formulation, *un plébiscite de tous les jours* [a daily referendum] – to maintain their collective commitment to social solidarity. In the words of political scientist Jeremy Jennings: 'Such a conception has no place for either race or ethnicity as defining characteristics for membership of the political community.'[7] Although sorely tested in the century and a quarter since Renan addressed his scholarly audience, this inclusive conception of national identity remains a core value of today's French polity. As Prime Minister Manuel Valls remarked in 2015, in a reference to the female figure who conventionally symbolizes the country: 'Marianne n'a pas de race, pas de couleur' [Marianne has no race, no colour].[8] While the practical implementation of the French state's official colour-blindness remains a matter of considerable debate, the sporting manifestations of the Republic's commitment to inclusivity will be central to the discussion that follows; as will the role of sport as a vector of integration, if not necessarily equality, in a society that has been characterized by no less a body than the national Musée de l'Histoire de l'Immigration as 'the oldest country of immigration in Europe'.[9]

The period highlighted by this collection of essays, 1995 to 2015, conveniently demarcates the 'open' or professional era in rugby union in France, just as it does elsewhere. However, professionalism actually has a much longer history in the French game, albeit in a variety of covert forms. Having been adopted by privileged Parisians in the 1880s, rugby would embark on a process of internal migration that saw its competitive nucleus and cultural core move in the 1900s to the Bordeaux region, and then in the years before the Great War to the deep southwest, with Toulouse emerging after the conflict as the game's principal hub. As rugby spread, it was popularized, democratized and, decisively, commercialized, with the amateur ethic so dear to its Parisian pioneers being lost as the sport was integrated into older systems of knowledge and power. The transformative energy of local business interests – and closely associated perceptions of civic prestige – may be traced back at least as far as the 1920s, when the poaching of players from established clubs by ambitious rivals intensified the already high levels of violence in the game, resulting in a number of deaths as a result of injuries inflicted during play. Such developments led to internal schism and then to international isolation: the establishment in 1930 of the Union Française de Rugby Amateur (UFRA) underlined, by virtue of its very name, the principal motive of traditionalists for breaking with the FFR; while, in 1931, the decision of the four 'Home Unions' (England, Ireland, Scotland and Wales) to sever relations with the French resulted in the country's exclusion from the Five Nations tournament, as well as in a ban on all contacts with touring sides. This situation was to last until the Second World War, when defeat, invasion and occupation served to exacerbate ideological and organizational cleavages within the French game, as a sporting reflection of the profound social divisions of those dark days. The primary victim of this process was the recently imported code of rugby league, which was forcibly incorporated into rugby union by the collaborationist Vichy regime.

Yet this unpromising period would be followed by the sparkling *rugby-champagne* of the 1950s and 1960s. Such was the appreciation of the technically innovative spectacle of 'French Flair' by the international television audience that also emerged at this time that the English term entered the French language. In this period, the game symbolized both abiding regional tradition and resuscitated national ambition as France embarked on the wholesale restructuring of *Les 30 Glorieuses* (1945–1975), the three decades of unprecedented economic growth that, with the decisive support of Marshall Aid, made possible the country's post-war renaissance. The increasing competitiveness and self-confidence of French rugby over this period was likewise dependent on external investment, exemplified by the 'social aid' provided to players by the construction company of Antoine Béguère, the president of the Lourdes rugby club, which with his support became a major force in the game.[10] Players from the Football Club Lourdais contributed significantly to the national side's first joint victory in the 1954 Five Nations Championship and its first outright triumph in 1959, which prepared the ground for the country's long-awaited first Grand Slam in 1968. France's inaugural overseas tour saw a series victory over South Africa in 1958, the first by any touring side, thereby effectively marking the country's arrival on the broader international stage. Yet that year would be primarily remembered by French society as the one in which the combined impacts of events in the country's troubled overseas empire led to the collapse of the post-war Fourth Republic and its replacement, under General Charles de Gaulle's visionary leadership, by today's Fifth Republic.

Although these two historical narratives may only rarely be juxtaposed, France's post-war modernization thus coincided with the country's reluctant retreat from overseas empire.[11] While this belated decolonization occurred relatively peacefully in France's territories in sub-Saharan Africa – with the notable exception of rugby-playing Madagascar, where the game was mobilized by nationalists as a marker of the island's autonomy[12] – the conflicts in Indo-China (1946–1954) and, especially, Algeria (1954–1962) were to mark a generation and, it may be argued, have still not been fully assimilated into the country's historical memory. This has major implications for a sport that, in contrast most notably to football and athletics, has come only recently to appreciate the competitive and symbolic potential of contemporary France's cultural diversity. With few exceptions, French rugby teams both at club level and in international competition had been characterized for most of the game's history by players originating in its south-western heartland or in a limited number of rugby-playing enclaves in the Massif Central and the south-east. The successful sides of the 1960s and 1970s were justifiably proud of their record of integrating players of Spanish and Italian heritage, as notably represented by the Herrero brothers in Toulon and the Spanghero clan in Narbonne. However, in the 1980s, the French game was belatedly obliged to engage with the broader challenges and opportunities of what was now an undeniably multicultural society, as well as with the processes of media-led globalization that would lead first to the creation of the Rugby World Cup in 1987 and then, inescapably, to the advent of professionalism in 1995.

We should not forget that residual suspicion of France and French ways was such that the International Rugby Board (IRB) had refused to admit the FFR as a full member until as late as 1978. Now, under the influence of both national and international broadcasters – such as France's first subscription television channel, Canal+, which was launched in 1984 – the combined competitive and communicative landscape was to evolve ever more rapidly. As so often before, Stade Toulousain, France's most successful and most iconic club side, led the way in this renegotiation of the game's structures and meanings, independently hosting its own international 'Masters' tournaments in 1986 and 1990, in spite of opposition from the traditionalists of the FFR.[13] More typically, as the rugby-playing world embarked on the professional era, older patterns of locally based participation and identification continued to dominate the game in France. Nevertheless, among other strategies, both the leading clubs and the national side responded to professionalism by expanding their recruitment among the country's ethnic minorities and by looking abroad to reinforce their squads. This new mobility is most visible in the reinvention of today's most successful clubs, the increasingly diverse origins of the playing elite and the evolving behaviours of supporters. The specificity of the French case may best be appreciated by considering rugby's transformation in the professional era from a strongly regionalized sport into an increasingly transnational phenomenon.

French rugby in the professional era: new actors, new structures, new meanings

When confronted with the onset of the 'open' era in 1995, the FFR initially looked to adopt the southern-hemisphere model of professionalized provinces as the preferred option for development. However, French rugby's embracing of openly commercial priorities was to result instead in the ending of the monopoly position hitherto enjoyed by the Fédération, as new bodies emerged to reflect sectional interests within the French game. These included the players' union, Provale, as well as the Ligue Nationale de Rugby (LNR), which was headed by former star Serge Blanco (himself born in Caracas, Venezuela) for a decade from its creation in 1998 to 2008. Established to represent the interests of the leading clubs, the LNR now entered into competition with the previously all-powerful FFR for control of players, competitions and media rights. With top French players henceforth under contract to individual clubs, where they played increasingly alongside imported foreign talent, a conflict of interest arose between their employers and the national side. As the power of the club presidents increased, the influence of the FFR, and particularly of the national coach, was proportionately reduced.[14]

Unsurprisingly, the leading role in rugby's post-1995 transformation in France has been played by the biggest clubs, including such established forces as Stade Toulousain, which has successfully adapted its time-honoured associative values to the demands of the new professional landscape. In playing terms, this process has been overseen by the peerless Guy Novès, who, having represented the club 189 times between 1975 and 1988, was destined to become a fixture as its head coach between 1993 and 2015, only leaving to take on the task of rebuilding the *XV de France* in the wake of RWC 2015. This continuity at the top has been rewarded by no fewer than eight victories (and two runners-up positions) in the reconfigured national championship, which after some experimentation in the early phase of professionalization settled into today's Top 14 competition. Stade Toulousain has also won the European Rugby Champions Cup on four occasions over the same period (again with two runners-up finishes), the strongest performance by any side to date.

Elsewhere, the historic Biarritz Olympique club has sought to reinforce its 'ethnic' specificity by rebranding itself as Biarritz Olympique Pays Basque, as well as by playing its European matches over the border in Spain, where local football stadiums allow for bigger gates as well as underlining the club's proclaimed Basque identity. Similarly, the Perpignan club has played European fixtures in the Spanish Catalan region, and in 2011 signed a twinning agreement with the celebrated FC Barcelona, thereby allowing it to play in the football club's landmark Nou Camp stadium.[15] Meanwhile, in Clermont-Ferrand, the club that was established in 1911 as the Association Sportive Michelin by the city's then main employer and still primary sponsor, and which was obliged by the national sports authorities to change its name in 1922 to the AS Montferrandaise, became ASM Clermont-Auvergne in 2004. In its current incarnation, and in common with several other leading clubs – such as 1997 Heineken Cup winners (and 1998 runners-up) CA Brive, now, in full, the Club Athlétique Brive Corrèze Limousin – the club has thus ensured its eligibility for regional subsidies offered by the French state, thereby both expanding the club's declared territorial base and enhancing its commercial viability.

Most dramatically, a number of sports associations with long and distinguished histories have been creatively reimagined by distinctly idiosyncratic and even consciously iconoclastic club presidents. These new actors are exemplified by Max Guazzini and Mourad Boudjellal, two entrepreneurs with a background in the creative industries (radio and publishing respectively), whose financial support and aggressive marketing have seen Stade Français and Toulon emerge as dominant forces in the modern French game. It is significant that these two clubs are based outside rugby's traditional heartland in the south-west, where, as we have seen, the professional era has tended to reinforce the territorially rooted traditions of the leading clubs, albeit inflecting them in new ways. Under Guazzini's stewardship, Stade Français, which last won the national championship in 1908, won it again in 1998, thanks to what *Le Monde* revealingly described as 'a team of mercenaries', recruited from competing French clubs as well as from abroad.[16] Another five championships were to follow between 2000 and 2015, together with two runners-up finishes in the European Champions Cup. Even more dramatically, the thoroughly internationalized playing squads and coaching teams assembled at the reinvented Racing Club Toulonnais led the club to finish the season as runners-up in the Top 14 in both 2012 and 2013, before taking the title in 2014. Based in a fervently rugby-playing enclave in the south-east of the country, the Toulon club has a proud tradition stretching back to 1908, having won the national championship three times in the amateur era, the last as recently as the 1991–1992 season. Having made his fortune as the publisher of *bandes dessinées* [comic books and/or graphic novels], including most notably the immigration-themed albums of his elder brother Farid,[17] local entrepreneur Mourad Boudjellal committed himself to a thoroughly modern business plan for the club upon becoming its principal shareholder in May 2006. Toulon's total dominance of the principal European competition for three years in a row between 2013 and 2015 is the clearest possible indication of its combined competitive and commercial muscle after a decade of Boudjellal's investment.

Central to this success has been the club's ability (like Stade Français before it) to recruit top players from both the northern and southern hemispheres, establishing itself as what the venerable French daily *Le Figaro* described in January 2008, less than two years into Mourad Boudjellal's reign, as 'the multinational of the rugby world'.[18] The club's successful policy of attracting influential figures from abroad is epitomized by the case of veteran goal-kicker Jonny Wilkinson. Between his recruitment in 2009 and his retirement in 2014, the former England star was a pivotal member of the Toulon operation, as reflected in the city's decision to make him an honorary citizen at the culmination of what was an authentically glittering career, and as part of the official celebration of the club's 2014 French and European championship double.[19] Other forms of appreciation include the short film 'Jonny Wilkinson: Merci', produced by the AMV BBDO advertising agency for Guinness as part of its 'Made of More' campaign to accompany the 2014 Autumn Internationals. Using clips of comments from anonymous supporters, as well as club owner Mourad Boudjellal, head coach Bernard Laporte and revered former player turned influential rugby writer Daniel Herrero, among others, the piece 'focuses on the great fly half's humility, dedication to the game, and relentless resolve to bounce back from a raft of injuries, leading to him being as well-loved in Toulon as he is in England'.[20]

More pragmatically, the Toulon club's dominance of the international transfer market suggests that it is likely to maintain its competitive advantage for the foreseeable future. The 2015–2016 Toulon squad is remarkable for its inclusion of some two dozen players recruited from all over the rugby world, from Argentina to Fiji, and including such international stars as Matt Giteau (Australia, who joined the club in 2011), Juan Smith (South Africa, since 2013) and Ma'a Nonu (New Zealand, who arrived in 2015). However, the current line-up is also noteworthy for its inclusion of an authentically home-grown talent, Mathieu Bastareaud, who is of Guadaloupean descent and was born in the Paris suburb of Créteil. The centre is the most successful product of the highly innovative Rugby Club Massy Essonne (RCME), with whom he played before being talent-spotted by Stade Français in 2007, going on to represent that club until his move to Toulon in 2011, as well as being a member of the French national side since 2009. The story of Massy's success is part of a broader return of Parisian rugby to the centre-stage that includes not only the accomplishments of Max Guazzini's reinvented Stade Français, but also the reconfiguration of its even older rival, Racing Club de France, first as Racing Metro and then as Racing 92, although with less conspicuous success.

Based in the Parisian *banlieue*, the Massy club was only founded in 1971, but has since established a national reputation not only for player development but also as a model of sporting inclusivity. The suburb has a population of around 40,000 people, of whom an estimated one-third are of immigrant origin.[21] With over 700 currently registered players, including no fewer than 280 children ranging from six to 14, the RCME is already the second-largest rugby club in France – after Montpellier, whose president, Mohed Altrad, is himself a self-made businessman and an immigrant from Syria.[22] Reporting on the club's success in 2015, Bruno Lesprit commented that pessimistic cultural commentators who believed that 'the French model of integration' was extinct could do no better than take a trip out to the Massy ground on a Wednesday afternoon, when its youngest members train, in order to see that Republican ethos splendidly in operation: 'Through the miracle of a sport, rugby, and its values, […] are still alive and well in spite of two decades of professionalization'.[23] The key to the club's success lies in its ability to combine an elite competitive project with a broader commitment to the educative values of sport as a vector of social cohesion. Thus, on the one hand, the senior side has managed, on two occasions, to be promoted to the Pro D2 league, the gateway to the Top 14 competition, thereby bringing the club into regular contact with the game's traditional powers, still predominantly based in the south-west. On the other, the club's rugby school is open to all-comers, which allows it to be supported by municipal funding, with its training sessions and matches attracting children from an exceptionally wide range of ethnic and cultural backgrounds, who are made aware of the club's activities through a programme of educational visits. The school's director, Bruno Ghiringhelli, explains that these children have typically had no previous exposure to the game through their families, with the result that the Massy club itself takes on the role of cultural intermediary in establishing contacts with the juniors' parents and older siblings, while the latter group also contains potential players who are particularly responsive to the success of the senior side.[24]

The club's commitment throughout its existence to consolidating its mass base means that, in the professional era, it has followed a very different path from the Parisian superstars of Stade Français and Racing Metro, who have concentrated on financing an elite model based on the importation of top players, whether from abroad or from elsewhere in France. The transnational mobility of its home-grown talent is of an altogether different kind, as Bruno Lesprit underlines, noting that a 2012 club survey revealed no fewer than 27 different nationalities (and double-nationalities), including both North and West Africans, as might be expected, but also everything from Angolans to Russians. 'A communitarian nightmare?' wonders *Le Monde*'s correspondent: 'Not really. The young learners, who all speak French, are not bothered about their respective origins.'[25] Altogether more important is educating children and their parents alike in the need for team-building, cooperation and, not least, modesty as regards the chances of any given apprentice player making it to the highest level. As is underlined by another of the club's educators, Philippe Meyrignac: 'To obtain one professional player, you need to start with 80 youngsters in the under-12s.'[26]

Significantly, media interest in the Massy phenomenon has spread beyond the national press. Reporting on the club's exemplary contribution to the transformation of the French rugby landscape, Gavin Mortimer highlights the key role played by Alain Gazon, 'now the director of Racing 92's rugby school, but for more than 20 years a tireless physical education teacher in the Paris suburb of Massy'.[27] In common with his counterparts at Parisian clubs from the mighty Stade Français to the altogether more modest Sarcelles club, Gazon highlights the importance of rugby as a vector for educating not only young players of migrant heritage but also their families: 'There are Malians, Ivorians, Algerians, Moroccans and Tunisians and, initially, it was a challenge to convince their parents to let their children play rugby because they knew nothing about the sport or its culture.'[28] That process of consciousness-raising through participation has been marked by the success of the Massy club in identifying talented players such as Mathieu Bastareaud and also Jimmy Marlu, Gazon's first major discovery, who was signed by Clermont in 1996. Marlu was additionally selected for the French squad that contested RWC 1999, when France finished as runners-up to Australia. He thus joined a truly emblematic figure in the evolution of the public perception of the *XV de France* – a player who had additionally been prominent in the country's 1991 and 1995 World Cup campaigns, and whose status as a harbinger of the future reconfiguration of the French game will be returned to in our conclusion.

Before drawing this discussion to a close, let us simply note the broader importance of professionalization, and the accompanying processes of internationalization and mediatization, in the evolution of the French national side, as of the broader rugby landscape. The comments of Jean-Paul Dispans, manager of Stade Français's rugby school, are telling in this regard, suggesting as they do an intriguing parallel with the much-discussed impact of the France 98 football World Cup:

> Professionalism has obviously played its part, but France's hosting of the 2007 World Cup was very important because, for the first time, rugby became mainstream in the media … people across France, not just from ethnic minorities, saw that it was a sport for everyone.[29]

Eight years on from the sociocultural watershed of RWC 2007, the competitive misfortunes of the *XV de France* clearly indicate that French rugby has not yet achieved its full potential. However, the various achievements of operations as different as Toulouse and Toulon, together with the three Parisian clubs highlighted above, suggest that a collective commitment both to the diversification of player recruitment and to the expansion of the game's public profile may, in time, reap dividends that are at once competitive, commercial and, most significantly, societal.

Conclusion: a 'rainbow nation' *à la française*?

The transnational diversity of the 2015 *XV de France* was already hinted at by the squad assembled for RWC 1995, the first of the professional era, although that non-traditional presence was overwhelmingly associated with a single player: Abdelatif Benazzi, who remains by far the best-known rugby player of Maghrebi heritage. Such was the contribution made by 'Abdel' to the French cause in South Africa that the tournament hosts, and eventual winners, nearly failed to make it to the grand finale of their own competition. Indeed, had the arms of the giant forward been a fraction longer, one of sport's most celebrated photo opportunities might never have occurred. For it was his disallowed try in the dying minutes of their rain-sodden semi-final in Durban that enabled the South Africans to progress to the final in Johannesburg, the culmination of which would be the spectacle of Nelson Mandela, clad in a Springbok jersey and cap, presenting the trophy to the winning captain, François Pienaar, in a symbolic gesture of profound significance for the newly post-apartheid home nation. Such is the stature of the French star, whose playing career spanned the transition from the amateur era to professionalism, that President Mandela himself supplied the preface for Benazzi's 2005 autobiography, commenting in the following terms on the player's contribution to the game and thus to its broader impact on the societies in which it is embedded:

> Sport has the power to change the world, because it has the power to inspire human beings. We rarely encounter actions capable of uniting peoples. Sport speaks to youth in a language it understands. It gives birth to hope where, previously, only despair existed. It is stronger than politics and governments in breaking down racial barriers, and in overcoming discrimination and prejudices.[30]

Subsequent events, not least the 2015 terrorist attacks in Paris, inevitably make for some scepticism as regards the transformative potential of even the most inspirational sporting achievements, up to and including the Springboks' apparently transcendent victory for a new 'Rainbow Nation' at Ellis Park in 1995, no less than the triumph of the multicultural French football team at the Stade de France in 1998.

Nevertheless, Benazzi's personal and professional itinerary undoubtedly provided an early indicator of the professionalized French game's emerging openness to diversity regarding both player recruitment and the evolving patterns of identification of its supporters. A native of Oujda in Morocco, Benazzi was talent-spotted by the Cahors club in 1988, before switching to the senior side Agen the following season. As the power-base of the then FFR president, the politically well-connected Albert Ferrasse, the Agen club was ideally placed to facilitate the fast-tracking of the player's naturalization,[31] allowing him to represent France a total of 78 times between 1990 and 2001. In 1997, he was appointed national captain, leading his adopted country to its first Five Nations Grand Slam in a decade. At least as significantly, the choice of Benazzi was far from being a matter of interest only to rugby fans. Ian Borthwick, a New Zealand-born journalist based at *L'Équipe*, captured the mood particularly effectively:

> At a time when the French nation is struggling to come to terms with Le Pen xenophobia and the recent passing of another town – Vitrolles on the Côte d'Azur – into the hands of the National Front, the presence of a Moroccan as captain of France is heavy with symbolism.[32]

The title of Borthwick's English-language piece for *The Independent*, 'A nation places its faith in Benazzi', hints at the primary reason for the particular importance of the player's selection as captain, namely his Muslim religion; while its subtitle 'A captain's talent and strength of character have lifted him above prejudice' also makes clear the real difficulties that Benazzi faced as a pioneering postcolonial presence in the French game:

> Abdelatif Benazzi, son of Zineb and Mohamed, is not only an Arab, but a practising Muslim, and proud of it. [...] Overcoming the racism and distrust which first greeted his arrival in this traditional bastion of French rugby became one of Benazzi's first major victories and now, six years later and with 51 caps to his credit, he has not only risen to the rank of captain of Agen, but also to that of a genuine local hero.[33]

Intended for an Anglophone audience, Borthwick's piece is striking for its tackling head-on of aspects of Benazzi's selection as national captain which French journalists would typically shy away from, preferring the sort of coded allusions which are also to be found in biographies devoted to the player.[34] In the wake of the *Charlie Hebdo* shootings and the November 2015 attacks, Islam and its perceived challenge to the Republican model of integration remain at the top of the political agenda. However, it is noteworthy that the inclusion in the French squad for RWC 2015 of Muslim players such as Rabah Slimani and Algiers-born Sofiane Guitoune, from the Bordeaux-Bègles club, was purely a matter of sporting, rather than sociological, discussion in the French media. This suggests that rugby, in its professionalized incarnation, may finally have joined the country's other major athletic disciplines in demonstrating that 'sports are boundary crossers in ways that few realms of social life are';[35] and, moreover, that this observation is as true of France, and of its oldest and most traditional team game, as it is of any other nation and sporting pursuit in an ever more globalized world.

Notes

1 Sébastien Fleuriel and Joris Vincent, 'A Profound Mutation: The Advent of Professional Rugby in France', *International Journal of the History of Sport*, 24, 1 (2007), 35–48; 35.
2 For a fuller statement of these arguments, see Philip Dine, *French Rugby Football: A Cultural History* (Oxford: Berg, 2001).
3 Adrien Pécout, 'Samedi noir pour le XV de France', *Le Monde*, 17 October 2015. All translations from French-language sources are my own.
4 Bruno Lesprit, 'XV de France: une déroute amère pour Philippe Saint-André', *Le Monde*, 18 October 2015.
5 Gavin Mortimer, 'A World Cup of hope stretches out its hand to France's rich culture', *Guardian*, 18 September 2015. This chapter was also published as 'French find strength in diversity', *Irish Times*, 19 September 2015.
6 Eugen Weber, *Peasants into Frenchmen: The Modernization of Rural France, 1870–1914* (London: Chatto and Windus, 1977).
7 Jeremy Jennings, 'Citizenship, Republicanism and Multiculturalism in Contemporary France', *British Journal of Political Science*, vol. 30 (2000), 575–98; 577.
8 Arthur Berdah, 'Marianne n'a pas de race, pas de couleur, lance Valls à Morano', *Le Figaro*, 30 September 2015.
9 Musée de l'Histoire de l'Immigration, 'Depuis quand la France est-elle une terre d'immigration?', www.histoire-immigration.fr/histoire-de-l-immigration/questions-contemporaines/les-migrations/depuis-quand-la-france-est-elle-une-terre-d-immigration (accessed 4 January 2016).
10 Alex Potter and Georges Duthen, *The Rise of French Rugby* (London: Bailey and Swinfen, 1961), 127–8.
11 On this linkage, see especially Kristin Ross, *Fast Cars, Clean Bodies: Decolonization and the Reordering of French Culture* (Cambridge, MA: MIT Press, 1995).
12 Évelyne Combeau-Mari, *Le sport colonial à Madagascar, 1896–1960* (Paris: Société Française d'Histoire d'Outre-mer, 2009), 193–208.
13 Jean Fabre and Pierre Capdeville, *Rugby: la quatrième mi-temps* (Toulouse: Cépaduès-Éditions, 1999), 36–8; Richard Escot, *Rugby pro: histoires secrètes* (Paris: Solar, 1996), 69–87.
14 For further details on these developments, see Philip Dine and Olivier Nier, '*La Vie en Rose*: Reinventing French Rugby in the Professional Era', in Greg Ryan (ed.), *The Changing Face of Rugby: The Union Game and Professionalism since 1995* (Newcastle: Cambridge Scholars Publishing, 2008), 20–40; also Olivier Nier, 'Les formes de professionnalisation dans le rugby d'élite européen', in Pascal Chantelat (ed.), *La professionnalisation des organisations sportives: nouveaux enjeux, nouveaux débats* (Paris: L'Harmattan, 2001), 221–40; and Olivier Nier, Pascal Chantelat and Jean

Camy, 'Les stratégies identitaires des clubs de rugby de l'élite européenne face à la professionnalisation (1987–1997)', *Science et Motricité*, 50 (2003), 103–25.

15 Arnaud Coudry, 'Perpignan fête le rugby catalan à Barcelone', *Le Figaro*, 8 April 2011.

16 *Le Monde*, 9 September 1998.

17 Cathal Kilcline, 'Representations of Rugby and Resistance in Toulon: from Literary Tradition to Televised Spectacle', *Contemporary French Civilization*, 39, 1 (2014), 93–110.

18 Arnaud Coudry, 'Toulon, la multinationale de la planète ovale', *Le Figaro*, 18 January 2008.

19 Bruno Vigoureux, 'Du délire pour fêter les champions', *L'Équipe*, 1 June 2016.

20 AMV BBDO, 'Jonny Wilkinson: Merci', produced for Guinness and available at www.amvbbdo.com/work/campaign/guinness/rugby/jonny-wilkinson-merci (accessed 4 January 2016).

21 Mortimer, 'A World Cup of hope'.

22 Gavin Mortimer, 'French rugby reacts to Charlie Hebdo tragedy', *Rugby World*, 16 January 2015.

23 Bruno Lesprit, 'Mêlée sociale à Massy', *Le Monde*, 23 January 2015.

24 Ibid.

25 Ibid.

26 Ibid.

27 Mortimer, 'A World Cup of hope'.

28 Ibid.

29 Ibid.

30 Abdel Benazzi, *Une vie à l'essai: autobiographie* (Paris: Flammarion, 2005), preface by Nelson Mandela, 7–8.

31 Michel Gardère, *Abdelatif Benazzi: l'homme aux trois patries: la France, le Maroc, le Rugby* (Paris: La Table Ronde, 1995), 105.

32 Ian Borthwick, 'A Nation Places its Faith in Benazzi', *Independent*, 1 March 1997.

33 Ibid. On the racist abuse endured by Benazzi, from both opponents and team-mates, following his arrival in Agen, see Donald McRae, *Winter Colours: Changing Seasons in World Rugby* (Edinburgh: Mainstream, 1998), 346–8.

34 Gardère, *Abdelatif Benazzi*; Abdelatif Benazzi, with Jean-Charles Delesalle, *Abdelatif Benazzi: la foi du rugby* (Paris: Solar, 2000).

35 Niko Besnier and Susan Brownell, 'Sport, Modernity, and the Body', *Annual Review of Anthropology*, 41 (2012), 444.

4 Cultural diversity in action

Developing and engaging effective responses within rugby union in Australia

Jioji Ravulo

Representation of diverse cultures is evident across the Super Rugby and sevens clubs in Australia, with near to 40 per cent of players identifying as being from a Pacific Island or Maori (NZ) heritage. To support the development and growth of such players, and to foster a greater understanding, awareness and inclusion of diversity in action, strategies have been developed through the Australian Rugby Union (ARU), the Rugby Union Players Association (RUPA) and Western Sydney University (WSU).

Since January 2014, the PATHE@RUPA programme has been implemented across the country, with various activities undertaken to enhance cultural competence in the game. This has included the rollout of cultural awareness training workshops and written resources, the development of Pacific leadership, and the profiling of possible pathways towards further education and training. This chapter will review various aspects of the partnership, taking an overview of the benefits of implementing such a model and its wider impact on the playing community – locally, regionally and globally. Additionally, the ability to enhance social and cultural capital through individual, team and organizational capacity building is explored.

Pacific people in rugby

Representation of Pacific people in rugby continues to create varied discussions globally. With the increased international mobility of players from a Pacific background, rugby clubs and teams around the world are experiencing the prevalence of an ethnic culture that strives to excel in teams sports – but may differ in the way in which Western ideals and perspectives are applied and understood, which in turn requires a more analytical approach to understanding.[1] Pacific players see the importance of engagement in rugby based on a variety of different anticipated outcomes. For some, it can be the sole means to promote social mobility, underpinned by financial gain to support both the individual and the family.[2] But, with this increased movement comes various challenges in the game's ability to address, or first recognize, how cultural difference may impact on a player's welfare and overall wellbeing.[3] For example, the lack of synergy between the ways in which Pacific players respond to expectations facilitated by coaches and playing staff, whilst they try to understand how to balance family and cultural commitments, may cause strain: not just in the team itself, but also across the community.[4]

In Australia, the number of professional players involved in Super Rugby who identify as coming from a Pacific background is growing, with 31 per cent listed in 2012,[5] and trends increasing to between 35 and 40 per cent across some teams. With this Pacific presence, a need to develop the cultural awareness, competency and inclusion across the game to assist all players and staff has become an important part of responding to the cultural context of Pacific players, rather than seeing them solely as a commodity for victory on the field[6] or a racialized cohort fit for labour migration.[7] Traditionally, Pacific players may also experience lower levels of educational achievement during and after their professional involvement, which can perpetuate a lack of positive career transition post-rugby.[8]

The need for cultural diversity inclusion in the professional era

An organization's ability to effectively engage with diversity in its workplace can be underpinned by the way in which it approaches diversity itself. Within a sporting context, 'The culture of sport organisations has typically been one of similarity in which members are expected to adopt a culture reflecting the values and assumptions of the dominant group of heterosexual, able-bodied, White males.'[9] People from diverse backgrounds may be greatly challenged to feel valued for their diverse characteristics, and may in turn feel pressured to assimilate to parochial and ethnocentric expectations, in turn diminishing the ability of staff and players within to experience diversity as valuable.[10] More so, when diversity is witnessed, a lowered tolerance towards overcoming possible challenges in a manner that promotes diverse perspectives and outcomes is also dismissed.[11]

Fink and Pastore suggest the need for sporting organizations to be proactive in their approach to diversity management, that is, offering more than a token gesture or workshop on diversity in their workplace.[12] Proactive diversity management promotes the ability to transform organizational policies and procedures to include differences, and embrace the diversity that currently exists or evolves over time. Striving to also understand deep-level characteristics[13] and features of diversity within a workplace is also an important part of effective and sustainable organizational change. This can include work ethic, spirituality, and personal and social skills.[14] Over time, sporting organizations may also actively recruit and reflect people of diversity in their workforce, rather than rely on external support to inform practices when challenged to adapt to changes brought on by diversity.[15] Flexible sporting organizations that embrace cultural diversity also empower individuals and groups to be autonomous, with a clear vision, expectations and boundaries provided to support the inclusion of difference.[16] In essence, this could include working parties or groups that facilitate the mobilization of effective ideas and strategies to further utilize diversity in action.

There is, therefore, a level of responsibility that should be taken by sporting organizations when it comes to valuing cultural perspectives, and the possible impact this has on an individual's professional aspiration to achieve alongside the subsequent personal pressure to perform. Rather than assume a Pacific player's motivation is individual self-fulfilment,[17] it may be important to understand the underlying cultural context in which a Pacific player is striving to develop a sporting identity whilst balancing family, societal expectations and stereotypes.[18] Various cultural competency programmes have been developed in New Zealand to develop individual and organizational capacity when working with Pacific communities.[19] However, I believe the focus of a sustainable, effective and engaging response needs to also work on developing a shared response to cultural awareness and inclusion – by not just building the capacity of others outside the Pacific community to understand what our shared values and beliefs are, but also for Pacific people to develop a greater understanding and awareness of how to work proactively with dominant Western perspectives and cultures. In essence, this reciprocal approach is based around building shared capacity in Pacific individuals, teams and organizations instead of relying on management within organizations to change exclusively. More so, the notion of Pierre Bourdieu's concept of Habitus – 'an unconscious process where wider culture is imbibed and embodied in individuals, and as a result informs their actions'[20] – can be challenged within a sporting context, promoting scope for changes in how we collectively approach diversity in a more purposeful and meaningful way.

The development of Pacific cultural inclusion in Australia

In 2010, I was approached by the newly appointed Pacific Welfare and Education Officer from the National Rugby League (NRL), Nigel Vagana, to develop a cultural awareness and inclusion training package from my recently completed ethnographic research on Pacific communities. Like rugby union, rugby league has also experienced a large increase in the representation of Pacific players across the game: it has grown to around 45 per cent of team compositions at some clubs. The Pacific Cultural Awareness workshop would be delivered to all Australian-based clubs, and designed for all NRL players and management, administration, coaching and playing staff. Within the presentation, an overview of the five key components that underpin the shared values of Pacific people from across Melanesia, Polynesia (including Maori people) and Micronesia was profiled. Following this, a comparison between Western and Pacific perspectives aims to provide a more practical understanding of some of the intercultural differences that may occur – across educational settings, career and vocational aspirations, financial responsibilities, personal and communication skills, alcohol and other drug usage, and health.

Two variations of the one-hour interactive workshop were developed, one for players, and the other for staff, with each presentation starting with Pacific values and intercultural difference. The format for players continued by gaining their feedback about how they could support each other and what additional resources the club could provide to celebrate cultural diversity. The staff presentation profiled the players' feedback for review and implementation, followed by an overview of key topics they could use to build a level of professional rapport with Pacific players. Over the following two years, the workshop was implemented, and received positive feedback from participants.

I then transitioned to an academic role at Western Sydney University in mid-2011, and Pasifika Achievement To Higher Education (PATHE) was created soon afterwards to promote the development of pathways towards further education and training in Pacific communities. My desire to see more Pasifika people engaged in striving for educational achievement came from an ongoing negative trend, where Pacific youth were not seeing the importance of further study to underpin other life successes. As a result, Pacific youth would participate in low-skilled employment, decreasing opportunities for social mobility as they got older. Mainly focussed on the area of Greater Western Sydney, where the largest cohort of Pacific people in Australia reside, PATHE strives to

- promote course retention, progression and completion for Pacific students currently enrolled in university
- outreach to primary and high schools to develop vocational and career aspirations amongst Pacific youth and families, and
- create sustainable resources and options through innovative projects, including engagement with Pacific parents and families.

Funded by the Office of Widening Participation within Western Sydney University via the Higher Education Participation and Partnerships Programme (HEPPP) grants provided by the federal government, the PATHE initiative continued this endeavour to increase Pacific cultural awareness and inclusion across various groups and stakeholders.

In late 2013, Rosemary Towner (National Player Development Manager – NPDM) and Greg Harris (CEO) from RUPA approached me to develop a partnership to further increase capacity across the game in working effectively with Pacific players and their families. After their consultation with Pacific players across the five Australian-based Super Rugby clubs and the national team, funding was sourced from the Collective Bargaining Agreement (CBA) negotiations to employ a part-time worker from January 2014 to December 2015. Capitalizing on the successes and positive reputation of PATHE, the PATHE@ RUPA initiative was created, formalizing a shared arrangement between Western Sydney University and RUPA to build cultural awareness, competency and inclusion in rugby union.

Programme model: PATHE@RUPA

In developing the specific model for the programme, considerations were made on how to work in complement with the existing Player Development Managers (PDMs), also funded by RUPA to work within each Australian

Super Rugby club. These roles were established to support the educational and welfare needs of players. To reflect a similar approach within a Pacific context, whilst also expanding the overall strategy on being culturally responsive and inclusive, the Cultural Diversity Development Manager (CDDM) was established as the key role under the PATHE@RUPA initiative. Moera Sakimi, who was previously employed as the first PATHE project officer in 2012, transitioned into this role. As a qualified social worker, and also from a Pacific background, the professional capacity, competency and skill set of the incumbent CDDM was imperative to developing and engaging effective responses.

In its initial stage of development, the PATHE@RUPA model was ideally constructed to have a similar three-pronged approach to PATHE, with a view to promote access, awareness and engagement of vocational aspirations for Pacific players whilst enhancing cultural competency and inclusion across the game.

1 Player support

From the previous work undertaken by PATHE, to the various trends associated with a professional sporting career, Pacific players had been less likely to participate in further education and training options. With the opportunity for professional players to access additional funds to assist in the enrolment and completion of study, the CDDM works with Pacific players individually to map and develop goals towards possible pathways. For Pacific players already engaged in study, this provided further opportunities to encourage completion amongst playing commitments, whilst providing such players with an opportunity to share their successes with other Pacific players with a view to encourage educational achievement.

However, player support also goes beyond nominating career aspirations – specific strategies are also developed to assist the underlying social and welfare needs of professional Pacific players. As the project is premised on a cultural context, the CDDM is also responsible for providing a case management approach to understanding the psychosocial wellbeing of the individual player, and the significant role family can play for a Pacific person. An initial assessment is undertaken when first meeting the player, highlighting possible issues alongside tangible solutions within a strength-based framework.

Through this component of player support, Pacific players are given the opportunity to feel valued for their prevalence in the game, whilst participating in service provision that strives to understand the cultural context in which they live. Further engagement with other support people in the club is also achieved by the CDDM liaising with, and empowering, PDMs and other team employees, such as medical and coaching staff, to approach Pacific players effectively. In turn, this promotes value around their contribution, as both an individual and a team member, in increasing cultural awareness and inclusion beyond an initial cultural awareness workshop.

2 Outreach

Within this component, we endeavour to build team and organizational capacity to embrace cultural awareness and inclusion. The Pacific Cultural Awareness workshop discussed above is a key feature to setting this tone for Super Rugby clubs and other stakeholders within the ARU. I personally travelled to each Super Rugby club and sevens squad (both male and female) across Australia to provide this workshop: first to the player cohort, followed by the coaching, management and administration staff. As the presentation was rolled out, scenarios specific to Pacific players being involved in rugby were further discussed, enhancing the practical nature of the presentation for both Pacific and non-Pacific people. Feedback from all players formed strategies for clubs to implement change that further promoted an ongoing commitment to diversity in action.

As a result of feedback collected during these workshops, and further enhanced by follow-up consultations specifically undertaken with Pacific players by the CDDM and NPDM, various leadership groups amongst Pacific players were formed to support the development of new knowledge and insight on what is expected when playing at an elite level. This form of peer mentoring, which may generally occur between a senior and a junior player, also broke down perceived barriers from young players who at first found it difficult to approach an older, more established and respected player, even from a cultural perspective between Pacific players. In forming this relationship, both players share their journeys, both professionally and personally, in navigating through the complexities of being an elite rugby player, whilst overcoming any challenges that come up. Additionally, this sense of collegiality assists young players to develop greater confidence in accessing other supports within the club, and to communicate more effectively due to their developing confidence in being and feeling included for their diversity.

3 Projects

Additional projects are developed to complement the first two components, which will promote the sustainability and impact of the programme. These include resources that further assist individuals, teams and organizational structures across rugby union in Australia. Such projects have been created to respond proactively to cultural diversity, and to further enhance inclusive approaches. An example is the set of Pacific grief and loss fact sheets. This was born out of feedback from non-Pacific staff interacting with Pacific players, who take leaves of absence from training and playing commitments to undertake cultural and family obligations related to the loss of a family member. The fact sheets provide a cultural context to Pacific protocols, whilst also providing practical strategies on how best to support players during these times.

A follow-up cultural awareness and inclusion workshop was developed to further explore other key Pacific concepts related to rugby, which also helps to leverage our desire to support ongoing conversations in the game about cultural diversity. This strategy emanates from the need for culturally inclusive practices of to continue the work on evolving knowledge in order to support the progress of individual, team and organization cultural capacity and competency.

Another project within this programme component is the whole of game approach to working with the ARU on their Pacific programme targeting the development of younger Pacific players. The project was pioneered by another Pacific staff member employed by the ARU, Manu Sutherland, who continues to work closely in developing respective knowledge directly within management to further assist in Pacific cultural approaches. The relationship between the work of PATHE@RUPA and that being undertaken by the governing body of rugby union in Australia highlights a shared effort in cultural inclusion, rather than working in silos that can perpetuate a lack of synergy and connection across the wider game.

Programme outcomes

Overall, each component operated in context of the larger vision of promoting a better understanding of cultural difference and how it can exist within an inter-cultural framework. Rather than diminish cultural difference as a barrier, the PATHE@RUPA programme is enabling professional sporting organizations to acknowledge the importance of collegiality through diversity.

Feedback from players, club staff and management continues to inform the delivery of the model, which is recorded in quarterly progress reports to ensure anticipated outcomes are achieved. Monthly supervision is also provided to the CDDM, to ensure professional practice and support for individual work with players is maintained within respective standards.

Enhancement of individual, team and organizational capacity has occurred through vocational planning for Pacific players, who are starting to increase their rate of participation in further education and training. Confidence in being able to access other support and resources is also supporting the endeavour to promote holistic responses to Pacific player welfare. Levels of interpersonal communication skills for Pacific players, who may at times come across as being reserved and withdrawn, and the confidence to approach people when needing additional support, have improved.

> I actually really enjoyed the cultural presentation. Speaking with a few of the boys since then also they have definitely learnt a lot from it. Especially socially and when in a working context how to address some of the more 'shy' Island boys. It gave a lot of insight into other areas and feedback within the group is that it is definitely worthwhile.
>
> (International/Super Rugby player)

Empowerment of Pacific and other culturally diverse players to feel valued for their difference is evident. Localized leadership initiatives in clubs are helping both Pacific and non-Pacific players to develop a stronger relationship, in which clubs are feeling more confident to respond to needs. Broader contribution to strategies that are also being developed in local clubs to assist in implementing the recommendations made by players during the Pacific Cultural Awareness workshop further supports deep-level engagement and purposeful connections.

> We will continue to uphold commitment to speaking/acknowledging/understanding diversity through cultural awareness training and reflection. To reflect cultural perspectives we will continue to support individuals and players to seek further support from staff. As a team we will factor in other religious commitments when needed.
>
> (Head coach – Super Rugby club)

Effective engagement through sustainable resources, which are being profiled across the wider game, is further evidence of organizational impact. With the development of new cultural workshop material and the ongoing use of cultural specific fact sheets on protocols, clubs are gaining momentum in creating other internal strategies to promote cultural inclusion. The Australian Rugby Union also continues to promote the need to work collaboratively, from Pacific resources being shared with coaches based in local communities, to elite Level 3 coaches striving to also gain a sound insight into working with cultural differences.

> I've sat in a number of PI presentations ... Jioji's presentation is by far the most effective in identifying those points of difference.
>
> (ARU staff member)

Concluding remarks and future possibilities

I have greatly enjoyed my contribution to rugby in Australia through the development of cultural awareness and inclusive practice approaches. The genuine and positive feedback received on the impact this continues to have on individuals, teams and organizations supports ongoing fervour to maintain such strategies. I am still pleasantly surprised by the willingness of both Pacific and non-Pacific players and staff to engage in conversations I hope will be continued by a real commitment to seeing the world beyond a monoculture lens. It is imperative that we maintain this commitment to cultural awareness and inclusivity to further enhance both off- and on-field performance.

Our need to provide a voice for Pacific players, who at times are personally challenged to remain in their countries of origin, or strive to succeed overseas, is important. This programme is providing a possible platform for Pacific players to be taken more seriously when it comes to overcoming transitional barriers when they move within or to Australia. However, more practical work needs to be done globally to truly understand the impact migration for rugby can have not just on the individual Pacific player, but on the family they desperately strive to maintain a connection with as part of their personal and cultural identity.

With such success achieved from enhancing social and cultural capital through initiatives such as PATHE@RUPA, there is now interest across the United Kingdom and Europe in implementing a similar programme, as they too continue to benefit from increasing Pacific mobility to that part of the world. I hope that this chapter can provide further support on the positive impact cultural differences can have in a game that embraces an international and professional identity.

Notes

1 P. Horton, 'Pacific Islanders in Global Rugby – A Growing Wave', *The International Journal of the History of Sport*, 31, 11 (2014), 1329–31.
2 N. Besnier, 'Pacific Island Rugby: Histories, Mobilities, Comparisons', *Asia Pacific Journal of Sport and Social Science* 3, 3 (2014), 268–76; P. Horton, 'Pacific Islanders in Global Rugby: The Changing Currents of Sports Migration', *The International Journal of the History of Sport*, 29, 17 (2012), 2388–404.
3 Y. Kanemasu and G. Molnar, 'Collective Identity and Contested Allegiance: A Case of Migrant Professional Fijian Rugby Players', *Sport in Society: Cultures, Commerce, Media, Politics*, 16, 7 (2013), 863–82.
4 G. Mumm and D. O'Connor, 'The Motivational Profile of Professional Male Fijian Rugby Players and Their Perceptions of Coaches' and Managers' Cultural Awareness', *Asia Pacific Journal of Sport and Social Science*, 3, 3 (2014), 202–21.
5 Rugby Union Players' Association, 'Cultural Diversity Program: Meet Moera Sakimi', *RUPA News* (2014). Retrieved 12 November 2015: www.rupa.com.au/news/archive/cultural-diversity-program-meet-moera-sakimi.
6 A. Grainger, 'From Immigrant to Overstayer: Samoan Identity, Rugby, and Cultural Politics of Race and Nation in Aotearoa/New Zealand', *Journal of Sport and Social Issues*, 30, 1 (2006), 45–61.
7 B. McDonald, 'Developing "Home-Grown" Talent: Pacific Island Rugby Labour and the Victorian Rugby Union', *The International Journal of the History of Sport* 31, 11 (2014), 1332–44.
8 L. Rodriguez and B. McDonald, 'After the Whistle: Issues Impacting on the Health and Wellbeing of Polynesian Players Off the Field', *Asia-Pacific Journal of Health, Sport and Physical Education*, 4, 3 (2013), 201–15.
9 A. Doherty, 'Managing Cultural Diversity in Sport Organizations: A Theoretical Perspective', *Journal of Sport Management*, 13 (1999), 288.
10 Ibid., 280–97.
11 Ibid.
12 J.S. Fink and D.L. Pastore, 'Diversity in Sport ? Utilizing the Business Literature to Devise a Comprehensive Framework of Diversity Initiatives', *Quest*, 51 (1999), 310–27.
13 G.B. Cunningham and J.S. Fink, 'Diversity Issues in Sport and Leisure', *Journal of Sport Management*, 20 (2006), 455–65.
14 Ibid.
15 C.M. Hanlon and D.J. Coleman, 'Recruitment and Retention of Culturally Diverse People by Sport and Active Recreation Clubs', *Managing Leisure*, 11, 2 (2006), 77–95.
16 A. Doherty, J. Fink, S. Inglis and D. Pastore, 'Understanding a Culture of Diversity through Frameworks of Power and Change', *Sport Management Review*, 13, 4 (2010), 368–81.
17 M. Schaaf, 'Elite Pacific Male Rugby Players' Perceptions and Experiences of Professional Rugby', *Junctures*, 7 (December 2006), 41–54. Retrieved 26 October 2016: www.junctures.org/index.php/junctures/article/viewFile/96/101.

18 G. Henning Presterudstuen, 'The Mimicry of Men: Rugby and Masculinities in Post-colonial Fiji', *The Global Studies Journal*, 3, 2 (2010), 237–47; P. Horton, 'Pacific Islanders in Professional Rugby football: Bodies, Minds and Cultural Continuities', *Asia Pacific Journal of Sport and Social Science*, December 2014, 1–14; B. McDonald and L. Rodriguez, '"It's Our Meal Ticket": Pacific Bodies, Labour and Mobility in Australia', *Asia Pacific Journal of Sport and Social Science*, 3, 3 (2014), 236–49.
19 J. Tiatia, *Pacific Cultural Competencies – A Literature Review* (Wellington: New Zealand Ministry of Health, 2008).
20 P.J. Kitchin and P. David Howe, 'How Can the Social Theory of Pierre Bourdieu Assist Sport Management Research?' *Sport Management Review*, 16, 2 (2013), 128.

5 Rugby union and Māori culture in Aotearoa/New Zealand 1995–2015

Farah Rangikoepa Palmer

Māori, the *tangata whenua* (indigenous people) of Aotearoa (New Zealand), have played a key part in how rugby union has developed in New Zealand during the process of colonisation, the formative years as a nation, during the game's amateur era and most recently during its professional era (1995–2015). Several historical accounts of New Zealand rugby and society refer to the influence Māori involvement had on the development of the game, the early years of Māori rugby, and in particular the role Māori rugby teams have played in reinforcing imaginary discourses around friendly race relations in New Zealand, an egalitarian ethos in rugby union, and evidence of Māori success in New Zealand society (Hokowhitu, 2005, 2009; Mulholland, 2009; Ryan, 1993).

Since the professionalisation of rugby union in the 1990s there has also been renewed interest in how the Māori rugby team (known officially since 2012 as the Māori All Blacks) and Māori symbols and rituals (such as the haka) have impacted on team culture, national identity, mega-sport events and branding (e.g. Falcous, 2007; Hapeta & Palmer, 2014; Hokowhitu & Scherer, 2008; Jackson & Hokowhitu, 2002). Predominantly Māori scholars have also examined what impact the game of rugby union has had on Māori aspirations, identity, wellbeing and culture (e.g. Erueti & Palmer, 2014; Hirini & Flett, 1999; Palmer & Adair, 2012). What this literature suggests is that over time, Māori rugby has been considered as either a *taonga* (treasure) to cherish, a burden to bear or a racist institution to abolish. For now the popular discourse is that the Māori All Blacks are of value to New Zealand rugby, to sponsors, to national pride and to the *mana* (prestige) of Māori as a people (Palmer, 2007; Te Puni Kōkiri, 2005; Watson, 2007). In 2014, for instance, the Māori All Blacks won Team of the Year at the Māori Sports Awards, and Māori rugby players such as Aaron Smith and Nehe Milner-Skudder are acknowledged regionally, nationally and internationally as highly capable athletes, leaders and role models. As Hokowhitu (2005) suggested ten years ago, rugby continues to be one of a few respected institutions where Māori are able to compete alongside *Pākehā* (New Zealand citizens of European descent) on what is presented as an 'even playing-field' (p. 90).

This chapter explores what role Māori rugby and in particular the Māori All Blacks play in the professional era. Who or what benefits from their existence?

What are some of the potential benefits and costs of recognising a racially selected team nationally and internationally? Do the Māori All Blacks contribute to the aspirations of Māori, New Zealand, the New Zealand Rugby Union (NZRU), sponsors and indigenous development?

Māori involvement in rugby during the professional era

Hokowhitu (2005) highlighted how early Māori rugby represented 're-imagined' *tino rangatiratanga* (self-determination), *mana* (prestige) building and re-masculinising of Māori manhood at a time when these were under threat. Does Māori rugby in the professional era still stand for these re-imagined benefits? In 2013, fewer than 15 per cent of New Zealand's population identified their ethnicity as Māori, 75 per cent as European, 11.8 per cent as Asian and 7.4 per cent as Pacific (Statistics New Zealand, 2013). This breakdown of ethnic groups is pertinent because of the 150,000 players registered in New Zealand rugby in 2014, 24 per cent of all players and 28 per cent of elite players identified as Māori. In 2015 there were 233 Māori players involved in the high performance programme. What this suggests is that Māori are highly invested and involved in New Zealand rugby at both the community and high performance levels, with a high conversion rate from amateur to professional rugby.

The Māori All Blacks – a high-performance team worth supporting?

Up until the end of 2015 the Māori team had won 305 of their 438 games, giving them a 69 per cent winning percentage. Their success rate has improved since the start of the professional era, and between 1994 and 2004 they lost only four of their 26 games (84 per cent win rate) which included wins against England, Argentina, Scotland and Fiji but also losses against Australia and the New Zealand Barbarians. Since 1995 the Māori team have regularly played against Pacific Island teams (Samoa, Fiji, Tonga) and Australia, participated in several Churchill Cup tournaments in Canada, had an historic win against the British and Irish Lions in 2005, replaced the Junior All Blacks in the Pacific Nations Cup in 2008 (only to be replaced by them a year later), played international and club teams on several occasions, and recently toured North America (2013) and Japan (2014).

Hokowhitu and Scherer (2008) argue that the value of the Māori rugby team has changed during the professional era because the team has been commodified to support the commercial imperatives of the New Zealand Rugby Union (NZRU), now branded as New Zealand Rugby (NZR). During this period, major sponsorship deals between NZRU and Adidas (since 1999) as well as AIG (since 2012) provided a mutually beneficial tripartite relationship between the sponsors (AIG and Adidas), the organisation (NZRU) and predominantly the All Blacks brand. Since 2012 the Māori team have also directly benefitted from these sponsoring relationships.

It is no coincidence, for instance, that the Māori team were rebranded as the Māori All Blacks in 2012, the same year that AIG announced they would sponsor the All Blacks and five other high-performance rugby teams (including the Māori team) under the auspices of New Zealand Rugby. When the partnership between AIG and the NZRU was announced, NZRU Chief Executive Steve Tew stated that the AIG sponsorship was 'the best option to sustain the future of New Zealand rugby and grow the global game' (AllBlacks.com, 2012). Bob Benmosche, AIG President and Chief Executive Officer, explained that associating the AIG brand with the legendary All Blacks and the other highly competitive and successful New Zealand Rugby Union teams was about aligning the attributes of these teams, such as a winning tradition and reputation for tenacity, integrity and performance, to attributes in AIG's own culture. Furthermore, AIG New Zealand Chief Executive Cris Knell indicated that AIG wanted to see the national teams play in new territories but explained they 'would never put the All Blacks up against a tier two nation. But I would love to see the Māori All Blacks play against someone like Japan, and that's something within our grasp' (see Hurley, 2012).

Other sponsors of the Māori All Blacks team have included the Bank of New Zealand (BNZ) from 2012 to 2014 and Aotearoa Fisheries Ltd/Sealord since 2010. They too benefit from the association, but their relationship is often subsumed by the major global sponsors, who expect more from their relationship with the Māori All Blacks, which includes their logo on the jerseys, but also an intimate relationship between the organisation, their staff, community-based initiatives and key stakeholders. This often involves cultural exchanges, as well as opportunities to mix and mingle with the team and learn more about their Māori values and practices such as the *haka*.

The haka in Māori rugby

Ever since the Natives team of 1888–89 introduced a haka (as well as the black jersey and the silver fern) to New Zealand rugby, rugby and things Māori have entered into a relationship that has varied between tumultuous and enamoured, especially when it comes to the haka (Hokowhitu, 2009). The form of haka most often associated with pre-game rituals in New Zealand rugby are war posture dances used to awaken the fighting spirit of the warrior (player), which is encapsulated by the saying '*kia kōrero te katoa o te tinana*', meaning 'the whole body should speak'.

During the professional era there have been several examples of the haka being commodified, exploited, misappropriated and sometimes resisted. Jackson and Hokowhitu (2002) examined the influence global forces have on local cultures via media technology by referring to the 'Adidasification' of the All Blacks and commodification of the haka. They concluded that new global technology is the saviour and enemy of indigenous culture because it is always seeking new signs and fresh cultural territory where nothing is sacred. Motion *et al.* (2003) examined the process of establishing a viable co-branded identity within a sponsorship relationship by examining the relationship between Adidas and the All Blacks during the 1999 Rugby World Cup (RWC) campaign. They examined television advertisements that embodied values and symbols associated with the All Blacks, which included a Māori warrior performing the haka. Motion *et al.* (2003) acknowledged that at an ideological level, this advertisement could be perceived as an example of cultural imperialism, but they also acknowledged that the subtle placement of logos, and emotional themes evoked, strengthened the articulation embodied by the All Blacks–Adidas co-brand within the discourse of national identity. It seems that when Māori symbols and rituals are used for purposes of national pride and identity, it is acceptable – but acceptable to whom?

The new haka (Kapa o Pango) performed occasionally by the All Blacks since 2006 was unacceptable to some for including a controversial throat-slitting gesture. Springbok coach Peter de Villiers claimed he was losing respect for the haka, which he felt was being over-exposed during RWC 2011 (see Watson, 2011) and several organisations, teams and spectators challenge the 'right' of the All Blacks, the Māori All Blacks and other New Zealand sports teams to perform the haka, which they perceive to give New Zealand teams an unfair advantage psychologically and physically (see Paul, 2014). What these scenarios highlight is, as Jackson and Hokowhitu (2002) conclude, that maintaining authority over representations of indigenous and other cultures is increasingly difficult in the professional era. One team that some would argue ideologically and culturally should have authority to represent Māori culture is the Māori All Blacks.

A significant moment in the recent history of the Māori team was their performance of the *Timatanga haka* introduced in 2001 and composed by team *kaumātua* (elder) Whetu Tipiwai (who has since passed away). The *Timatanga* (beginning) haka recounts the Māori view of creation from the void (the nothingness and the darkness) to what we have at the present (enlightenment) – namely a Māori rugby team idealistically representing Māori and New Zealand from the four winds (directions) of Aotearoa/New Zealand. Other aspects of *tikanga Māori* (Māori culture) are also incorporated into the symbols, artefacts, protocols, rituals and spaces associated with the team, which will be discussed in more detail later in this chapter.

Celebrating Māori rugby

Another special moment in the recent history of Māori rugby was the centenary games and celebrations in 2010. After scrapping the NZ Māori programme in favour of the Junior All Blacks in 2009, the NZRU was under pressure from Māori stakeholders to reinstate the team for 2010, a year that also happened to mark the centenary year of the NZRU-sanctioned Māori team that first played in 1910. After confirming test games would take place, the NZ Māori Rugby Board (NZMRB) and NZRU proceeded to invite past players and their *whānau* (extended family) to luncheons and games hosted in Whangarei, Rotorua and Napier. As if sticking to the script, the Māori team won all three games against the New Zealand Barbarians, Ireland and England, providing an excellent platform for provincial players such as Aaron Smith (incumbent All Black half back) to demonstrate their skill in front of Super Rugby and All Black selectors. It also provided a platform for the Māori community and rugby stakeholders to acknowledge the rich and varied history and stories associated with Māori rugby that evoked emotions of pride and elation as well as of sorrow and regret.

Māori rugby as a political tool

Perhaps as a result of heightened media attention, the significance of the year 2010 to Māori rugby stakeholders, and the coinciding publication of a book on the history of Māori rugby by the politically savvy Malcolm Mulholland (2009) titled *Beneath the Māori Moon*, the call for an apology to Māori players excluded from tours to South Africa during its Apartheid regime started to be roused (Bidwell, 2010). Initially, the NZRU did not respond immediately or favourably to such a request, which only intensified demands. Eventually the New Zealand and South African rugby unions caved in to public and international pressure and apologised to Māori players who were excluded from All Black teams touring South Africa in 1928, 1949 and 1960. As a postscript to the apology, however, the NZRU explained that it had not apologised earlier because of advice from the NZMRB that it would be inappropriate to be critical of Apartheid-era decisions made in particular by Māori administrators.

The role of Māori culture in mega-sport events

A year later, RWC 2011, hosted in New Zealand, provided Māori culture and initiatives with exposure to a captive international audience. Māori symbolism and cultural elements were incorporated into several aspects of the tournament, including advertising, promotions and the opening ceremony. There were over 200 public events and projects with strong Māori content spread across all 15 host regions throughout the country. For instance, the Waka Māori pavilion on the Auckland waterfront, the New Zealand Rugby exhibition titled 'Ake Ake Kia Kaha: The Spirit of Māori', and free-to-air coverage of games on Māori Television provided real focal points for the Māori contribution to this mega-sport event and surrounding activities. Ironically, although Māori culture played a dominant role in representing a distinct image of New Zealand identity to a worldwide audience, the resources necessary to make RWC 2011 a success on and off the field meant that the Māori rugby team had no games or tours that year. This raises once again the question, 'Who benefits from Māori culture and a Māori rugby team and when?'

Māori rugby – a site for *tino rangatiratanga* and *mana*?

Hokowhitu (2005) suggests that rugby is a site of cultural resistance fraught with contradictions in the postcolonial and neocolonial world, where Māori both gain and lose *mana* (prestige and power):

... the notion of a nationalistic New Zealand Māori team runs counter to New Zealand's egalitarian ethos, yet the control of the New Zealand Māori under the auspices of the NZRFU has left little room for it to be a tool for *tino rangatiratanga.*

(Hokowhitu, 2005, p. 89)

The NZMRB for instance, is largely an advisory board to the New Zealand Rugby Union (NZRU) Board. The NZMRB has limited power in decision-making and allocation of resources, especially with regard to the Māori All Blacks. The paternal relationship between the two boards is best represented by the alignment of the NZMRB's vision to the NZRU vision, which is 'inspiring and unifying New Zealanders' (NZMRB Annual Report, 2015). A Māori flavour is added to this vision by including a well-known *whakataukī* (proverb) with regard to collective *mana*: '*Ehara taku toa, i te toa takitahi; engari taku toa, te toa takitini*', which translates as 'It is not through the strength of one, but of many, that we will succeed.' Thus the NZMRB is 'committed to making an effective and valued contribution to New Zealand rugby through its parent body, NZ Rugby' and functions 'to promote the game of rugby at all levels amongst Māori and to be guardians of *tikanga* Māori [Māori culture and customs] for NZ Rugby' (NZMRB Annual Report, 2014, 2015).

The fluctuating status of the Māori All Blacks and the NZMRB illustrates how power struggles play out in the increasingly businesslike approach taken in New Zealand rugby. Hokowhitu and Scherer (2008), for instance, argue that in the era of multinationalism, the Māori All Blacks have largely become a farm team for the All Blacks. They base this claim on the coinciding periods of selection, games and tours for both teams (i.e. during the windows for international rugby fixtures in June and November) and suggest that those players who are next in line for the All Blacks are kept match-fit and within the sights of All Black selectors through playing for the Māori All Blacks.

To some extent, this is an accurate claim, considering Christian Cullen's controversial inclusion in the Māori team in 2003 (when he had never previously played for the team or publicly identified as Māori (Hokowhitu & Scherer, 2008) – many saw it as a desperate attempt to get international rugby exposure and regain his lost form and, subsequently, a position in the All Black 2003 World Cup squad), the chopping and changing of support for the Junior All Blacks and Māori All Blacks to represent New Zealand rugby in the Pacific Nations Cup between 2008 and 2009, and the observation that three new caps in the 2016 All Black squad (Elliot Dixon, Liam Squire and Damian McKenzie) were selected for the Māori All Blacks in the previous two seasons while two players from the New Zealand Barbarians team (Ofa Tu'ungafasi and Seta Tamanivalu) who faced the Māori All Blacks in 2015 were also named as new caps in the June 2016 All Black squad. This suggests that arranging high-performance games (such as the Māori All Blacks versus the New Zealand Barbarians) does give selectors another chance to compare players on the verge of All Black selection, and gives players the chance to impress. Players, coaches and administrators are also aware of this privileged pathway, which can create resentment but also appreciation. Ian MacRae, New Zealand Rugby President, reiterated this in the 2014 Māori All Blacks Media Guide when he stated that the Japan Tour 'provides players from both sides with valuable exposure to international rugby'. Head Coach for the Māori team in 2010, Jamie Joseph, explained that playing against international teams gave 'players the chance to really make their mark' (*Sydney Morning Herald*, 2010); and Colin Cooper, who took over the role in 2013, stated in 2016 that

> Having the Maori All Blacks as a key part of the high-performance pathway to other honours has been a great motivator for players.... Seeing them named as All Blacks is a great recognition of what the Maori All Blacks bring.
>
> (Planet Rugby, 2016)

Māori players interviewed by the author in 2014 expressed awareness of how much being selected for the team meant to members of their *whānau*, which created a sense of pride in being a Māori All Black for them:

> I just always wanted to play for this team. And my family wanted me to. This is probably the All Blacks for them.
>
> When I told her [his partner] that I got selected she screamed and then I told my dad and my little sister. And I think I could see a little bit of a tear from Dad, him being so proud.
>
> It's how much it means to Māori people to represent them ... every year I've left I am sort of glad I can represent a group of people like that, and how much it means to them.

So, the value of the Māori team to New Zealand Rugby, to sponsors and to the *whānau* of players has been presented loud and clear. Is there still room for the Māori team to challenge the status quo with regard to race relations in New Zealand?

Hokowhitu (2009) examined modern Māori rugby through the lens of decolonial subversion to determine whether rugby had the capacity to disrupt dominant discourses surrounding race in New Zealand. He concluded that the subversive element of Māori rugby has historically been reflected through creativity and 'unorthodox play', but that this aspect of Māori rugby has recently been domesticated, lain latent and reconfigured to oppress (Hokowhitu, 2009, p. 2315). It could be argued, however, that the unorthodox and creative style of play associated with Māori rugby and embodied by the Māori All Blacks in the professional era is still valued by New Zealand Rugby and its stakeholders. During the 2010 Māori Rugby Centenary celebrations, for instance, Jamie Joseph, then the team's Head Coach, stated that the games against teams such as Ireland and England would give players the chance to 'play the style of rugby the New Zealand Māori team is famous for' (*Sydney Morning Herald*, 2010). More recently, in the Māori All Blacks 2014 Tour to Japan Media Guide, the New Zealand Rugby President, Ian MacRae, highlighted that internationally there is a 'huge appetite to see the exciting style of rugby for which the Māori All Blacks are famous' (p. 2), a statement that rang true when more than 20,000 spectators filled stadiums in Kobe and Tokyo to see the 'men in black jerseys' playing against the Brave Blossoms (Japan).

Spectator surveys were conducted during these two games by Professor Makoto Nakazawa and his students from the University of Tsukuba. The respondents associated New Zealand with rugby, Māori, Kiwi and outdoor activities (in that order). Sixty-three per cent of the Kobe respondents and 69 per cent of those in Tokyo were fans of the All Blacks, and slightly fewer (53.2 per cent in Kobe and 58.6 per cent in Tokyo) were fans of the Māori All Blacks, whom they associated with the haka, a strong team and New Zealand. Commonalities between the two nations mentioned by participants included being island nations, the natural environment, politeness, rugby, earthquakes, tradition and pride (World in Union (New Zealand): Rugby Conference 2017, forthcoming). What this demonstrates is the close association between the All Blacks and the Māori All Blacks, and between New Zealand, rugby and Māori.

Māori rugby tours – connecting and commodifying the Māori rugby brand to an international market

The Māori All Blacks tour to Japan in 2014 gave the NZRU and its sponsors an opportunity to display their co-brand to a new international market 'up close and personal'. Māori culture played a significant part in this through strategic use of stories and symbols associated with the haka, the jersey, the team culture, the history of Māori and Māori rugby, and the Māori style of play. In collaboration with senior Māori players, Adidas enlisted the help of renowned Māori artist Dave Burke, the team's *kaumātua*, Luke Crawford, and Rugby Development Manager of New Zealand Rugby Māori Tiki Edwards, to deliver a design that not only showcased authentic Māori images and stories, but also paid respect to traditional Māori and Japanese cultures. The black of the jersey represented the beginnings (*Te Kore*) of Māori and Japanese cultures. The spiral patterns (*Takarangi*) on the shoulders represent growing out of the darkness and descending down the *whakapapa* (genealogy) lines from the godly realm (*Te Ara Poutama*) into two *manaia* (guardian figures) on the *puku* (stomach) region. These *manaia* deliver to the players traditional weapons in the form of a *taiaha* and a samurai blade. The weapons urge the player wearing the jersey to give of their very best in the task they have before them on the field. Burke stated, 'we wanted to show our Japanese friends that we're very similar. Part of the design pays tribute to Maori moko art form and its similarity to Japanese culture and rituals around body tattooing' (Stuff, 2014).

Does Māori rugby benefit Māori players and society?

Durie (2003) affirms that access to the Māori world is imperative to foster a secure Māori identity, but warns that it still remains a relative impossibility for many Māori. The latest New Zealand Census results (Statistics New Zealand, 2013), for instance, suggested that more than half of Māori (53.5 per cent) identified with two or more ethnic groups, compared with 46.5 per cent who identified with Māori only. Māori was the only major ethnic group in which people were more likely to identify with two or more major ethnic groups than with just one. The Māori All Blacks tend to reflect this range of experiences with regard to cultural influences during their upbringing, as revealed in interviews with the author during their tour of Japan in 2014:

> We lived with our Pākehā dad so we kind of left the Māori culture behind … it's one of the things I wish I could go back on … getting a bit more Māori influence and learning about the culture.
>
> I wouldn't say we were brought up Māori, but my grandad was quite proud. It's one of those things you don't realise how much it means to other people until you make the team and someone tells you about it.
>
> I had *te reo* [Māori language] the majority of my life and especially with being around that *kapa haka* [Māori performing arts] environment. All the practices were at a *marae*, pretty much grew up on the *marae* [traditional meeting house].

The rhetoric surrounding the Māori team as something 'for Māori', however, is constantly under threat (Hokowhitu & Scherer, 2008). The existence of the team relies on gaining support (and funding) from New Zealand Rugby and its sponsors. There is always a sense among the players, therefore, that there is no certainty with regard to the future of Māori rugby, as expressed by one player during the 2014 Japan tour:

> I had to ask my coach if I could go on tour, and one of the big things for me is that the Māori programme isn't set in stone so we don't know what's going to happen in the future. This might be my only opportunity to play.

There have been some studies suggesting that the Māori rugby team can be a tool for reaffirming and strengthening Māori identity and wellbeing by providing those involved in rugby with access to the Māori world. Hirini and Flett (1999), for example, surveyed the 1999 Māori rugby team, a high-profile group of Māori men, to determine how strong their cultural identity as 'Māori' was. By using self-identification, *whakapapa* (genealogy), *marae* participation (participation with ancestral meeting house), *whānau* associations, *whenua tipu* (sacred lands), contact with Māori people, and use/knowledge of Māori language as cultural indicators, the survey brought some interesting findings to light:

- 95 per cent of the players identified as Māori, but only 42 per cent described themselves as Māori.
- 90 per cent could identify two or more generations of *whakapapa*, and had been to a *marae* at least a few times in the past year.

- 58 per cent knew Māori at a very basic level.
- 42 per cent had good knowledge of *marae tikanga*.
- 21 per cent had a secure Māori profile.
- 10 per cent had a notional or compromised Māori profile.
- 26 per cent experienced some stress in formal Māori contexts.

As a result of this study, the NZMRB and the management of the Māori rugby team put strategies in place to increase the knowledge players had of their own *whakapapa* (genealogy), Māori culture, *kawa* (protocol) and language. It was hoped that this would reduce the amount of stress players felt in Māori contexts, which would inevitably improve performance, pride, health and their ability to inspire other Māori. As a member of the Māori Rugby Board, I became aware of an internal review of the Māori All Blacks' North American tour in 2013 that produced an overwhelmingly positive response from the players, coaches and support staff. Highlights included the successful performance on and off the field, positive team environment, team unity and camaraderie, galvanising and Māori cultural sessions. The only areas of concern related to a lack of time together prior to the tour; the busy schedule while on tour, with games as well as sponsor responsibilities; and the desire of many of the players for more time to learn about Māori culture from *kaumātua* Luke Crawford, as expressed in a player's response to the review:

> Everything was amazing. Lukey was awesome at bringing out the Māori side of the players. I really learnt a lot from him about my people which I never knew but loved it. Without Lukey there, we wouldn't have been as close as we were.... The Māori side bound us together.

As a researcher and board member, these evaluations and studies piqued my interest to explore what issues Māori rugby players may have with regard to cultural identity and wellbeing. As a result, I conducted research with the Māori All Blacks during their two-test tour of Japan in 2014. The focus of this research was to examine the cultural identity, wellbeing and leadership perspectives of the players through surveys (before and after the tour) and semi-structured face-to-face interviews during the tour. The pre-tour survey revealed that there were 11 new caps, there was a range of years playing professional rugby (from two to 13 years) and the average age of the players was 24. Thirteen of the 26 players surveyed had participated in the regional Māori rugby tournaments that are hosted annually in three regions: the Northern region (Te Hiku o te Ika), the Central region (Te Tini a Maui) and the South Island region (Te Wai Pounamu). Players were also asked to respond to questions regarding parameters of Māori cultural identity, adapted from the Te Hoe Nuku Roa project (Durie *et al.*, 1995; Stevenson, 2004) and markers of Māori identity developed and tested more recently by Houkamau and Sibley (2010). These Likert-scale questions were asked before and immediately after the tour to determine whether the players' responses to the following 'markers' of cultural identity changed:

- Knowledge of Māori culture
- Involvement in Māori culture

- Association with other Māori
- Level of comfort in Māori contexts
- Knowledge of Māori language
- Strength of Māori identity
- Feelings toward Māori culture
- Knowledge of *whakapapa*/genealogy.

Responses in the post-tour survey indicated that all but two of these markers significantly improved for the players. Feelings toward Māori culture and knowledge of *whakapapa*/genealogy remained constant from pre- to post-tour. This may be so because their pre-tour responses to these two markers were already positive. Furthermore, it is worth noting that players are encouraged to learn about their *whakapapa* prior to the tour in preparation for the *mihi whakatau* (welcome and introductory ritual), where their *pepeha* (personal introduction) is recited to all present including players, coaches, team management, NZRU staff, Māori Rugby Board members, sponsors and *whānau*/family. One player talked about how this process helped him to reconnect with his *whakapapa* and Māori *whānau*: 'I was obviously doing it [researching my whakapapa] because I had to do my *pepeha* and I didn't know my river or my *maunga* [mountain] or anything. It was quite interesting and it was cool.' Another valuable source of learning about their Māori culture and identity were the daily *kapa haka* (Māori performing arts) sessions, which are an integral part of the Māori All Blacks culture programme that all team members – both players and management – attend. These sessions, often led by the *kaumātua* (Luke Crawford), cover a range of activities, which can include:

- Team *tikanga* (customary Māori practices)
- Haka practice – including the meaning and importance of the haka
- *Waiata* (Māori song) – practice to support team speakers on formal occasions, and to sing for team bonding (after games on the bus and in the team room)
- *Te reo* (Māori language) – pronunciations and phrases that can be used within the team environment or a rugby context
- *Wananga* (Māori school of learning) – discussing matters pertaining to the Māori world, *whakapapa*, *iwi*/*hapū* (tribal) stories and details
- *Whakataukī* (tribal sayings) and what they mean, and the significance these may have for the team and the *kaupapa* (purpose)
- *Rangatiratanga* – stories about Māori leaders and their contributions
- *Tuakana-teina* – past players come in and share their stories/*pepeha*/*mihi*.

Players shared their experiences of how they were inspired by past players (*tuakana-teina*), other players and the *kaumātua* (Lukey) during these *kapa haka* sessions:

Hearing a past player speak [Māori] last night was like, 'Oh, look, I gotta get my *reo* [language] back.'

You get to learn a bit more about the other *iwi* [tribes] and where everyone else has come from. You get so locked into what you do in your own *iwi* ... you forget about everyone else. I enjoy it.

Lukey knows his stuff so I just keep listening to what he has to say. I love it so after this I think I'll be getting into my own books and trying to carry on from there.

Māori values are also incorporated into the team culture, and are reinforced to the players during *kapa haka* sessions, are visually included in the team room and poster, and are infused in various symbols, stories, proverbs and scenarios before, during and after a tour. Their relevance to rugby performance is also emphasised when appropriate. The values include:

- *Pepeha* – tribal connections: where *whakapapa* is the door into the team, *pepeha* is the key to that door; no one enters the team without a *pepeha*
- *Maunga* – sacred mountain: *me hoki ki to maunga, kia pūrea ngā hau o Tawhirimātea* – urging players to return home to their ancestral homelands and to learn from their old people – who they are
- *Awa* – sacred waters: *me hoki ki to awa, kia pā mai ngā wai o Tangaroa* – urging players to return home to their ancestral waterways and to learn from their old people – who they are
- *Tapuae* – rugby connections; the team follows in the footsteps of many former players, administrators and fans who built the legacy that is Māori All Blacks rugby
- *Rangatira* – chiefly connections: *He toa rangatahi, he toa rangatira, piki ake ... ki ngā taumatatanga e*; words in the team haka, urging players to be the very best they can
- *Wairua* – spiritual connections: the MABs connect with the unseen spiritual realm through *Karakia* (incantation), *Waiata*, haka and Jersey
- *Whēnua* – land connections: we are *tangata whenua*, people of the land of the long white cloud; as we sustain the land, the land sustains us and we draw strength from it
- *Whānau* – family connections: as a team, we place huge importance on the support we receive from our genealogical family but also from our rugby family and fans
- *Whakapapa* – ancestral connections: *whakapapa* allows the MABs to connect through our tribal affiliations; each with the other through blood; *whakapapa* is the doorway into the MAB team
- *Ihi / Wehi / Tapu* – excellence: urging the team to draw on their inner potential and to actualise this in their performance; to reach the upper levels of performance is to become *tapu*.

In summary, the players expressed an appreciation for the team and what it represented to Māori and in particular their *whānau*. They also learnt about aspects of Māori culture and developed their sense of Māori identity as a result of being in the team. They all felt pride in being selected for the Māori All Blacks, which made them want to 'deliver' on the field, as expressed by one player: 'You just grow another arm and a leg, another heart and lung. I don't know what happens, you just do it.'

Conclusion

The existence and support of the Māori rugby team embodies the principles of the Treaty of Waitangi (the Treaty), a covenant signed in 1840 between the *tangata whenua* of Aotearoa (now known collectively as Māori) and the representatives of the British Crown. Because the two texts (Māori and English) of the Treaty have led to different understandings, and because of the need to apply the Treaty to present-day circumstances and issues, Treaty principles are often applied that inter-pret the Treaty as a whole: its intention and its spirit. The Royal Commission on Social Policy (1988) popularised the three Ps: Participation, Partnership and Pro-tection. These have been applied in a variety of contexts, including sport. The prin-ciple of Partnership encourages a collaborative process between groups to achieve a common purpose (i.e. equal access to decision-making and power positions). The Participation principle refers to the enablement of individuals or groups to access pathways and opportunities to participate at all levels of society. The Protection principle is akin to fiduciary duty to recognise, respond to and protect Māori cul-tural beliefs, values and practices. The intent and spirit of the Treaty can be applied to Māori rugby through the principles of partnership (is there a genuine partnership between the NZMRB and the NZRU?), participation (are Māori given opportun-ities to engage in rugby at all levels?) and protection (are Māori rugby and the Māori rugby team recognised and protected?).

How should rugby in New Zealand embrace Māori culture without losing sight of Māori aspirations and rights to participation, partnership and protection? During a national conference titled 'Te Pae Roa 2040: Pathways for Māori development into the future', hosted by Massey University in Auckland, respected Māori scholar and leader Sir Mason Durie (2014) challenged those present to ask, 'What is the future destination we seek as Māori?' His thoughts on what we should seek including the following:

- All Māori thriving as Māori
- Flourishing *whānau*/families
- Forward-looking and globally connected *iwi*
- Strong and vibrant language, culture and communities
- A booming economy
- A regenerated natural environment
- Consideration for the constitutional arrangements/aspirations of indigenous people.

This chapter suggests that Māori rugby in the professional era of the game may not rock the boat enough with regard to power relations in New Zealand society or rugby because it reasserts the hegemonic national imaginary regarding race ideologies and egalitarianism in particular. In addition, the impact that Māori rugby has on the holistic wellbeing of Māori individuals and communities in systemic and tangible ways is yet to be examined. There is plenty of scope for studies exploring, for instance:

- What happens to Māori players (and their *whānau*) when they retire?
- Are Māori rugby players effective role models for Māori youth?
- Are Māori players with a strong sense of Māori identity coming through the professional rugby pathways?
- What has the greatest impact on Māori communities: investing in the Māori All Blacks or investing in Māori rugby at the flax-roots level?
- What are the lost opportunities for Māori as a result of committing to the dream of getting a black jersey?

There are many questions to be asked, and there is more that could be done, to explore the relationship between Māori, rugby union, and the personal and collective advancement of indigenous peoples. This chapter has outlined the potential of rugby union to assist Māori with their future aspirations by:

- helping Māori rugby players, coaches and leaders to thrive
- helping Māori families to feel a sense of pride
- giving Māori players a chance to be globally connected
- strengthening the use of Māori language, rituals and cultural values in a rugby context
- enabling *iwi/hapū* and Māori businesses to leverage off Māori rugby to gain exposure to international markets, thus enhancing the Māori economy
- putting into practice Treaty principles and the rights of indigenous peoples in a sporting context.

In closing, Hokowhitu (2009) suggests discourse associated with Māori rugby may remain outwardly constant (the team) but its 'value' can change to collude with, at times, seemingly conflicting discourses (p. 2315). The debate about whether the existence of a Māori rugby team provides Māori with more 'bites at the black jersey' is ongoing, but the value of the Māori All Blacks to New Zealand Rugby, sponsors, Māori rugby players and the Māori community ensures the team's existence as a *taonga* (treasure) for now. This is best summed up in the words of a 2014 Māori rugby player, interviewed by the author:

Tū Māori mai – don't be afraid to stand up and be who you are. Just be proud of where we've come from and who we are. I think that's the best thing I've got out of this. No matter what anyone says they can't really take it away from us – embrace it.

References

AllBlacks.com (2012). AIG to become major global sponsor of New Zealand Rugby Union. Retrieved from www.allblacks.com/News/20786/aig-to-become-major-global-sponsor-of-new-zealand-rugby-union.

Bidwell, H. (2010). NZ rugby 'owes Maori apology'. *The Press*, 5 May. Retrieved from www.stuff.co.nz/sport/rugby/news/3674410/NZ-rugby-owes-Maori-apology.

Durie, M. H. (2003). *Nga Kahui Pou: Launching Māori Futures*. Wellington: Huia Publishers.

Durie, M. (2014). *Conference Summary for Te Pae Roa 2040: Hui Taumata Commemoration 1984–2014*, Massey University, Albany campus, Auckland, 2–3 September 2014. Retrieved from www.massey.ac.nz/massey/maori/events/te-pae-roa/te-pae-roa-2040-review/closing-address/closing-address_home.cfm.

Durie, M. H., Black, T. E., Christensen, I. S., Durie, A. E., Fitzgerald, E. D. & Taiapa, J. T. (1995). Te Hoe Nuku Roa framework: A Māori identity measure. *The Journal of the Polynesian Society, 104,* 461–470.

Erueti, B. & Palmer, F. R. (2014). Te Whariki Tuakiri (the identity mat): Māori elite athletes and the expression of ethno-cultural identity in global sport. *Sport in Society: Cultures, Commerce, Media, Politics, 17* (8), 1061–1075.

Falcous, M. (2007). The decolonizing national imaginary: Promotional media constructions during the 2005 Lions tour of Aotearoa New Zealand. *Journal of Sport and Social Issues, 31* (4), 374–393.

Hapeta, J. & Palmer, F. R. (2014). Māori Culture Counts: A case study of the Waikato Chiefs. In Black, T. (ed.) *Enhancing Mātauranga Māori and Global Indigenous Knowledge* (pp. 101–116). Wellington, NZ: New Zealand Qualifications Authority.

Hirini, P. & Flett, R. A. (1999). Aspects of the Māori All Black experience: The value of cultural capital in the new professional era. *He Pukenga Korero: A Journal of Māori Studies, 5* (1), 19.

Hokowhitu, B. (2005). Rugby and tino rangatiratanga: Early Maori rugby and the formation of traditional Maori masculinity. *Sporting Traditions, 21* (2), 75–95.

Hokowhitu, B. (2009). Māori rugby and subversion: Creativity, domestication, oppression and decolonization. *International Journal of the History of Sport, 26* (16), 2314–2334.

Hokowhitu, B. & Scherer, J. (2008). The Māori All Blacks and the decentering of the white subject: Hyperrace, sport, and the cultural logic of late capitalism. *Sociology of Sport Journal, 25* (2), 243–262.

Houkamau, C. A. & Sibley, C. G. (2010). The multi-dimensional model of Māori identity and cultural engagement. *New Zealand Journal of Psychology, 39* (1), 8–28.

Hurley, B. (2012). $80m for rugby in AIG deal. *New Zealand Herald*, 4 November. Retrieved from www.nzherald.co.nz/sport/news/article.cfm?c_id=4&objectid=10844989.

Jackson, S. J. & Hokowhitu, B. (2002). Sport, tribes and technology: The New Zealand All Blacks haka and the politics of identity. *Journal of Sport and Social Issues, 26* (2), 125–139.

Māori All Blacks 2014 Tour to Japan 2014 Media Guide. Wellington, NZ: New Zealand Rugby Union.

Motion, J., Leitch, S. & Brodie, R.J. (2003). Equity in corporate co-branding. *European Journal of Marketing, 37* (7/8), 1080–1094.

Mulholland, M. (2009). *Beneath the Māori Moon: An Illustrated History of Māori Rugby.* Wellington, NZ: Huia Publishers.

New Zealand Māori Rugby Board (2014). *Annual Report*. Wellington, NZ: New Zealand Rugby Union.

New Zealand Māori Rugby Board (2015). *Annual Report*. Wellington, NZ: New Zealand Rugby Union.

Palmer, F. (2007). Treaty principles and Māori sport: Contemporary issues. In Collins, C. & Jackson, S. (eds). *Sport in Aotearoa/New Zealand Society* (2nd edn) (pp. 307–334). Melbourne: Thomson Dunmore Press.

Palmer, F.R. & Adair, D. (2012). Indigeneity, race relations and sport management. In Leberman, S., Collins, C. & Trenberth, L. (eds). *Sport Business Management in New Zealand and Australia* (3rd edn) (pp. 54–80). Melbourne: Cengage Learning Australia.

Paul, G. (2014). All Blacks: Haka arousing second thoughts. *New Zealand Herald*, 29 June. Retrieved from www.nzherald.co.nz/sport/news/article.cfm?c_id=4&objectid=11283849.

Planet Rugby (2016). Cooper reappointed as Maori All Blacks coach. Retrieved from www.planetrugby.com/news/cooper-reappointed-as-maori-all-blacks-coach/.

Royal Commission on Social Policy (1988). *The April Report*. Wellington, NZ: Royal Commission on Social Policy.

Ryan, G. (1993). *Forerunners of the All Blacks. The 1888–89 New Zealand Native Football Team in Britain, Australia and New Zealand*. Christchurch, NZ: Canterbury University Press.

Statistics New Zealand (2013). *2013 Census QuickStats About National Highlights*. Wellington, NZ: Statistics New Zealand. Retrieved from www.stats.govt.nz/Census/2013-census/profile-and-summary-reports/quickstats-about-a-place.aspx?request_value=13170&tabname=Culturaldiversity.

Stevenson, B. (2004). Te Hoe Nuku Roa: A measure of Māori cultural identity. *He Pukenga Korero, 8* (1), 37–46.

Stuff (2014). NZ Maori rugby jersey pays tribute to Japan. Retrieved from www.stuff.co.nz/sport/rugby/news/10630309/NZ-Maori-rugby-jersey-pays-tribute-to-Japan.

Sydney Morning Herald (2010). Six All Black discards in Maori squad. Retrieved from www.smh.com.au/rugby-union/union-news/six-all-black-discards-in-maori-squad-20100531-wpvt.html.

Te Puni Kōkiri (2005). *Te Māori i te whutupōro: Māori in rugby* (Fact Sheet 23). Wellington, NZ: Te Puni Kōkiri.

Watson, G. (2007). Sport and ethnicity in New Zealand. *History Compass, 5* (3), 780–801.

Watson, M. (2011). Haka losing respect – Springboks coach. *The Dominion Post*, 19 September. Retrieved from www.stuff.co.nz/dominion-post/news/5646179/Haka-losing-respect-Springboks-coach.

World in Union (New Zealand: Rugby Conference 2017 (forthcoming). Hosted by Massey University, Palmerston North, NZ.

6 The impact of the professional era on Pacific Islands rugby

Robert Dewey

Introduction – David versus Goliath

On 8 July 2015, the New Zealand All Blacks played their first 'official' Test Match in the Pacific Islands, against Manu Samoa at the National Stadium in Apia. The recurrence of the term 'historic' in media previews of a match between two geographically proximate, competitively ranked teams from countries linked by indigenous and colonial histories, migration, trade, regional organizations and overlapping player bases was particularly revealing. The novelty of the occasion heightened its symbolic importance in the eyes of most of the overseas press. An accompanying, and, at the time, patronizing, subthread focused upon awestruck locals and visiting All Black celebrity. Headlines from TV One New Zealand and the *Guardian* hailed a 'historic' match 'that stopped a nation', the latter casting All Black stars Dan Carter and Richie McCaw as 'rock stars from another planet'.[1] From that journalistic perspective, this was rugby's core visiting the periphery, First World journeying to Third or, in the old International Rugby Board (IRB) parlance, a 'Tier I' nation on a charitable visit to a 'Tier II' one. For its part, the Manu Samoa and local media commentary focused rather more on the game at hand, with 'David versus Goliath' providing a slogan for team talks, editorials and television promotions. As Manu Samoa captain Ofisa Treviranus told the *Samoa Observer*,

> Samoa is a small country just like David. New Zealand is a big country and they have a lot of money to develop their rugby. I think they are the Goliath. It's a good analogy to have, it motivates and encourages us that even though we are up against all the odds, we can do it.[2]

The David and Goliath trope has long animated both Samoan and Pacific Islands rugby. As a point of reference it melds ability and improbability at the intersection of *lotu* (religion) and history. But, as is invariably the case in Test Match rugby, Goliath triumphed, on this occasion by a score of 25–16.

With the passing of the historic moment came a return to historical realities. 'The All Blacks may never return to Samoa', Gregor Paul noted in the *New Zealand Herald* the following day. In light of financial considerations, 'The whole business of another visit has been fudged, gently rebutted with non-committal statements.'[3] Ten days later, the Prime Minister and chair of the Samoa Rugby Union (SRU), Tuilaepa Sailele Malielegaoi, announced that ST\$3.4 million had been spent to host the event. The result was a ST\$1.5 million loss and a search for assistance from government agencies. Of particular note was an admission that the greatest single expense was incurred by player allowances for a match-day squad that included only one domestically based player.[4]

For anyone familiar with the popularity and plight of international rugby in the Pacific, there was little surprise in either the welcome accorded the All Blacks or the financial hangover. The three Pacific unions' player-to-population ratios are the highest in the sport. According to World Rugby statistics compiled in 2014, there are more rugby players in Fiji (156,140) than in New Zealand (148,483),[5] a country whose population is five teams larger. Those statistics fail to convey the sport's socio-economic, political and cultural significance. In the unlikely event the All Blacks choose to play Test Matches in Nuku'alofa or Suva, they can expect similar receptions. But the resulting financial losses to the SRU were equally predictable. Expenditure on the All Blacks match equalled the SRU's 2013 incoming receipts (ST\$3,401,968) from sponsors, merchandising, and government and IRB grants.[6] As such, the All Blacks in Apia episode was emblematic of both Samoa's and Pacific rugby's place in the professionalized rugby landscape.

This chapter partially surveys the fortunes of the Fiji, Tonga and Samoa rugby unions during the first two decades of the professional era. Historically at the margins of international rugby, union officials and national team coaches shouldered professionalized burdens with the resources of an amateur era. Indeed, in the minds of its own officials, Pacific rugby administration remained a distinctly 'amateur' affair for much of the past two decades. Amidst high public expectations and mobile player aspirations, a performance gap widened between under-resourced Tier II Pacific nations and their Tier 1 counterparts. On rare occasions, the Pacific trio punctuated otherwise predictable Rugby World Cup (RWC) competitions with occasional moments of drama. Wales yielded to Samoa in 1999 and Fiji in 2007, while Tonga beat France in 2011. But in most encounters with Tier I by the early 2000s, the Pacific nations suffered losses by record margins. In a belated response, the International Rugby Board (IRB) implemented a three-year, £30 million global strategic 'development' plan for Tier II nations, including Fiji, Tonga and Samoa. That funding, and its renewal in 2009, led to the creation of High Performance Units (HPU) and regional competitions. Just how far those programmes helped close the gap remains an open question.

As I have argued elsewhere, the advent of professionalism in 1995 represented less a sea-change in the fortunes of Pacific Islands rugby than an extension, and in some cases an amplification, of longstanding structural inequities in the international game.[7] Yet, whatever their origins, changing circumstances demanded imaginative union responses. The results were mixed. But of all the challenges faced by the Islands' rugby administrators in the professional era, none was more disruptive than the intensification of player movement. Thus, what emerged for Pacific rugby in the late 1990s and 2000s was a bewildering synthesis of increased aspiration and vulnerabilities for the national rugby unions intertwined with enhanced global opportunities for the region's most talented athletes. For the sake of convenience, those trends might be described as self-reinforcing processes of exclusion and inclusion. Thus, while the national unions remained largely excluded from the most profitable competitions and highest levels of international governance, the inclusion of mobile Pacific Islanders in elite club and national teams overseas became a defining feature of the newly monetized landscape. Paradoxically then, Pacific rugby has never enjoyed a higher profile but its constituent nations look only somewhat more likely to contest a RWC final than they did 20 years ago.

Local histories and regional connections

Any broad discussion of the impact of professionalism in the Pacific must concede the dangers of oversimplification in a regional approach to Fiji, Tonga and Samoa rugby. Amidst shared experiences and interests there are countless points of divergence. The most obvious of these relate to historical, economic and political relationships within and outside the Pacific, religious affiliations, regional and ethnic divisions, and more nuanced differences in constructions of social hierarchies, gender and cultures of tradition. For the sake of brevity, three rugby-centric points of difference can be explored by way of example.

First, rugby has been played in the Pacific for more than a century, with tri-angular Test competitions between Fiji, Tonga and Samoa dating from 1924 and matches with the New Zealand Maori teams from 1938. Those contacts fostered cooperation as well as deep and at times violent rivalries. But each country's emergence into the realm of international touring and hosting occurred at different stages. Fiji first toured New Zealand, with great success, in 1939, and filled stadiums in Australia and New Zealand on subsequent tours in the 1950s. By the early 1960s, Europe beckoned with tours to Wales and France in 1964. During the 1970s Fiji hosted Australia and the British Lions as well as national 'XV' sides from England, France and New Zealand. Mean-while, Tonga first visited New Zealand in 1969 and Australia in 1973, achiev-ing notable victories on both occasions. Samoa, by comparison, did not tour New Zealand until 1976 and was omitted from the first Rugby World Cup in 1987.

Perceived differences are also evident in the stereotypical renderings of playing styles. Thus, whereas *palagi* (foreign) commentaries conflate 'flair' and 'physicality' within a racialized trope of Pacific Islander rugby,[8] those terms are sometimes inscribed as divergent characteristics within indigenous rugby dis-courses. Most often proposed with tongue firmly in cheek by an older generation steeped in the triangular rivalry of the amateur era, such observations purport to differentiate between the comparative physiologies and abilities of Fijian backs and Polynesian forwards. Thus, according to one such version, the Fijians always relied on their flair, fitness and athleticism to run rings around Samoa and Tonga in the past, the Tongans and Samoans played a slower, more sluggish, physical game. Consequently, contests between Samoa and Tonga were always more difficult and closely fought.[9]

Further sub-categorizations appear on a local basis. In Fiji, for example, the stereotypical ascription or empowering embrace of the term *kai colo* (people from the hills) to describe teams from the highlands of Viti Levu carries meanings associated with a historical version of warriorhood and by extension, a specific playing style.

Finally, obvious differences in operational capacities among the three unions derive from advantages of scale. Fiji's population of roughly 850,000 includes a 'registered' player base of 65,980, while Samoa's population of 191,000 and Tonga's population of 104,000, include 20,845 and 13,965 registered players respectively.[10] Accompanying differences in economic productivity and comparative national wealth are also evident in the availability of private sector sponsorship and pledges of government support. Thus, Fiji's annual operating budgets and union staffs were sometimes larger than those available in Tonga, for example, which lacked a union headquarters building before 2000. According to a former Tonga Rugby Board member, 'there were no administrative funds; we were borrowing from people for paper and telephone calls'.[11]

Yet there are valid reasons for treating the impact of professionalism on Fiji, Tonga and Samoa as a regional proposition. As Epeli Hau'ofa and Albert Wendt, among others, have argued, 'Oceanic' identities are evident in ancestral pasts and within trends of the globalizing present that run counter to the divisions and boundaries imposed by colonialism and perpetuated by neo-colonial structures.[12] Given its colonial roots and national basis of organization, rugby's potential as a vehicle for regional consciousness is likely limited. Within the Fiji–Tonga–Samoa crescent, however, historic and competitive links developed over the past century fostered the emergence of what might be loosely described as a 'Pacific rugby culture' or, to its most ardent proponents, a unifying 'secular religion'. Those bonds in turn facilitated coordinated responses to the challenges posed by the new era.

Professionalism and the structures of exclusion

Islands rugby administrations fully understood the national and regional implications of television-driven professionalization before its formal adoption in late August 1995. In a Fiji v. Samoa match programme published the previous month, SRU President Tupua Tamasese Efi wrote of his fears for the future of rugby in the region and the need for cooperation among its constituents. 'Commercial value', he observed, 'is the only language which the Murdoch proponents understand.... The future of South Pacific rugby is in the balance and it does not become any of us to be parochial.'[13] Clarity about the future derived in part from earlier anxieties about international performances and preparations for the 1995 RWC. In 1992, coach Feleti Wolfgramm decried the lack of 'professionalism' in Tonga's approach to rugby and his union's failure to implement player development programmes. 'It is all hope,' he said, 'and in most cases it is only a fluke if we win.'[14] Meanwhile in Fiji, criticisms emerged amidst inquests into the national team's failed bid for RWC qualification. After proclaiming the 1990s 'a disaster', *Fiji Sport* bemoaned competition from rugby league and devotion to rugby sevens, and criticized players for insufficient dedication to training and excessive consumption of alcohol and *yaqona* (kava).[15] Those shortcomings took on greater significance when combined with the likelihood of player movements overseas. 'The new fully professional environment', the magazine warned, 'looms like a hurricane on the horizon of Fiji Rugby. It has the potential to destroy the local game.'[16]

Pacific rugby escaped the most ominous forecasts, including predictions that the Islands might abandon Test rugby in the early 2000s. But a catalogue of obstacles, too numerous to list here but ranging from major budgetary shortfalls to the minutiae of RWC match scheduling, undermined attempts to field competitive teams. Among the most intractable barriers, best categorized as hegemonic structural exclusions, were the absence of matches against Tier I opponents, marginalization within IRB governance and omission from SANZAR (South Africa, New Zealand and Australia Rugby) competitions.

Over the past two decades, Pacific rugby officials consistently bemoaned the lack of international fixtures, and matches against top-flight opponents in particular. Between 1995 and 2014 the number of non-RWC matches played by England (196), Australia (223) and New Zealand (212) was nearly double that played by Tonga (107), Fiji (120) and Samoa (105).[17] Thanks to more effective IRB calendar management, the November Test windows provided for regular Northern Hemisphere tours by Pacific teams. But corresponding opportunities to host visiting sides during the June tours were uncommon for two primary reasons. First, Tier I countries either refused to send teams or focused all energies and resources on tours of Australia and New Zealand. Second, international rugby's tour financing model, in which ticket sales and television revenues offset hosting costs, were completely incompatible with the economic realities of life in the Pacific Islands. Thus, infrequent visits from Tier I powers during the amateur era became scarce in the era of professionalism. Australia, who last went to Fiji in 1984, have never played in Tonga or Samoa. Before the All Blacks' recent Test in Apia, no senior New Zealand side had played in the region since a New Zealand 'XV' visited Fiji in 1984. Argentina and South Africa have never played a Test Match in the Pacific. England last visited Fiji in 1991 but have never competed in Samoa and called on Tonga once, in 1979. Wales last visited the region in 1994 and duly lost to Samoa. In the professional era, the only Tier I visitors to the Pacific were France (1998, 1999), Italy (2000, 2006, 2014), Ireland (2003) and Scotland (2012).

Meanwhile, for those inclined to view international rugby governance as parochial at best and neo-colonial at worst, the IRB (now World Rugby) Council provided a wide target. In the deliberations of rugby's highest legislative body, the eight 'foundation unions' (England, Wales, Scotland, Ireland, France, Australia, New Zealand, South Africa) retained two votes apiece while four additional unions (Argentina, Canada, Italy, Japan) each held a single vote. In a limited expansion, the IRB created six Continental bodies in 2000 to represent the interests of global rugby, including a Federation of Oceania Rugby Unions (FORU). Each 'regional organization' was subsequently granted a single Council vote in 2004. That brought Fiji, Samoa and Tonga to the table not as individual unions, but rather as part of a dozen-member FORU organization that included Australia and New Zealand. In other words, the single regional vote represented interests drawn from all three tiers of Oceania rugby. Complaints about a lack of democracy increased as IRB attempts to enforce or amend its rules on player availability regulations proved ineffective. Nor were the Pacific unions alone in their criticism. As *Putting Rugby First*, an independent report published in 2008, calculated, 'With a seventy-five percent majority required for key decisions, it takes just four Foundation unions to veto a proposal that might have been agreed by the other 111 members.'[18] On the eve of RWC 2015, however, a belated measure of reform looked likely. According to senior rugby officials, the three Islands unions had rejected the offer of a 'rotating seat' and were hoping for full Council membership as part of a broader World Rugby governance restructure.[19]

In retrospect, perhaps the most significant regional episode in early professionalism was the exclusion of the Pacific nations from the creation and subsequent expansions of the SANZAR Super Rugby and Tri-Nations (later Rugby Championship) competitions. Their omission was especially poignant because the Pacific Tri-Nations champions participated in Super Rugby's late-amateur forerunner, the provincial Super 10s, between 1993 and 1995.[20] Looking back on those events, FORU President Harry Schuster concluded, 'There is a selfishness about the professional game, it is an inherent characteristic … it was obvious right from the outset that when the game went professional, Fiji, Tonga and Samoa were going to be left out.'[21] The addition of Super Rugby sides in Australia, South Africa and, more recently, Japan and Argentina revealed the economic calculus at the heart of SANZAR decision-making. As New Zealand Rugby Union CEO Steve Tew conceded in 2013,

> It comes down to the ability of a team to have an economic base. There's no point having a team in Fiji, Samoa or Tonga, or a combined team, if you don't have the financial power to make it work.[22]

Tew's suggestion that Pacific entry into Super Rugby might hinge upon support from a rich benefactor ignored the fact that Manu Samoa had restructured as Manu Samoa Rugby Limited (MSRL) between 1995 and 2007 with the assistance of investment banker Sir Michael Fay. During those years MSRL's lobbying for the inclusion of a Pacific team in Super Rugby expansions went unheeded.

Recruitment and inclusion overseas

The converse of international rugby's structural exclusivity was a commodified inclusivity or active overseas recruitment of Islander athletes. Their journeys to schools, development programmes, clubs and, by unstated design or convenient default to other national teams, became a centrepiece of many commentaries on professionalization after 1995. In academic research, multi-directional mobilities attracted attention[23] in part because pursuit of the 'rugby dream' resembled the Global South to North pathways in other sporting landscapes. In the Australian and New Zealand media, examples of exoticized interest and racialized anxieties were propelled by discourses on the 'browning' or 'Polynesianization' of clubs and national teams in both codes.

Recent developments in professional rugby union should not obscure deeper precedents. 'Code-swapping' from rugby union to rugby league, for example, began attracting Pacific athletes more than 50 years ago. In 1961 two ageing Fijian rugby union stars, Orisi Dawai and Iosefa Levula, signed with Rochdale Hornets in England. Other Fijian players soon followed to Rochdale, Wigan, Blackpool and Huddersfield.[24] For the Fiji Rugby Union (FRU), which counselled its players to avoid all contact with rugby league scouts, there was profound nervousness about code defections. Concerns about the attractions of rugby league peaked again in the early 1990s when Culden Kamea organized a Fiji rugby league competition that soon grew to include eight clubs and 200 players. Those developments coincided with the battle for influence between the Australian Rugby League and Rupert Murdoch's Super League, which had already extended to Papua New Guinea, Tonga and Samoa. By 1995, according to one estimate, 33 Fijians were playing rugby league in Australia, with other notables including Noa Nadruku considering lucrative offers.[25] Meanwhile New Zealand-based players with Tongan backgrounds including, Emosi Koloto and the Sorenson brothers, signed contracts with Australian and English league clubs. By the late 1980s, the New Zealand Kiwis Test sides included half a dozen players of Samoan descent.[26]

On the eve of rugby union professionalism, player mobility also flowed in the opposite direction. In the late 1980s, Manu Samoa began drawing New Zealand-based players into their Test side, including France Bunce, Peter Fatialofa and, later, stars such as Pat Lam and Va'aiga Tuigamala. Fiji and Tonga followed suit. In the Fijian case, the FRU amended its constitution in 1992 to facilitate selection of overseas-based players after a poor showing in RWC 1991.[27] Those movements 'home' intensified after 1995, even though players were now departing professional club settings overseas to compete for essentially amateur national teams. By the 2003 and 2007 RWCs, only a handful of players representing Fiji, Tonga and Samoa were actually based in the Pacific Islands.

Much of the initial outward movement flowed along the colonial corridors. New rugby migrants joined local 'Pasifika' players whose families had journeyed to Australia and New Zealand in the 1950s and 1960s. By the early 2000s nearly one-third of the All Blacks squad could claim ancestral connections with the Islands. Tana Umaga became the first Pacific Islander to captain New Zealand, in 2004. George Smith crossed a similar threshold in Australia in 2007. Pacific player movements to Japan were more serendipitous, but increased in part because Japanese corporate clubs regarded the migrants as 'cheap labour'.[28] Over the past decade, those flows shifted toward higher-paying destinations in the United Kingdom and France. It is difficult to establish just how many Pacific Islander players compete overseas, particularly at lower levels, in part because the Islands unions have struggled to track movements with precision. However, scholars at Massey University in Auckland estimate that at elite level, Pacific Islander player numbers increased by 100 per cent in Super Rugby between 1996 and 2013, and by 33 per cent in Australia's National Rugby League between 2008 and 2013.[29] Similar growth was apparent in the Northern Hemisphere. According to statistics compiled by *Teivovo Rugby* magazine at the start of the 2014 Northern Hemisphere season, there were 60 Pacific Islanders playing in the French Top 14 and another 85 in D2; 41 in the Aviva Premiership; 23 in the Guinness Pro 12; and another 16 in the Greene King IPA Championship.[30]

The earliest conversations surrounding 'code-swapping' and transnational mobility were frequently characterized as instances of 'poaching'. Invocations of 'theft', as used by some Pacific rugby administrators and local journalists, spoke to frustrations at the loss of age-grade athletes to overseas scholarships and club development programmes. In the international press, however, 'poaching' allegations tended toward rugby at international level, particularly when athletes born in the Pacific began appearing in Australian Wallaby and New Zealand All Black uniforms. Heated journalistic exchanges erupted, as in the responses to Steven Jones' claim that New Zealand were 'arch-poachers'[31] of the Pacific. The 'poaching' terminology was useful because it spoke to stark inequalities and pointed toward transgressions that were underhanded and opaque. But its use as a descriptor was limited precisely because of that opacity and the complexities it obscured. Perhaps as a consequence, the term 'poaching' appears less frequently in current analyses of player movement.

A variety of factors may account for the decline of 'poaching' allegations. First, both broad assertions and statistics, including those cited in this chapter, fail to distinguish between players born in the Pacific Islands and those born in Australia, New Zealand and beyond. Greater complexity can be read, for example, in social scientific attempts to categorize player movements as 'amateur, scholarship, nomadic and transnational'.[32] But for every category there are clear exceptions. Second, there is significantly more agency in the decision to pursue a career overseas than the poaching discourses suggest, even if those choices are shaped by comparative economic deprivation and the immediate needs of family, village and church. A recent study conducted by Dr Rochelle Stewart-Smithers and Koli Sewabu concluded that Pacific Islander players overseas were sending home remittances totalling NZ$21 million per year.[33] If anything, this figure may be too conservative. The scale of remittances helps explain why so many Pacific rugby authorities have resigned themselves to player mobility. During interviews I conducted between 2005 and 2015, Pacific coaches and administrators emphasized they would never stand in the way of individual 'opportunity'. Third, if we extend Kanemasu and Molnar's analysis of Fiji, there are clearly instances in which individual achievement overseas is grasped as a source of local and national pride.[34] Finally, it may be the case that what is described as poaching by faceless agents is actually a matter of 'soft recruitment'.[35] In other words, Pacific Islanders already based in professional leagues overseas facilitate overtures to brothers, cousins and former teammates.

If the application of 'poaching' terminology inadequately captured complexity, the issues that phrase sought to express were no less real or serious. Ironically, with the recent rise of academies targeting young players, the allegations of 'poaching' are now more valid than ever. For FORU President Harry Schuster, the academy system constitutes 'the biggest threat to Pacific Islands rugby... it is a drain we cannot afford'.[36]

Given the precedents set elsewhere by Major League Baseball and European soccer, the application of the academy model to the Pacific was predictable, if not inevitable. Among the first in the region was Clermont-Auvergne's relationship with Nadroga in Fiji, which began in 2010 and was renewed in 2014. Another French club, Brive, recently revealed similar plans for an academy based at Ratu Navula College in Nadi. The statements of its Director of Rugby, Nicholas Godignon, revealed the depth of sensitivities over player development. 'We are not here to poach players,' he pledged, 'but we are thinking of their future and if they go through the programme, they can also do further studies in France and follow in the footsteps of some well-known players.'[37] In Samoa, former Manu Samoa rep and SRU critic Mo Schwalger started Rugby Academy Samoa, targeting talent in the 15–17 age groups and promoting them for scholarships to schools in New Zealand and overseas clubs.[38] Meanwhile in Tonga, Saracens established the Toa Saracens Rugby Academy in August 2013 with a focus on students aged 14 and above. Another report claimed that the small local rugby academy at Tonga College had steered 60 students to scholarships in New Zealand and Japan during the past two years. Figures like that may have drawn the interest of the Essentially Group (NZ), a sport management company which claims to have represented half of the All Blacks and Super 15 athletes in New Zealand since 2007. In June 2015, its senior staff met with Tongan officials to discuss setting up an academy in Nuku'alofa.[39]

Player agents were especially busy in Fiji during 2014–15.[40] In May 2015 the *Fiji Times* reported that seven members of Fiji's team from the World Rugby U-20 Championship were likely to depart overseas, two of them to Toulon. Soon afterwards, Fiji sevens coach Ben Ryan complained about overtures made to members of his squad and requested that overseas and local agents be regulated. 'There are some terrible agents around here who have no experience and knowledge,' he noted. 'No one is going to stop them [players] if they are going for the right reasons. But often some of the players go too early for small salaries and it is a loss to the Fiji national teams forever.'[41] In all likelihood Ryan's comments were directed at the Process Rugby Foundation, based in Nadi. Founded in 2014, and carrying the slogan 'Mentioned,

Mentored and Monitored', non-profit Process Rugby has facilitated the movement of promising U-18 Fijian schoolboy athletes to French clubs and academies, where, they claim, the young players receive allowances of €2000 to €3000 per month. To its critics, Process Rugby stands accused of 'recruiting the cream of Fiji second school rugby' for French clubs.[42]

For some officials, the silver lining in rugby migration rested in a presumption that movement to rugby's professional core represented the lone viable 'development' pathway for national teams. As FRU CEO Keni Dakuidreketi warned in his 2010 report, 'In the absence of a local professional competition ... we have to acknowledge that getting them professional contracts is the only option open.'[43] Accordingly, players exposed to professionalized coaching, training methods, facilities and medical care overseas enhance national team performances upon return. In the most optimistic versions of this formula, the player, his family, agent, club, and ultimately, nation benefit. Others questioned this approach. Current Manu Samoa coach and former All Black Alama Ieremia, for example, characterized the developmental benefits of overseas professionalism as overstated. From his perspective, European club coaches chasing short-term results have little interest in 'developing' new players. Moreover, athletes who do not regularly start games lack fitness and in some cases have been coached into Northern Hemisphere habits that Ieremia regards as ill-suited for Manu Samoa's style of play.[44] The other obvious question is: if you let them go, can you get the players back? Too often the answer has been 'no', particularly when Fiji, Tonga and Samoa attempted to assemble full-strength World Cup squads. This is partly a matter of eligibility statutes enshrined in IRB regulation 8.2, the so-called 'one country for life rule', and the accompanying issues surrounding three-year residencies and other nations capping young Pacific Islands players at sevens and 'A' levels.[45] Above all, player availability was compromised by the failure of professional clubs to abide by, and the IRB to enforce, player release regulation 9.

'Controlling what we can control'

While this chapter primarily addresses international rugby, it is important to note that the unions carry other responsibilities including oversight of women's rugby, development programmes through High Performance Units, youth and schools rugby, national/provincial competitions and rugby sevens, among others. Former FRU CEO Manasa Baravilala described his job as a mix of long hours, diplomacy, conflict resolution, media relations, sponsorship searches, creative thinking, faith in tradition and 'controlling what we can control'.[46] Perhaps because of endless wrangling over releases for overseas players, the Pacific development models after RWC 2007 increasingly emphasized local pathways. But as *Teivovo* editor Culden Kamea observed in 2014, the absence of funds and structures, and the continued hollowing out of local competitions by player departures, turned the development enterprise in Fiji into a 'mission impossible'. 'The sad reality', he wrote, is that most of our professional rugby players around the world are being used as cheap labour … our young players have rushed off overseas on the whiff of an airline ticket and nothing much else, only to find life on the other side a lot tougher to endure.[47]

The dynamics of exclusion and inclusion outlined above placed severe administrative strains on the Islands unions and were accompanied by chronic indebtedness that at times bordered on insolvency. As FRU Board Chairman Bill Gavoka told attendees at the 2011 AGM, 'When we stand shoulder to shoulder with international sides in foreign stadiums, I sometimes wonder how we managed to be there. Turning up at all have in many ways been miracles in themselves.'[48] In their better moments, officials framed ambitious development plans, restructured local competitions, implemented administrative reforms and extended fundraising activities. Fruitful collaborations with the IRB facilitated a dramatic increase in the global profile of rugby sevens, the incremental growth of women's rugby and the reinvigoration of triangular play in the Pacific Nations Cup and Pacific Rugby Cup competitions. Infrastructural improvements included aforementioned HPU facilities and enhancements of national union offices and communications capacities. Behind those facades, union administrations gradually shifted from 'amateur' to 'professional' in their expectations and management systems, albeit with the growing pains seen elsewhere in the rugby world.

Rugby officials also contested what they saw as the most glaring injustices in the sport. Samoan Prime Minister Tuilaepa Sailele Malielegaoi took complaints about exclusion from Super Rugby and Tests against Australia and New Zealand to the level of regional diplomacy at the Pacific Islands Forum and meetings with senior politicians. The Pacific Islands Rugby Alliance forged a new regional path on the British and Irish Lions model with the creation of the Pacific Islanders side. But its tours in 2004, 2006 and 2008 demonstrated that composite Pacific teams were liable to the same disruptive international forces as their national constituents, and the project was abandoned in 2009.[49]

Union administrations, which underperformed at crucial moments and became particularly unstable in Fiji and Tonga, must shoulder their share of blame for fractures that appeared in their relations with national boards, players and the IRB. Most of the problems that emerged in the past decade stemmed from allegations of financial improprieties and failed management systems. Instabilities in Tongan administration appeared most dramatically in the context of violent political protests in Nuku'alofa in 2006. Union board infighting and alleged financial mismanagement destabilized rugby administration to the point that the Ikale Tahi's presence at RWC 2007 was in doubt. Administrative reforms followed, but turnover in CEO and board positions remained high. Turnover was even higher at Rugby House in Fiji. Since the departure of FRU CEO Pio Bosco Tikoisuva in 2005, more than half a dozen men have held the CEO position, with few tenures lasting more than 18 months. Following its strategic development and HPU investments in the Pacific, the IRB began using its funding as leverage for reforms in governance and financial practices. Threats of financial suspensions were followed up in 2014 in Fiji, when the IRB temporarily suspended £1.1 million in funding until the FRU demonstrated progress in implementing reforms. One of the first instances of direct action by Manu Samoa players occurred in 2000 when a dozen team members chose not to join a UK tour in disputes over pay and tour arrangements. Manu Samoa player dissatisfaction with management at the 2011 RWC dramatically reappeared in November 2014, when the team threatened to boycott its match against England. The appearance of organized player efforts, as in the Manu Samoa cases, is significant because they point to a rise in player agency. Indeed, with the creation of the Pacific Islands Players Association in 2013, Pacific rugby may be on the verge of a new era of player power.

Conclusion

When set in broader contexts, the positions of Fiji, Tonga and Samoa rugby after two decades of professionalism take on deeper if at times contradictory hues. International rugby discourses, for example, continue to set dynamic style expectations within hierarchical stasis. In the weeks leading up to RWC 2015, the UK media revived descriptions of Fiji, Tonga and Samoa as gallant underdogs and possible 'X factors'. In a tired version of the phrase that has appeared in previews of every RWC since 1987, one journalist wrote, 'The Islands bring colour to the World Cup.'[50] Without underestimating the empowering significance of the David versus Goliath allegory for Manu Samoa, we should nonetheless interrogate the rugby world's willingness to accept a crystallized trope that imprisons Pacific Islanders as entertainers rather than potential champions. In other words, external judgements of Pacific rugby still privilege 'flair' and spectacle in a sport that measures 'progress' through narrowing margins of loss rather than prospects of victory in a World Cup semi-final.

The ways in which the Islands unions frame expectation and manage the forces of professionalism, however, are anything but static. In his study of a society positioned 'at the edge of the global', Niko Besnier analysed the manner in which Tongans 'see themselves as occupying the margins of globalization at the same time they engage with it.' Confronted by anxiety-inducing global flows, Besnier described how such societies approach 'possibilities' and 'constraints' in ways that 'reconfigure modernity' and reshape traditional assumptions.[51] By extending his analysis to include rugby as a site of modernity, this dynamic becomes evident in the Pacific rugby encounter with professionalism. Echoes of the process can be heard in the FRU CEO's emphasis on 'controlling what we can control' or in discussions of development schemes that emphasize the global potentials of 'our' local players.

In an ironic dilemma posed by this situation, the Islands unions are engaging World Rugby power structures that speak the language of the global but remain embedded in the national, hegemonic and neo-colonial interests of its most powerful constituents. And yet, if we follow the imaginative geography of hegemonic rugby categories, the strands of globalization are readily apparent. Thus below a Northern Hemisphere Anglo-French 'economic core' and a Southern Hemisphere SANZAR 'power core'[52] it is possible to identify a third diasporic node best characterized as a 'Pacific performative web'. Driven by economic necessity, ambition and individual mobility, extending from Fiji, Tonga and Samoa to all corners of the rugby globe, the sinews of Pacific Islanders provide unifying threads for a frail 'World in Union'.

Acknowledgements

I am most grateful to rugby officials, players and coaches in Fiji, Tonga and Samoa for their kindness, hospitality and time during multiple visits to their unions over the past decade. I am also grateful to DePauw University for providing resources from the Professional Development Fund in support of research travel.

Notes

1 'The Test that Stopped a Nation', TV One News, www.tvnz.co.nz/one-news/sport/rugby/the-test-that-stopped-a-nation-all-blacks-battle-past-passionate-samoans-in-apia-q00471, accessed 13 July 2015; R. Maharaj, 'Samoa vs All Blacks: The Game that Stopped a Nation', *Guardian*, www.theguardian.com/sport/blog/2015/jul/08/all-blacks-samoa-the-game-that-stopped-a-nation, accessed 10 July 2015.
2 M.K. Lesa, 'David vs. Goliath', *Samoa Observer*, 8 July 2015, www.samoaobserver.ws/home/headlines/13883-david-vs-goliath, accessed 10 July 2015.
3 G. Paul, 'The All Blacks May Never Return to Samoa', *New Zealand Herald*, 9 July 2015, www.nzherald.co.nz/sport/news/article.cfm?c_id=4&objectid=11478274, accessed 15 July 2015.
4 '$1.5 Million Loss in Hosting All Blacks', *Samoa Observer*, 19 July 2015.
5 World Rugby, 'Mapping the Popularity of Global Rugby', www.worldrugby.org/development/player-numbers.
6 SRU receipts total, excluding IRB High Performance Unit grant, *Samoa Rugby Union Incorporated Statement of Receipts and Payments*, for the year ended 31 December 2013.
7 R. Dewey, 'Pacific Islands Rugby: Navigating the Global Professional Era' in G. Ryan (ed.), *The Changing Face of Rugby* (Newcastle: Cambridge Scholars, 2008), 82–108. That chapter includes more densely researched analysis of professionalism up through 2008 but shares many of the same conclusions.
8 See for example, J. Clement, 'Participating in the Global Competition: Denaturalizing "Flair" in Samoan Rugby', *The Contemporary Pacific* 26, 2 (2014), 369–87; B. Hokowhitu, 'Tackling Maori Masculinity: A Colonial Genealogy of Savagery and Sport', *The Contemporary Pacific* 15 (2004), 259–84; A. Grainger, 'Rugby Island Style: Paradise, Pacific People and the Racialization of Athletic Performance', *Junctures* 12 (2009), 45–63.
9 L.T. Simi, 'Traditional Rivals, Traditionally Difficult', Manu Samoa vs. Tonga Match programme, 28 June 1997.
10 2014 statistics from United Nations Population Fund, Pacific Sub-Regional Office, http://countryoffice.unfpa.org/pacific/ and World Rugby, www.worldrugby.org/development/player-numbers.
11 Author interview with Drew Havea, Nuku'alofa, Tonga, 11 July 2005.
12 See for example, E. Hau'ofa, 'Our Sea of Islands', *The Contemporary Pacific* 6, 1 (1994), 147–61 and 'The Ocean in Us', *The Contemporary Pacific* 10, 2 (1998), 391–410; A. Wendt, 'Towards a New Oceania', *Mana Review* 1, 1 (1976), 49–60.

13 T. Tamasese, 'Message from the President', Manu Samoa vs. Fiji match programme, 1 July 1995.

14 'Tonga Must Beat Manu Samoa', *Matangi Tonga*, 17, 3 (May–June 1992), 42.

15 S. Singh, 'All the Way to Hell and Back', *Fiji Sport* (July 1995), 8–12.

16 A. Raganivatu, 'Eye of the Hurricane', *Fiji Sport* (December 1995), 19.

17 Statistics cover the period 1 January 1995 – 1 January 2015. Figures acquired from Statsguru, http://stats.espnscrum.com/statsguru/rugby/stats/index.html. accessed 11 May 2015.

18 Q. Smith and W. Field, *Putting Rugby First* (London: Addleshaw Goddard, 2008), quoted in P. Ackford, 'Rebels Attack "Undemocratic" IRB in Crusade for Global Revolution', *Daily Telegraph*, 14 September 2008, www.telegraph.co.uk/sport/rugby-union/2911031/Rebels-attack-undemocratic-IRB-in-crusade-for-global-revolution-Rugby-Union.html, accessed 11 May 2015.

19 Personal comments to author, June 2015.

20 For comments on the regional importance of the Super 10s to Pacific rugby, see 'Message from the Prime Minister', Otago vs. Manu Samoa match programme, 8 May 1993.

21 Author interview with Harry Schuster, Apia, Samoa, 6 June 2015.

22 A. Soames, 'Super Rugby Expansion Likely to Exclude Islands', 27 January 2013, www.superxv.com/super-rugby-expansion-likely-to-exclude-islands/, accessed 17 August 2015.

23 For extensive discussions of Pacific rugby and sporting mobility see relevant chapters in the following special journal issues: P. Horton (ed.), 'Regional Issue: Australasia and the Pacific Islanders in Global Rugby Football', *International Journal of the History of Sport* 31, 11 (June 2014), 1329–31; G. Molnar and Y. Kanemasu (eds), 'Special Issue: Playing on the Global Periphery: Social Science Explorations of Rugby in the Pacific Islands', *Asia Pacific Journal of Sport and Social Science* 3, 3 (December 2014); L. Uperesa and T. Mountjoy (eds), Special Issue: Global Sport in the Pacific', *The Contemporary Pacific* 26, 2 (2014).

24 T. Collins, *The Oval World: A Global History of Rugby* (London: Bloomsbury, 2015), 347–8.

25 S. Singh, 'Jewels in the Crown', *Fiji Sport* (July 1995), 16–19.

26 D. Lomas, 'Flying Samoans Take Off in League', *Islands Business* (December 1988), 42.

27 'Planning a Comeback', *Fiji Sport* (July 1995), 13–14.

28 N. Besnier, 'The Athlete's Body and the Global Condition: Tongan Rugby Players in Japan', *American Ethnologist* 39, 3 (July 2012), 491–510; D. Scheider, 'Fiji Islander Rugby Union Players in Japan: Corporate Particularities and Migration Routes', *Asia Pacific Journal of Sport and Social Science* 3, 3 (2014), 250–67.

29 Radio NZ, 'Pacific Rugby Team Would be a Boost', 3 February 2016, www.radionz.co.nz/international/pacific-news/295639/sport-pacific-super-rugby-team-would-be-a-boost-on-and-off-the-field-ex-players, accessed 17 February 2016.

30 Statistical charts in *Teivovo*, 58 (2014), 58–61.

31 S. Jones, *Midnight Rugby* (London: Headline, 2002), 89.

32 G. Molnar and Y. Kanemasu, 'Playing on the Periphery: Social Scientific Explorations of Rugby in the Pacific Islands', *Asia Pacific Journal of Sport and Social Science*, 3, 3 (2014), 183.

33 Massey University, 'Research Explores Winning Off the Field in Samoa', 3 March 2015, www.massey.ac.nz/massey/about-massey/news/article.cfm?mnarticle_uuid=FD2ECFAD-C42D-850B-19AC-AD0CE25677D2, accessed 20 August 2015.

34 Y. Kanemasu and G. Molnar, 'Pride of the People. Fiji Rugby Labour Migration and Collective Identity', *International Review for the Sociology of Sport* 48 (2013), 706–19.

35 Author interview with Culden Kamea, Suva, Fiji, 16 June 2015.

36 Author interview with Harry Schuster, Apia, Samoa, 6 June 2015.
37 A. Kumar, 'Deal to Benefit Fiji Rugby', *Fiji Times*, July 16 2014, www.fijitimes.com/story.aspx?id=274548, accessed 15 August 2015.
38 'A Man with a Heart for Samoa', *Samoa Observer*, 19 October 2014, www.samoaobserver.ws/home/headlines/11909-a-man-with-a-heart-for-samoa, accessed 15 August 2015.
39 'Essentially Group (NZ) Rugby Academy for Tonga', Nepituno – Tonga On-line News, 5 June 2015, www.nepituno.to/sports/item/384-essentially-group-nz-rugby-academy-for-tonga.
40 For a discussion of difficulties in player–agent relationships from a Fijian perspective see S. Raiwalui, 'No Messin' column, *Teivovo*, 48 (June 2013), 54.
41 Z. Singh, 'Deals Pour in for Seven', *Fiji Times*, 30 May 2015, www.fijitimes.com/story.aspx?id=307843, accessed 8 July 2015; P. Narain, 'On the Radar', *Fiji Times*, 6 July 2015, www.fijitimes.com/story.aspx?id=312641, accessed 8 July 2015.
42 P. Narain 'France Treat', Fiji Times 17 June 2015, www.fijitimes.com/story.aspx?id=310166; Process Rugby Facebook Page, www.facebook.com/processrugby/info?tab=page_info; M. Malo, 'Process Rugby Foundation Denies Claim', *Fiji Times*, 21 June 2015, www.fijitimes.com/story.aspx?id=310676, accessed 8 July 2015.
43 K. Dakuidreketi, 'CEO's Report for 2010', Fiji Rugby Union Meeting Papers, 30 April 2011.
44 Author interview with Alama Ieremia, Apia, Samoa, 4 June 2016.
45 For a full discussion of these issues see A. Grainer, O. Rick and D. Andrews, 'Bound to the Nation: Pacific Islands Rugby and the IRB's new "One-Country-for-Life" Eligibility Rules', *Sport in Society* 17, 7 (2014), 977–91.
46 Author interview with Manasa Baravilala, Suva, Fiji, 19 June 2015.
47 C. Kamea, 'McKee Flies Out on Mission Impossible', *Teivovo*, 58 (2014), 50.
48 B. Gavoka, 'Chairman's Report 2010', Fiji Rugby Union Meeting Papers, 30 April 2011.
49 R. Dewey, 'Pacific Islands Rugby Alliance (PIRA): Rugby in "Our Sea of Islands"', *International Journal of the History of Sport*, 31, 11 (2014), 1406–20.
50 P. Rees, 'Pacific Islanders Quick to Arrive for the World Cup and Hopefully Not the First to Leave', *Guardian*, 27 August 2015, www.theguardian.com/sport/2015/aug/27/pacific-islanders-arrive-for-world-cup-and-hopefully-will-not-be-first-to-leave, accessed 2 September 2015.
51 N. Besnier, *At the Edge of the Global: Modern Anxieties in a Pacific Island Nation* (Stanford: Stanford University Press, 2011), 231–2.
52 J. Harris, 'Definitely Maybe: Continuity and Change in the Rugby World Cup', *Sport in Society* 16, 7 (2013), 857–8.

7 The globalization of rugby sevens

From novelty to the Olympic Games

Jeremy Stewart and Marc Keech

Introduction

In 2009, the International Olympic Committee (IOC) approved rugby (union) sevens at the Rio de Janeiro and Tokyo summer Olympic Games of 2016 and 2020.[1] Since rugby union turned professional in 1995, seven-a-side (hereafter called 'sevens') rugby has notably increased in importance and popularity, shedding the old view of it being simply an end-of-season celebration.[2] There is an established Rugby World Cup Sevens, which was first held in 1993; sevens has been included in the Commonwealth Games since 1998; and there is an annual World Series that began in 1999. Most elite players are now sevens specialists, with noticeable differences in the physiological characteristics required for the game compared with the fifteen-a-side game.[3] These competitions have arisen from a number of influential tournaments created in the amateur era.[4] In over twenty years of professionalism, the international governing body, World Rugby (formerly the IRB (International Rugby Board) and before that the IRFB (International Rugby Football Board)), has developed strategies to ensure sevens is part of the vision of 'making rugby a truly globalized sport',[5] although this has been a challenge to an historically elitist sport traditionally associated with a power structure where there is a dominance of the Tier 1 unions: Australia, England, France, Ireland, New Zealand, Scotland, South Africa and Wales. Not only does the hierarchy allow the foundation unions greater power and autonomy, but it has also established the sport as, habitually, a globally insular practice.[6]

The study of the influence and impact of sevens is under-researched, with occasional histories cited, and rarely considered in the context of history or the power relations of rugby union. But, not only is it the chosen format to reintroduce rugby union to the Olympics, after an unsuccessful involvement between 1900 and 1924:[7] sevens has also become core to the global strategy in developing the newer unions, known as Tier 2 and 3 unions. Transnational processes are clearly evident in sevens, and as a spectacle and sporting practice, the game is considered an easier format to comprehend. Sevens is allowing the lower-tier nations to host and compete in major events, where they would not previously had have the same opportunity in the fifteen-a-side game.[8] This chapter traces the development of sevens to the extent that it is now an opportunity for World Rugby to showcase the sport to a worldwide audience and the key to which is a positive Olympic reintroduction.[9] The chapter examines the conception of the sevens format in 1883 and its development until the beginning of the professional era in 1995. The process of the game's globalization in international sport is presented as a significant factor in leading to the Hong Kong Sevens, rugby union's first truly global competition, which raised the standards of rugby sevens and allowed Tier 2 and 3 unions the opportunity to compete on the global stage for the first time. The chapter concludes with an overview of contribution of sevens to the promotion of rugby union as a global game.

The game within a game

Rugby sevens literature is relatively scarce, with the format having often been seen as little more than end-of-season fun. Allan provides a strong reconstruction of the conception of sevens in *The Official History of the Melrose Sevens*.[10] There are further accounts relating to the social and global success of the Hong Kong Sevens. The context of rugby in different cultures does provide indications of how sevens has played a part in rugby history and its position in global sport. Global accounts of the game, whether analytical or nostalgic, do make regular short references to sevens competitions.[11] Scottish rugby history, and in particular Borders rugby history,[12] recognizes the cultural importance of sevens in a region where identity is of great importance.[13] The development of, and challenge for, improving opportunities for Tier 2 and 3 unions has become recognized as a critical issue for the sport in the context of the dominance by the traditional foundation unions.[14] Harris incorporates historical and global analysis to underpin an examination of contemporary worldwide rugby issues, including a rare reference to sevens and Olympic participation (referred to as 'Olympianization') and the development of lesser unions. He rightly recognizes and identifies important but lacking subject areas in rugby and highlights the requirement for greater study.[15]

A part of the 'Sacred Seven' English schools that included Eton, Winchester, Westminster, Harrow, Charterhouse and Shrewsbury, Rugby School was a leader in applying sport as a pedagogic tool.[16] Immortalized in former pupil Thomas Hughes' novel *Tom Brown's Schooldays*, Dr Thomas Arnold, an ex-headmaster of the school, was a reformist of education and advocate of muscular Christian ideology. Arnold utilized sport to nurture pupils' moral and spiritual development in conjunction with their physical growth, ready for the duties of the Empire. The 'real' British gentleman was one of faith, discipline, imperialism, chivalry, leadership and bravery, all of which, Arnold believed, were encompassed in the right sporting practice. Sport at Rugby School embodied the muscular Christian ethos under Arnold. It was the school's football code that truly personified its imperialist values.[17]

The codified laws of Rugby School football arrived in Scotland through educational rivals Edinburgh Academy and Merchiston School. Embracing elitist, muscular Christian ideals, the initial diffusion of rugby in Scotland was rarely recognized outside of these middle- or upper-class institutions. After the formation of the English governing body, the Rugby Football Union (RFU), and the first international rugby match, in which Scotland beat England, both in 1871, rugby acquired a measure of approval outside the Scottish elite. The formation of the Scottish Football Union (later to become the Scottish Rugby Union – SRU) followed in 1873, and club rugby eventually extended to the Scottish Borders.[18] Physical textile and agricultural industries dominated Borders employment, and physical leisure, which recreated and complemented this corporal nature, was enthusiastically engaged with by the male working population of Scotland. The process of rugby's diffusion in the Borders was testament to Rugby School and the application of codified rules as a diffusional paradigm. Many towns only held a population large enough to support one code of football and were influenced by privately educated mill owners who favoured rugby over association football. Sporting culture in the Borders, however, conflicted with the traditional ideals of the RFU and a similarly conservative SRU.[19]

There were a number of established folklore forms of football in the Borders. In a society so influenced by distinctly classed systems, some activities were deemed too violent and destructive.[20] But with town pride already placed in the traditional games, rugby, which bore many similarities, captured the imagination of the region. Borders rugby was essentially a working-class sport, tempered by a diversifying working-class population that now included a number of emigrated mill workers from Yorkshire, a rugby stronghold of the era, conveying their knowledge of the game.[21] Border towns began regular fixtures, which were watched by partisan spectators of both sides and continued the passion and interest witnessed and celebrated in the old folklore games. Such was the passion on the playing field, it was commonplace for a number of players to settle individual disputes with a fistfight behind the hosting club pavilion during the game, returning to play once finished. Matches were closely followed by intrigued spectators, with town bands intensifying the atmosphere. The matches were attended for leisure and a demonstration of town pride. It was an unintended show of identity and opposition to the elitist hierarchy that had established rugby as a moral and physical pursuit for the individual. Borders rugby was a part of life that exhibited pride, physical ability and a spectacle that represented a parochial Border character often in conflict with Scottish identity. There was a clear aptitude for innovation and making the most of what was to be had in the Borders, as was the case in the Northern unions of England, but it was the Edinburgh-based SRU that reinforced RFU philosophy. Tensions intensified when a Borders regional league competition was initially rejected by the SRU. Grievances ran high, with the suggestion of a Borders union being established to protect the region's game.

A new innovation followed in 1883. In an attempt to raise desperately needed funds, Melrose Rugby Club, inspired by local butcher and club member Adam 'Ned' Haig, conceived a football and athletics tournament at a club meeting. Unable to host a full rugby tournament in one afternoon, but convinced that rugby would be the main attraction, a seven-a-side format with full rules in fifteen-minute matches was agreed. The full extent of Haig's contribution varies by account, but he, assisted by teammate and co-worker David Sanderson, was credited with inventing sevens.[22] The tournament caught the imagination, with invitations sent to all of the clubs in the Borders. On 29 April 1883, the first sevens tournament was held, attracting around 1600 spectators from across the region.[23] Melrose won the inaugural tournament, beating bitter rivals Gala in the final. Tied without score, both captains agreed to play an additional fifteen minutes, but with five minutes remaining Melrose scored and left the field claiming victory. The decision was upheld by the referee, much to the confusion of the crowd, and the first score in extra time remains a deciding rule in contemporary rugby sevens. A year later, the controversially beaten Gala hosted a tournament of the same format, and other Border clubs followed, leading to an annual sevens circuit hosted by five clubs by 1909, now known as 'The Kings of Sevens'.[24] The open and more expansive game was in line with the exciting passing game for which Scottish rugby was recognized in the fifteen-a-side format, utilizing speed, precision and a full back line. But rugby sevens had little recognition outside of the Borders, a circumstance that probably favoured the format's continuation. The SRU did not endorse rugby sevens until 1905, when it took control of the format after fears over travel expenses.[25] But, importantly up until this point, it did not oppose sevens either. The SRU's alignment with RFU governance, together with the English stance taken against professionalism and another shortened format developed in Northern England, highlighted the evident tensions.

Preceding the Melrose Sevens, in 1879, Huddersfield Cricket and Athletic Club, in Yorkshire, hosted a six-a-side tournament with matches played over twenty minutes, originally applying full rules. The popularity of the format spread in the following years, with many other clubs in the Northern English unions hosting tournaments. By the 1880s a further nine-a-side format was introduced, attracting large crowds and media interest. The RFU deemed the tournaments as a breach of rugby's code. The Yorkshire and Lancashire unions placed a full ban on the formats by 1890, citing the hosting of tournaments outside of the regular season, and modified scoring, as undermining RFU authority. The greatest opposition was in relation to the well-known rewards, which players received from prize money and trinkets of substantial monetary value.[26] Cases of players receiving financial reward in rugby were a perceived evil in Northern England and strictly dealt with through bans or even expulsion.[27] Class hierarchy was restricting the development of rugby in Northern England and the Scottish Borders.[28] A key difference in the shortened formats was seen in the Borders' innovation of upholding amateur status but rewarding hosting clubs rather than players. The Borders game was not exceptional in its format, but the survival of its invention and spectacle was unique. For rugby in the Borders, town passion and team pride had outweighed any desire for financial reward and instead expressed ideals that represented Borders people and innovation.

The Middlesex Sevens

In the late nineteenth century, association football (hereafter referred to as 'football') became the premier winter sport in Britain. Whilst football embraced ideas of professionalism and crowd spectacle, rugby's authorities remained troubled that sport could be for any other reason than the moral and physical development of the 'self'. Such notions were to the detriment of the sport, as football continued to grow both in Britain and globally.[29] The moral myopia of the RFU, even in the wake of declining popularity, alienated those advocating modernization to save the game. Muscular Christian ideals were widely challenged in the early twentieth century as the physical fitness of British men became a major concern following the Boer War in 1899–1902. A 1904 government report on the Interdepartmental Committee on Physical Deterioration linked imperial decline to British masculinity, and sport was a reflection of the concern. Defeats were experienced in a number of traditionally British sports, including rugby.[30] Rugby tours by New Zealand and South Africa to Britain in 1905 and 1906 respectively were a contradiction, in confirming on the one hand the physical decline of British men, but on the other, reminding how a strong, healthy nation can be built on muscular Christian ideals.[31] The report, however, deemed rugby as the best sporting preparation for the trials of military combat.

The First World War was a significant test of the muscular Christian ideals inherent in rugby, but renewed confidence in British masculinity invigorated English rugby and the founding ideals.[32] The RFU cemented rugby as the game of choice within elite schooling in the early 1920s, and the imperial confidence of the era was emphasized by its refusal of support for Olympic rugby competition that eventually ended in 1924.[33] The ethos of amateurism was unmoved, but rugby sevens, nearly forty years after the format's conception, finally made an impact on the RFU. Sevens competitions had slowly dispersed from the Borders into the elitist rugby areas of Edinburgh and Glasgow, and even to Argentina and Western Samoa, by 1920. In 1921, sevens was first played in England, at the Percy Park tournament, followed by competitions in Rockcliffe in Northumberland in 1922.

The tournaments eventually led to RFU approval of a sevens competition hosted at Twickenham, but only under the stipulation put forward by the London-based Scot, tournament founder and Middlesex Union member Dr J. A. Russell-Cargill that proceeds would go to the Middlesex Hospital restoration fund. After preliminary rounds between Middlesex-based teams to reach a last sixteen, the main tournament took place on 24 April 1926, and raised over £1,180.[34] The star was England captain and RAF Officer William Wavell Wakefield, who had led England to a famous victory over New Zealand in the fifteen-a-side format a year earlier. Wakefield himself had been heavily involved in the creation of the Middlesex tournament, and led a distinguished Harlequins team to the first Middlesex Sevens.[35] Credited as an innovator of forward game play, with great strength and pace, as well as forward-thinking tactical play, Wakefield also held the position of Middlesex Union representative on the RFU board. In his co-written 1927 book *Rugger*, Wakefield showed desire for the game to expand and develop, but he was also a champion of the amateur code.[36]

Wakefield was ahead of his time, advocating the transfer of rugby law governance to an impartial 'Imperial Board'. He had rallied support, sometimes unsuccessfully, but control was passed to the international governing body, the International Rugby Football Board (IRFB) in 1930.[37] It was not surprising that Wakefield became a member of the IRFB. His book recognized the potential development of new unions in international rugby, a view in opposition to the hierarchical outlook of the time.[38] His support for and participation in the Middlesex Sevens enhanced the enthusiasm about the shortened format that was new to English rugby. Wakefield also put forward the motion, seconded by RFU Chairman Roland Hill, that declined a sevens tournament proposed to be played outside of the season in Halifax.[39] A man possessing a sense of duty, Wakefield, along with the Middlesex Union, reinforced the charitable importance of the tournament when calling on all associated with rugby union to consider the 'ravages' of cancer and to support the sevens tournament as advertised in the London weekly newspaper *The Saturday Review*.[40] Further correspondence was also sent to affluent persons, appealing for further assistance, with Wakefield's signature prominent on each request.[41] The continued success of the Middlesex Sevens in the name of charity, strong social ties with the London elite, and an all-day end-of-season rugby celebration established the shortened format as an acceptable form of rugby philosophy.

The Hong Kong Sevens: changing the nature of the game

Despite the continued success of sevens in Britain, there was slow dissemination of the game globally. Rugby union broadly resisted global and commercial interest, rejecting international competition beyond bilateral matches and/or 'test' series, and any kind of sponsorship, until 1970. Rugby sevens slowly spread to new destinations, but continued as a festivity and was rarely played outside of Britain and its former colonies. In 1973 the SRU celebrated its centenary by hosting an international sevens tournament at Murrayfield – the first of its kind. Through sevens there was considerable excitement at the possibility of all of the leading nations being involved in a single competition, although the IRFB was quick to insist that this was merely a celebration of the SRU and not a prelude to a much sought-after World Cup.[42] The use of sevens was an acknowledgement to the SRU regarding where the format had started. The tournament was a one-off celebration: exactly the format for which sevens had now been established. It was not to be taken too seriously, and, in the eyes of the IRFB, would not demonstrate a natural progression towards a fifteen-a-side world tournament. Sevens was a format of rugby without the same connotations of national pride and masculinity. A legacy from the tournament would not, at the time, have been a threat to the fifteen-a-side game's status. England won the tournament, and were regarded by many English, facetiously, as the first rugby world champions, but the IRFB firmly noted there would be no repeat of the tournament.[43]

Global competition sat uncomfortably with the IRFB. For example, it can be argued that IRFB control of the sport, and rejection of globalization in favour of amateurism, was highlighted with the refusal of Canada's admission to the IRFB board.[44] But, in 1975, a lunchtime meeting in Hong Kong between two rugby lovers, Hong Kong Rugby Football Union (HKRFU) President Tokkie Smith and Ian Gow, an executive of Rothmans Tobacco, was to inadvertently challenge old-guard hegemony and open rugby up to international competition.[45] Gow approached Smith with the idea of creating an international rugby tournament in Hong Kong, with Rothmans prepared to sponsor. The ambitious idea was well received by other businessmen, as Cathay Pacific Airlines and the Hong Kong Bank (later HSBC) were to back the tournament.[46]

Like with the Melrose tournament, the logistics of hosting so many teams led to the conclusion that sevens would best serve the tournament. Financially it was a shrewd decision. Fewer players, coaches and support staff were required, allowing costs on accommodation and travel to be minimized. British imperialism and 'Old Boy' influence may have brought rugby to the colony, but Hong Kong did not suffer from the same colonial reservations found elsewhere. It was 'the world's least parochial place'.[47]

Rugby's hierarchy, however, still held heavy sway. After the idea had been ratified by the HKRFU, approval was sought from the RFU.[48] In response, the RFU reminded tournament organizers that a multi-team international competition was against the rules at that time. Highlighting the changing culture, however, the RFU submitted a proposal, approved by the IRFB in 1976, changing the wording of Rule 20, resolution 4.7 of the IRFB handbook, to allow a tournament consisting of teams from two or more countries, so long as approval of any unions concerned was given before invitations were sent.[49] With permission obtained, the first tournament was held at Happy Valley, home of the Hong Kong Football Club. Two representative sides from Australia and New Zealand, alongside national teams from Fiji, Hong Kong, Indonesia, Japan, Korea, Malaysia, Singapore, Sri Lanka, Thailand and Tonga all competed. The New Zealand 'Cantabrians' defeated the Australian 'Wallaroos' in the maiden Cup competition, but in a tournament structure emphasizing the logistical adaptability of sevens, Hong Kong won a Plate competition comprising the losing sides from the first round.

Fiji became the stars of the Hong Kong Sevens, with the local population adopting them as their favoured team. With a first win in 1977, Fiji repeated the success in 1978 in an enlarged tournament now including Bahrain, Papua New Guinea, Western Samoa, a full international Australian team and the American state of Hawaii. The quality of rugby backed the carnival atmosphere of the tournament, and the Fijians advanced the game with their high-class pace, skill and flair. Players became noted for world-class ability in the shortened format.[50] In 1982, the tournament moved to the Hong Kong Stadium, allowing greater capacity and an eventual expansion to twenty-four teams. The now fully established tournament was an interactive spectacle for the crowd and provided serious competition on the pitch. New Zealand followed Australia's example and sent a national team, a move that led New Zealand to take on the game in the same serious manner as the Fijians.[51] The involvement of British Isles and other European nations was rare however, until in 1990, Wales sent a national team. However, Hong Kong had established itself without the need of the Tier 1 unions, and the emergent tournament resembled the global sports industry of a free commercial market, advocating global competition in rugby union and recognizing the potential of Tier 2 and 3 unions. Overall playing standards rapidly improved in sevens, with regular upsets adding to what many in rugby considered world-class sporting entertainment. The growth of the Hong Kong Sevens was a reflection of rugby union's conflict with commercialization and globalization. Commercial consumption of sport in the 1970s and 1980s challenged the traditional values of insular, elitist and ideological sports.[52] Those recognizing the global potential of rugby demanded international competition and spectacle similar to other sports. The international character of the Hong Kong Sevens had set it apart from other rugby union competitions in any format, presenting Asian rugby with a foothold in the international game. Japanese rugby chief Shiggy Konno, despite being a guardian of amateurism, recognized the impact of the Hong Kong Sevens as popularizing rugby in the Far East, and applied for funding from the IRFB to assist Asian rugby tournaments, with little success.[53] The applications were further examples of the growing pressure the IRFB faced in developing global rugby. The Australian and New Zealand unions produced a report on the prospect of a fifteen-a-side World Cup in 1985, and the IRFB ultimately consented to two sixteen-team World Cups in 1987 and 1991.

The global spectacle

The creation of a World Cup tournament led to a new application criterion for Tier 2 and 3 unions, with Argentina, Canada, Italy, Japan, the USA and Zimbabwe becoming associate members of the IRFB. A new international voice had been negotiated, but the IRFB clung on to amateur ideals. The 'fear' of professionalism had also seen the creation of an 'Amateurism Committee' to work and report on the safeguarding of negotiated traditional ideals of rugby.[54] The success of the 1987 and 1991 fifteen-a-side World Cups continued rugby's global initiative to expand and revised the image of the sport. Rugby World Cup Limited, a wholly owned subsidiary of the IRFB, was established to manage the competitive and commercial interests of the tournament and led to players receiving indirect material benefit. With new rules encouraging a quicker, more continuous and attractive game that spectators could enjoy as well as players, the game was finally responding to global trends in other sports. Rugby sevens naturally fitted into this new ethos. The successes in Hong Kong and the World Cups saw a number of new proposals, in particular an application by the SRU to host a sevens World Cup twenty years after its centenary tournament.[55]

The proposal was consequently accepted, and responsibility for a twenty-four-team tournament was passed to Rugby World Cup Limited, who organized the first Rugby World Cup Sevens in 1993. The IRB invited the established rugby union nations but also was keen to involve emerging nations in the event, recognizing the fact that sevens was providing the bridge between developed rugby nations and those whose rugby union traditions were less established. Nineteen nations were invited and five had to pre-qualify. Hosted at Murrayfield, the tournament exemplified the growing status of sevens, with the trophy named as the Melrose Cup. Exceptional players, attracted by the possibility of partici- pating in a World Cup sooner than anticipated after the 1991 fifteen-a-side tour- nament in the British Isles and France, were in abundance. Laurent Cabannes and Phillippe Bernat-Salles of France, Rob Howley and Neil Jenkins from Wales, Michael Lynagh, Willie Ofahengaue and David Campese of the Walla- bies, and Springboks Johann Van der Westhuizen and Chester Williams all were in attendance. England, despite only meeting up for one brief get-together in preparation, had the air of play around them and whilst scrum-half Dave Scully of Wakefield was an inspired choice, future British and Irish Lions players, such as Lawrence Dallaglio and Tim Rodber, exemplified the class of the unheralded England team. Despite previous low expectations and frustrations relating to the gruelling format over three days, it proved to the IRFB to be another success fol- lowing the fifteen-a-side World Cups.[56] Commercial success and the prospect of a new international tournament in an ever-evolving climate, losing the shackles of fading elitist authority, led to a Rugby World Cup Sevens in Hong Kong in 1997 and the serious consideration and subsequent acceptance of Common- wealth Games participation from 1998.[57]

In 1994, the IOC accepted an application from the IRB to become a non- participatory member. But rugby was evolving, and trying to appease the growing demands for new development and professionalism was proving impossible. The pressure of both internal and external forces was abundant, and in particular, commercial interest from media mogul Kerry Packer and his busi- ness rival Rupert Murdoch. The pair unsettled the Australian (rules) football and rugby league codes by battling for power and placing huge investment into rugby league.[58] This made professionalism in rugby union all the more likely and needed. The acceptance of rugby union into the Olympic movement was swiftly followed by an adamant domestic governing body that wanted rugby league included in the 2000 Sydney Olympics. At the same time, the IRFB requested the Australian Rugby Union (ARU) apply for the sport to be included in the Games in 'any format',[59] appearing to suggest that sevens would be considered suitable. It transpired that neither rugby code was to be included, but the episode highlighted the fears for the survival of the sport in a country increasingly chal- lenged by the commercial impact of other sports.

Despite uncertainty, the IRFB, alongside its union members, pushed forward with new commercially viable competitions and in 1995 published an official set of rules solely for sevens.[60] The format had been recognized for its appeal and ability to host a large number of teams over a short period of time. A spectacle that over a day or weekend created a party atmosphere for spectators, but pro- vided important and meaningful competition on the field, was welcomed. Since the introduction of professionalism in 1995, World Rugby has encouraged the development of non-traditional rugby-playing nations through sevens in particular, illustrating the increasing awareness of the format as a catalyst for the evolution of the sport.[61] The Sevens World Series, currently comprising ten tournaments played around the world, is televised globally. Each tournament consists of sixteen international teams based on qualification criteria, which includes the recognized nations (other than Ireland) and also emerging nations such as Kenya. The World Series was used as the qualification mechanism for the 2016 Olympics.

After a troubled start to the professional era and despite the success of the quadrennial fifteen-a-side World Cup, the desire for the game to expand globally and develop lesser unions was cited as crucial in rugby's strategy in order to safeguard the future of the sport, increase its popularity, develop competition and promote commercial success.[62] Although the fifteen-a-side World Cup, for men and women, remains the global pinnacle of the game, the central development in the process of globalizing rugby has been the growth of sustainable sevens programmes. World Rugby has firmly placed sevens Olympic participation at the core of global strategy and sees it as a tool to open rugby up to new audiences. Sevens illustrates increasing transnational elements that suggest the sport can be considered a global sport, with an increasing number of international competitions, the growth of the sevens women's game and individual contests between teams. The nature of sevens provides a competitively equalizing format that has allowed, and continues to allow, Tier 2 and 3 unions the prospect of beating the Tier 1 unions. Reduced time and playing numbers permit quicker and less technically demanding breakdowns of play, more space for athletic players to exploit, and different tactical set-ups that generally require an exciting and expressive spectacle that is easier for newcomers to comprehend. A fast-moving and flexible tournament schedule also provides for the completion of a large number of games over a short period of time. The differences in the sevens format and its fast-paced nature lead to unpredictability, and provide the capacity to include leading world teams over a weekend in multiple worldwide destinations that do not require specialist facilities to host tournaments. This emphasizes not only the use of sevens as a globalizing tool, but also its compatibility for serious competition within multi-sport events.

The success of the first two editions of the Rugby World Cup Sevens, in 1993 and 1997, led the IRB to seek participation in continental multi-sport events, and then further competition with the annual World Series. Aided by the Commonwealth Games Federation's decision to permit the introduction of team sports, the 1998 Commonwealth Games saw the first sevens tournament take place at a multi-sport event, with players such as Jonah Lomu and David Campese participating. The development demonstrated how rugby could, for the first time, contribute to global multi-sport events and laid the platform for applications which eventually resulted in the IOC's vote for Olympic participation in 2009, debuting sevens in Rio de Janeiro in 2016.[63] The inclusion potentially opens rugby to new audiences and prosperous new partnerships.[64] Utilizing support to increase funding and the sporting and structural development within a union, sevens or

'Olympic rugby' provides new opportunity and increased potential for any tier of rugby union. With the 2016 Olympics and the 2018 Commonwealth Games also hosting a women's tournament, the successful implementation of World Rugby's current strategy will intentionally position rugby as a truly transnational sport.

Conclusion

The chapter illustrates that the global development of rugby sevens should always be seen within the context of the fifteen-a-side format, but, contrarily, has also embraced innovation and encouraged further participation. Sevens entertainment challenged much of what rugby stood for, but amateurism was respected. A fund-raising spectacle with the intention to keep a club and its members playing rugby, whether with the desire for the overall goal of moral self-improvement or not, provided no challenge to hegemony. It can be argued that the conception of sevens in such a scarcely populated area as the Scottish Borders, with little outward influence, was a deciding factor in the format's survival there. The formation of the Hong Kong Sevens was the catalyst for developing the global potential of the sport. New nations were competing in rugby union's first international tournament. The competition proved rugby had commercial appeal and did not need to rely on the foundation unions to develop and popularize the game. Rugby sevens has led modernization, embraced new talent, and embodied the changing ideology and power relationships of the sport.

The full impact of Olympic rugby will not be understood until the competition has taken place and been evaluated over the course of several cycles. Questions have been asked as to whether rugby sevens will enhance the fifteens game or become a global sport in its own right.[65] A number of players in the Sevens World Series are sevens specialists, and are physically and tactically conditioned to the format, evolving from the earlier identified tournaments, which have become increasingly demanding and important. However, such is the tactical, technical and physiological sophistication required by the format, even the most skilled fifteen-a-side players have to make adjustments to its specialized requirements. Add in already demanding season schedules, and concessions have to be made to accommodate these ambitions. This also asks questions of the future role of senior club rugby across the world as to whether it can support the game.

In the advent of the era of Olympic rugby, a noticeable omission is made in forecasting about the potential growth and influence of clubs. Greater commercialization in the men's game, in Super Rugby, the Top 14, the English Premiership and the Pro 12, has already entrenched it at franchise and club levels in both hemispheres. Players are brought in from around the world on large salaries to improve a team and attract spectators. The possibility of an 'Olympic hero' who could be brought into a leading club, even if a sevens specialist, may prove too tempting to resist for an ambitious club. It raises the possibility of expanding and developing domestic rugby sevens. Like with fifteen-a-side rugby, a global outlook could see teams building squads of international sevens superstars not bound by nationality, similar to cricket's Indian Premier League. The governance of World Rugby will be key to any successful globalization of rugby in both formats. Keen to impress, World Rugby needs to ensure that the Olympic participation in 2016 and 2020 exemplifies the extent to which rugby sevens is a global game. It would certainly be a failure, and leave no legacy for the sport, if sevens were not included in Olympic competition far into the future.

Notes

1 International Rugby Board (IRB) (2011), *Rugby Sevens Plan: 2011–2020*, Worldrugby. org, http://pulse-static-files.s3.amazonaws.com/worldrugby/document/2014/11/15/1da4d 777-5ec0-416d-a03a-645b01d2cd4c/120327LJRugbySevensPlanFINAL.pdf (accessed 23 July 2014).
2 M. Blackburn, *Coaching Rugby Sevens* (2nd Ed) (London: Bloomsbury, 2009).
3 R. Meir, 'Training for and Competing in Sevens Rugby: Practical Considerations from Experience in the International Rugby Board World Series', *Strength and Conditioning Journal*, 34, 4 (2014), 76–86.
4 See S. Chadwick, A. Semens, E. Schwarz and D. Zhang, *Economic Impact Report on Global Rugby Part III: Strategic and Emerging Markets*, Centre for International Business of Sport, Coventry University (2010), https://pulse-static-files.s3.amazonaws.com/worldrugby/document/2014/11/16/9a57db49-4160-4ffb-9912-2ae-ae873260e/2042288_PDF.pdf (accessed 21 October 2016); J. Harris, *Rugby Union and Globalization: An Odd Shaped World* (Basingstoke, UK: Palgrave Macmillan, 2010); IRB, *Rugby Sevens Plan: 2011–2020* (2011).
5 B. Lapesset, 'The Future is Bright', in IRB (International Rugby Board), *International Rugby Board: Year in Review 2013*, IRB.com (2014), http://pulse-static-files.s3. amazonaws.com/worldrugby/document/2014/11/16/dcccc735-59b3-402f-8749-6126ec 1ab174/IRBYearinReviewLR100.pdf, p. 3 (accessed 18 January 2016).
6 See T. Chandler, 'The Structuring of Manliness and the Development of Rugby Football at the Public Schools and Oxbridge, 1830–1880', in J. Nauright and T. J. L. Chandler (eds), *Making Men: Rugby and Masculine Identity* (London: Routledge, 1996), 13–31; and R. Kitson, 'Global Leaders Face Battle to Satisfy Rugby Union's Impatience for Growth', *Guardian* 16 September 2014 www.theguardian.com/sport/blog/2014/sep/16/global-leaders-rugby-union-impatience-growth (accessed 16 September 2014).
7 Harris, *Rugby Union and Globalization*; M. Ryan, *Try for Gold: America's Olympic Rugby Medals* (New York: AI, 2009).
8 J. Harris and N. Wise, 'Geographies of Scale in International Rugby Union', *Geographical Research*, 49, 4 (2011), 375–83.
9 IRB, *Rugby Sevens Plan* (2011); B. Rumsby, 'International Rugby Board Chief Says Olympic Rugby Sevens Debut at Rio 2016 Could be Compromised by Delays', *Telegraph* 16 April 2014, www.telegraph.co.uk/sport/rugbyunion/10770411/International-Rugby-Board-chief-says-Olympic-rugby-sevens-debut-at-Rio-2016-could-be-compromised-by-delays.html (accessed 16 April 2014).
10 W. Allan, *The Official History of the Melrose Sevens* (Edinburgh: Mainstream Publishing, 1994).
11 S. Barnes, 'Made in Hong Kong', in S. Barnes and M. Seabrook (eds), *Nice Tries: An Anthology of New Rugby Writing* (London: Victor Gallancz, 1995); S. Jones, *Midnight Rugby: Triumph and Shambles in the Professional Era* (London: Headline Book Publishing, 2000).
12 N. Drysdale, *Southern Comfort: The Story of Borders Rugby* (Edinburgh: Birlinn, 2011).

13 See, for example, F. Gill, 'Public and Private: National Identities in a Scottish Borders Community', *Nations and Nationalisms*, 11, 1 (2005), 83–102; D. Douglas, *The Thistle: A Chronicle of Scottish Rugby* (Edinburgh: Mainstream Publishing, 1997); S. Thorburn, *The History of Scottish Rugby* (Edinburgh: Johnston and Bacon, 1980).

14 P. Horton, 'Pacific Islanders in Global Rugby: The Changing Currents of Sports Migration', *The International Journal of the History of Sport*, 29, 17 (2012), 2388–404; J. Overton, E. Warwick and J. Heitger, 'Pass the Passport! Geographies of the Rugby World Cup 2011', *New Zealand Geographer*, 69, 2 (2013), 94–107.

15 Harris, *Rugby Union and Globalization.*

16 M. Bose, *The Spirit of the Game: How Sport Made the Modern World* (London: Constable, 2011).

17 J. Corsan, *For Poulton and England: The Life and Times of an Edwardian Hero* (Leicester: Matador, 2009).

18 See Allan, *The Official History of the Melrose Sevens*; E. Dunning and K. Sheard, *Barbarians, Gentlemen and Players: A Sociological Study of the Development of Rugby Football* (2nd edn) (London: Routledge, 2005).

19 See, for example, Douglas, *The Thistle;* Drysdale, *Southern Comfort.*

20 T. Collins, *Sport in Capitalist Society: A Short History* (London: Routledge, 2013).

21 See H. Richards, *A Game for Hooligans: The History of Rugby Union* (Edinburgh: Mainstream Publishing, 2006); R. Holt, 'Heroes of the North: Sport and the Shaping of Regional Identity', in J. Hill and J. Williams (eds), *Sport and Identity in the North of England* (Cornwall: Carnegie Publishing, 1996), 137–64.

22 R. J. Phillips, *The Story of Scottish Rugby* (Edinburgh: T. N. Foulis, 1925) Rugby Football History available via www.rugbyfootballhistory.com/scottish_rugby_0.html (accessed 12 August 2014); M. Williams, *Rugby Sevens* (London: Faber & Faber, 1975).

23 See, for example, Allan, *The Official History of the Melrose Sevens*; Douglas, *The Thistle.*

24 See, for example, Drysdale, *Southern Comfort.*

25 For a more detailed account see Thorburn, *The History of Scottish Rugby.*

26 For a more detailed account see T. Collins, *The Oval World: A Global History of Rugby* (London: Bloomsbury, 2015).

27 See, for example, G. Ryan, *The Changing Face of Rugby: The Union Game and Professionalism since 1995* (Newcastle: Cambridge Scholars Press, 2008).

28 See, for example, T. Collins, *A Social History of English Rugby Union* (London: Routledge, 2009).

29 See, for example Collins, *Sport in Capitalist Society* or W. J. Murray, *Football: A History of the World Game* (Aldershot, UK: Scholar Press, 1994).

30 J. Nauright, 'Sport, Manhood and Empire: British Responses to the New Zealand Rugby Tour of 1905', *The International Journal of the History of Sport*, 8, 2 (1991), 239–55.

31 I. Zweiniger-Bargielowska, 'Building a British Superman: Physical Culture in Interwar Britain', *Journal of Contemporary History*, 41, 4 (2006), 595–6.

32 See, for example, T. Collins, 'English Rugby Union and The First World War', *The Historical Journal*, 45, 4 (2002), 797–817; and Richards, *A Game for Hooligans.*

33 See, for example, Ryan, *Try for Gold.*

34 Middlesex Union, Statement of Accounts: Middlesex Sevens Tournament, April 1926 (held at the archives of the World Rugby Museum, Twickenham, London, hereafter referred to as 'World Rugby Museum').

35 Middlesex Union, *Official Middlesex Sevens Programme* (London: Middlesex Union Publication, 1927), World Rugby Museum.

36 W. W. Wakefield and H. P. Marshall, *Rugger* (London: Longmans Green & Co, 1927).

37 Rugby Football Union (RFU), Annual General Meeting, 1930, *RFU Minutes Collection: 1920–1934*, Rugby Football Union Publications, World Rugby Museum.

38 See Wakefield and Marshall, *Rugger.*
39 RFU, Annual General Meeting, 1925, *RFU Minutes Collection: 1920–1934,* Rugby Football Union Publications, World Rugby Museum.
40 P. Royds, E. T. Gurdon, R. Cove-Smith and W. W. Wakefield, 'Seven-a-side Rugby Football', *The Saturday Review of Politics, Literature, Science and Art,* 145, 3783 (1928), 520, Published 28 April 1928 (accessed 8 August 2014).
41 Middlesex Union, Letters appealing for monetary support, April 1928, World Rugby Museum.
42 International Rugby Football Board (IRFB), Annual General Meeting, 1972, *Minutes of the Meetings of the International Rugby Football Board: 1970–1979,* International Rugby Board Publications (1972), World Rugby Museum.
43 C. Thau, 'Sevens Rugby World Cup Preview', *Rugby World Magazine Monthly,* April 1993, 60–2.
44 IRFB, Annual General Meeting, 1972, *Minutes of the Meetings of the International Rugby Football Board: 1970–1979,* International Rugby Board Publications (1976), World Rugby Museum.
45 K. Sinclair, *The Hong Kong Sevens: A Book to Celebrate 10 Years of Rugby Sevens in Hong Kong* (Hong Kong: Arden Publishers, 1985).
46 R. Skeldon, 'Hong Kong: Colonial City to Global City to Provincial City?' *Cities,* 14, 5 (1997), 265–71.
47 Barnes, 'Made in Hong Kong', 14.
48 See, for example, Sinclair, *The Hong Kong Sevens.*
49 IRFB, Annual General Meeting, 1976, *Minutes of the Meetings of the International Rugby Football Board: 1970–1979,* International Rugby Board Publications (1976); RFU, Annual General Meeting, 1976, *RFU Minutes Collection: 1972–1979,* Rugby Football Union Publications (1976). Both held at World Rugby Museum.
50 For more detailed accounts see, for example, Collins, *The Oval World* or Richards, *A Game for Hooligans.*
51 H. Richards, 'The Tournament: Great Place to Try Your Best', *The Financial Times,* FT.Com, posted 30 March 2007 www.ft.com/cms/s/0/7972d1da-de5b-11db-afa 7-000b5df10621.html (accessed 21 October 2016).
52 G. Sage, *Globalizing Sport: How Organizations, Corporations, Media and Politics are Changing Sports* (London: Paradigm Publishers, 2010).
53 J. Blondin, *Hong Kong, The Sevens: Celebrating 20 Years* (New South Wales: The National Publishing Group, 1995).
54 IRFB, Annual General Meeting, *Minutes of the Meetings of the International Rugby Football Board: 1986,* International Rugby Board Publications (1986); IRFB, Annual General Meeting, *Minutes of the Meetings of the International Rugby Football Board: 1987,* International Rugby Board Publications (1987); IRFB, Annual General Meeting, *Minutes of the Meetings of the International Rugby Football Board: 1988,* International Rugby Board Publications (1988). All held at World Rugby Museum.
55 IRFB, Annual General Meeting, *Minutes of the Meetings of the International Rugby Football Board: 1991,* International Rugby Board Publications (1991), World Rugby Museum.
56 S. Jones, *Endless Winter* (Edinburgh: Mainstream Publishing, 1994).
57 B. Gallagher, 'Jumping at the Sevens, Slumping at the Cricket', *The Rugby Paper,* 20 July 2014, 22–3.
58 M. Phillips and J. Nauright, 'Sports Fan Movements to Save Suburban-based Football Teams Threatened with Amalgamation in Different Football Codes in Australia', *International Sports Studies,* 21, 1 (1999), 23–38.
59 IRFB, Annual General Meeting, *Minutes of the Meetings of the International Rugby Football Board: 1994,* International Rugby Board Publications (1994), World Rugby Museum.

60 IRFB, Annual General Meeting, *Minutes of the Meetings of the International Rugby Football Board: 1995*, International Rugby Board Publications (1995), World Rugby Museum.
61 IRB: Year in Review 2013, IRB.com (2014), www.worldrugby.org/strategic-plan?lang=en (accessed 21 October 2016).
62 Ibid.
63 IRB Strategic Plan: 2010–2020, IRB.com (2010), www.historyworkshop.org.uk/the-modern-olympics-and-the-triumph-of-capitalist-sport/ (accessed 21 October 2016).
64 See, for example, J. Boykoff, *Celebration Capitalism and the Olympic Games* (London: Routledge, 2014); J. L. Chappelet and B. Kubler-Mabbott, *The International Olympic Committee and the Olympic System: The Governance of World Sport* (London: Routledge, 2008); J. Nauright, 'The Modern Olympic Games and the Triumph of Capitalist Sport', History Workshop Online, *Histories of the Present*, posted 6 August 2014 (open access), www.historyworkshop.org/the-modern-olympics-and-the-triumph-of-capitalist-sport/ (accessed 7 August 2014).
65 N. Cain, 'IRB's Lack of Sevens Plan Could Spell Chaos', *The Rugby Paper*, posted 16 July 2014, www.therugbypaper.co.uk/features/columnists/nick-cain/17353/nick-cain-irbs-lack-of-sevens-plan-could-spell-chaos/ (accessed 18 January 2016).

8 The Rugby World Cup as a global mega-event

Kamilla Swart

Contemporary mega-events are considered to have significant consequences for host cities, regions and nations due to their scale and the significant media coverage that they attract. New developments in the technologies of mass communication, the formation of the sport–media–business alliance and the positioning of mega-events as valuable promotions tools for destinations have contributed to the growth of sport mega-events.

Mega-events are considered to be large-scale events that have mass popular appeal, international significance and extensive media coverage, and that have major consequences for the host destinations.[1] However, there is much ambiguity as to what constitutes a mega-event, and while the Olympic Games and FIFA World Cup are generally recognizable as mega-events due to their sheer size and scale, the Commonwealth Games, Cricket World Cup and Rugby World Cup (RWC) have also been included as second-order mega-events, whereas continental championships such as the African Games, Asian Games and UEFA European (soccer) Championship are considered to be third-order mega-events.[2] Mega-events generally do not occur on annual basis but occur every four years for a fixed duration in a different host destination, and are therefore transient. Although more regularly occurring events such as the National Football League (NFL) in the USA enjoy many millions in viewership for regular season matches, what seems to distinguish the mega-event from other sporting events is its international significance.[3] This relates to the dollars brought into the local economy by significant numbers of mega-event tourists, the television (and corporate sponsorship rights) that are sold outside the local area, and the consequent image effects on a host destination. It is further contended that the best available proxy for visitor attractiveness is the number of tickets sold.[4] Mega-events are also distinguished based on the huge costs, with large parts of the infrastructure required publicly funded, and sizeable impacts associated with hosting these events.[5]

It is contended that in the second half of the twentieth century, sport mega-events surpassed other types of mega-events in terms of the frequency and financial investment, a development linked to increasing media coverage and global reach.[6] Additionally, when one reviews the global distribution of mega-events, it is evident that the intense pursuit of the growing capital linked to sport consumption has made the pursuit of sport mega-events especially attractive to emerging and semi-peripheral nations that are seeking increased visibility and prestige within the context of globalization.[7] Mega-events are increasingly being used by these countries as a generally easy way to overcome their marginality globally, as well as to potentially achieve a range of beneficial spin-offs domestically.[8]

Thus it is not surprising that the BRICS (Brazil, Russia, India, China and South Africa) countries have been dominating the mega-event landscape in recent years (e.g. the 2014 FIFA World Cup in Brazil and 2016 Olympic Games in Rio de Janeiro; the 2012 Winter Olympic Games in Sochi and 2018 FIFA World Cup in Russia; the 2008 Olympics in Beijing; the 2010 FIFA World Cup in South Africa; the 2010 Commonwealth Games in Delhi; and the 2022 Commonwealth Games in Durban). Similarly, Japan will be hosting the 2019 RWC – the first time it will be staged in an Asian country – as well the 2020 Olympic Games.

The RWC is a major international sport event which is owned by World Rugby (formerly the International Rugby Board – IRB). It is now considered by some as the third biggest global sport event, after the Olympics and FIFA World Cup. The RWC first took place in 1987 and has since been held every four years. The year 1987 was chosen so as not to clash with the Olympic Games to be hosted in 1988 and the FIFA World Cup™ in 1990.[9] Twenty-five nations participated in the first edition, in a primarily amateur era, and the number of participating unions has grown from 16 in 1987 to 95 (with 20 qualifying for the main tournament) in 2015, in a highly commercialized and professional context. It is interesting to note that for the inaugural event all 16 teams were invited, and there was no qualification process.[10] The 1991 edition took place across five countries in the northern hemisphere, with a discernible increase in television viewership. The potential commercial gains of the RWC came to the fore in this edition, especially in relation to television.[11] Although the staging of the 1995 event in South Africa was considered a high-risk choice, given the sport's connection to the country's apartheid past – as elaborated upon further in this chapter – the fact that the event was lauded as 'the most significant trans-racial moment of celebration since the 1994 elections'[12] gave the RWC a further boost. The fourth edition of the World Cup in 1999 was hosted by Wales and took place in England, France, Ireland and Scotland, and is considered to have been the first World Cup in the openly professional era.[13] This edition was marred by poor scheduling and the overall economic impact was less than generally claimed, as discussed later in the chapter.[14] Up to this point, other than the 1995 RWC, all the previous editions had been hosted in more than one country, and the 2003 RWC was due to follow suit with Australia and New Zealand as joint hosts. However, a dispute around 'clean stadiums', with no conflicting advertisements or sponsorship agreements, resulted in matches only taking place in Australia.[15] In 2007, the RWC returned to the northern hemisphere with France as host, but matches also took place in the UK. While it was anticipated that the 2011 RWC would be hosted in Japan in order to develop and further internationalize the game, New Zealand was awarded host nation status and Japan had to wait until the 2019 edition for the event to be held for the first time in an Asian nation, as the event reverted to the northern hemisphere for the 2015 edition in the UK. The tournament now lasts for about six weeks, attracting large numbers of international visitors and worldwide television coverage.

It is contended that only the FIFA World Cup attracts more attendance and cumulative television audiences for a single sport event in comparison to the RWC.[16] Furthermore, it is evident from the direct economic contribution of tournaments in recent years that the proximity of host destinations to the traditional rugby-playing nations in the North plays an important role in attracting large numbers of visitors. It is interesting to note, though, that a study which examined the effects of several mega-events, including the Summer and Winter Olympic Games, FIFA World Cup Cricket World Cup and RWC (1995, 1999 and 2003), on the flows between 200 countries between 1995 and 2006 found that on average tourism increased by 8 per cent.[17]

However, there were major differences between the events, with the Winter Olympics and RWC displaying less positive impacts. Possible reasons for this could include tourism displacement, but also the smaller scale of these events and the fact that some of them were in countries with an already strong tourism demand.[18] The authors acknowledge that the results of the 2003 RWC in Australia were surprising and could be a result of the effect of the boost to tourism following the success of the 2000 Olympics, which displaced 'normal' tourism and had a consequent negative effect on the RWC.[19] The study further found that tourism from participating countries increased more than the number of tourists from countries not participating in the mega-event, which supports the finding above that in more recent editions of the RWC it is clear that traditional rugby playing can attract large numbers of visitors to host destinations, especially when they are in close proximity. The results further indicate that events held during the off-peak tourism season attract significantly higher numbers and have lesser displacement effects, as was the case for the 1995 RWC, albeit off a low base.

Arguably, the RWC has grown in stature and has evolved to be perceived as a mega-event over a relatively short period of time as illustrated in Table 8.1. However, due to its narrow reach and the inability of World Rugby to develop the game in the largest economies and population bases, the claim that the RWC is the third biggest global event is problematic.[20] Similarly, Muller contends that the 2011 RWC qualifies as a mega-event in terms of visitors and media rights but not in relation to the associated costs and urban transformation opportunities.[21] He argues that although costs vary widely amongst the different types of mega-events, none is below US$1 billion. Share of capital investments in total costs is used as an indicator of the transformative element of mega-events, and is especially large in emerging economies.[22] Neither of these aspects is included in Muller's further categorization of the RWC as a major event on a continuum, with the FIFA World Cup™ as a mega-event and the Olympic Games as a giga-event.[23] However, as the following case studies (1995 RWC in South Africa, 1999 RWC in Wales, 2011 RWC in New Zealand and 2015 RWC in England) illustrate, the RWC demonstrates key features and attributes of a mega-event.

Table 8.1 The growth of the Rugby World Cup

Year	Official host nation(s)	No. of countries	Ticket sales	Cumulative TV audience	Broadcast hours (and territories)	Direct contribution to GDP (£ million)	Net surplus (£ million)
1987	New Zealand and Australia	16	0.6 million	0.3 billion	103 (17)	unknown	1.0
1991	Great Britain, Ireland and France	31	1 million	1.75 billion	1,100 (103)	unknown	4.1
1995	South Africa	52	1.1 million	2.67 billion	1,180 (124)	unknown	17.6
1999	Wales	69	1.7 million	3 billion	2,425 (209)	unknown	47.0
2003	Australia	82	1.9 million	3.4 billion	5,414 (194)	169	64.3
2007	France	94	2.25 million	4 billion	8,500 (202)	380	122.4
2011	New Zealand	100	1.35 million	4 billion	10,000 (238)	289	90
2015	England	95	2.47 million			464*	95

Sources: Adapted from Deloitte and Touche LLP, *Potential Economic Impact of the Rugby World Cup on a Host Nation* (Dublin: IRB, 2008); Jackson (2012); S.J. Jackson and J.J. Scherer, 'Rugby World Cup 2011: Sport mega-events and the contested terrain of space, bodies and commodities', *Sport in Society: Cultures, Commerce, Media, Politics*, 16:7 (2013), 883–898; Ernst and Young, *The Economic Impact of Rugby World Cup 2015* (2014), www.ey.com/Publication/vwLUAssets/EY-rugby-world-cup-final-report/$FILE/EY-rugby-world-cup-final-report.pdf; and rugbyworldcup.com.

Note
* Forecasted figure – official figures are not available publicly to date.

The RWC, although to a lesser extent than the Olympic Games and FIFA World Cup™, has been used as a platform to reimage nations and signal their arrival on the world stage,[24] as was the case of South Africa in relation to hosting the 1995 RWC. South Africa, having emerged from the apartheid era, used a variety of image-boosting strategies, one of which was the bidding and hosting of mega-events.[25] These mega-events, and sport more broadly, were also employed to unite a racially divided society and provide a focal point for national identity.[26] Rugby – a traditionally 'White' sport favoured by Afrikaans males and a symbol of the apartheid state – was used, through the hosting of the 1995 RWC and the slogan 'one team, one nation', to unite the 'Rainbow Nation'. An important aspect of this nation-building project was Nelson Mandela's use of the opportunity to 'advance his own priority of national reconciliation'.[27] Although there were risks in white South Africans holding on to apartheid symbols and anthems that were strongly associated with rugby, Mandela was seen to be able to use rugby in a way that all races were able to embrace, albeit fleetingly. The fact that the South African team was successful, beating New Zealand in the final, also contributed to the reconciliatory, nation-building effect that the World Cup had on South African citizens. It is contended that as the Springboks won all their matches, public interest was maintained, and if the results had not been as successful, there would not have been less nationwide celebrations.[28] The 1995 RWC served as an affirmation and emergence of the 'new' South Africa and heralded South Africa's re-entry into the international community. As mentioned previously, although tourism arrivals increased off a low base, the psychological and emotional benefits ('feel-good' effects) to the host nation, albeit transitory, far outweighed the tangible benefits of hosting the 1995 RWC.[29] The successful hosting of this second-order mega-event was also used as a springboard for South Africa to host other mega-events, including the 2003 Cricket World Cup as well as the 2010 FIFA World Cup™. South Africa is also one of the four current contenders for the 2023 RWC, along with Ireland, France and Italy, with the US withdrawing from the race.[30]

The 1999 RWC presents an illustrative case as to how Wales had to pay the price for this mega-event being spread across the UK, Ireland and France, and the implications of this for the impact of the event.[31] Rugby's prominent position in the culture of Wales assisted in securing the bid for Wales and resulted in widespread support. However, the event was marred by political compromises, with exclusive contracts between RWC Ltd and overseas tour operators, which limited the visitor expenditure and commercial impact to the host economy.[32] The division of profits after the event was also a concern, with more than half of the profit retained by RWC Ltd and the rest split by the respective national rugby unions, with the Welsh Rugby Union having little or no control over some of the costs, which were primarily the responsibility of RWC Ltd.[33]

There were also several negative social impacts associated with hosting the 1999 in Wales. These included inconvenience to residents in relation to the construction of the Millennium Stadium, such as noise and road closures. Access to and participation in the event was also contentious, as 50 per cent of the tickets were distributed outside the host region to tour operators and corporate sponsors, making it difficult to access tickets locally. While one of the positive social impacts of the 1999 RWC was the stadium itself and the related transport infrastructure, the economic impact was limited, as only eight of the 41 games took place in Wales, and there were long periods where no matches took place, resulting in a lack of atmosphere and loss of potential additional spending by visitors.[34] The economic impact was further reduced in that four of the games involved the home team: the majority of the spectators were locals and therefore did not capture new spending by visitors. It is further reported that the media coverage of the event was mixed, and in some instances quite negative relating to the standard of organization.[35] Seemingly, however, there were successes for Cardiff and Wales both in the short and the long term, in showcasing a multipurpose legacy stadium that attracts a myriad of different types of events.

The 2011 RWC in New Zealand further underscores the significance of the politics and economics associated with hosting this mega-event.[36] Before and after the 2011 RWC, concerns were raised about the costs of staging the event, but these were overshadowed by the more positive forecasts about the legacy benefits to the host nation.[37] At the time of bidding for the event, an assessment of the economic impact estimated that it would add NZ$408 million to the GDP and more than NZ$90 million in tax revenue; although a year after it won the right to host the event, the New Zealand Government indicated that it was anticipating a loss of about NZ$35–40 million due to the monopolization of broadcast rights by the IRB.[38] Furthermore, the linkage between sport and national identity was to permeate the bid and the overall RWC promotional campaign, 'New Zealand as a stadium of four million'.[39] Through this campaign, the New Zealand Government and its partners sold the nation's attributes to the IRB and its corporate sponsors. It was also used as a mechanism to garner support from New Zealanders to support the bid and the event, and New Zealanders who were resistant to the campaign were alienated from the dominant discourse.[40] A leveraging and legacy project was launched and was claimed to 'alleviate fears, garner support and manage resistance'.[41] The building or upgrading of the stadia was not without contention either. There was opposition to the building of a new stadium on the waterfront in Auckland due to environmental concerns as well as opportunity costs, whereas Dunedin, a city of only 120,000, built a costly, state-of-the-art, covered stadium. There was much opposition in Dunedin too, with the emergence of 'Stop the Stadium', a local opposition group.[42] It is argued that the shortfall for the 2011 RWC was more than $NZ200 million over and above the $NZ555 million of public spending on the stadia,[43] despite the surplus illustrated in Table 8.1. The fast-tracking of infrastructure-related projects associated with mega-events was also evident with the planning and processes of the 2011 RWC. For example, the RWC 2011 Empowering Act 2010 was used by the New Zealand Government to accelerate planning and approvals for event-related infrastructure and time-critical activities.[44] Provision was also made for the 2011 RWC organizers to override normal planning processes and grant approvals where necessary.

An aspect that has increasingly received attention in recent years is the legacy of a mega-event. It is argued that the literature and media focus on mega-event legacy has increased along with the investments involved in hosting these events.[45] The case of the RWC is no different. A commonly accepted definition of 'legacy' is that it consists of 'planned and unplanned, positive and negative, intangible and tangible structures created through a sport event and remain after the event'.[46] Five types of legacies have also been identified: urban, infrastructural, economic, social and sport legacy.[47] More recent studies have also identified environmental and governance/institutional legacies.[48] Several examples are presented to illustrate how legacy featured in recent editions of the RWC.

There is much debate as to whether a mega-event can successfully deliver on claims regarding a legacy of sport participation, with the current evidence base seemingly poor.[49] Hence a study was conducted on sport participation levels as a result of Australia's hosting of the 2003 RWC.[50] It specifically examined participation data for rugby union in Australia between 2000 and 2008, which indicated a positive trend, with a greater increase in junior male registration in comparison to senior male registration over the 2003–2004 period.[51] The study further found that the hosting of the RWC was not the only reason for increased participation, and that the Australian Rugby Union had been investing in rugby development programmes since the late 1990s, which was considered a more effective, long-term approach. Although the study was limited to male junior and senior participation only (it excluded women, sevens and social rugby), the case study does provide some evidence for how rugby leveraged the media and the profile of the RWC to promote the sport.[52]

The 'Stadium of Four Million' report, which captures the RWC 2011 experience from the perspective of the New Zealand Government, demonstrates the most comprehensive report on a RWC to date. The two primary objectives of hosting the event were to host a successful tournament and to maximize the opportunities and ensure lasting benefits for New Zealand.[53] The related themes that emerged in relation to the objectives included demonstrating New Zealand's major event capability to the world, providing a stimulus to the country's economy in 2010 and 2011; promoting 'Brand New Zealand' to achieve tourism and business benefits; and building social cohesion by engaging the nation in the event.[54] Specific legacy aspects reported on relate to the tourism legacy: rugby tourists indicated that they were likely to recommend New Zealand as a holiday destination and that they would consider visiting New Zealand again in the future.[55] In terms of positioning New Zealand as an investment destination, the Business Club database obtained 4,500 overseas members; it was hoped that this may be used to drive future business growth and investment opportunities.[56] Promoting Auckland as major host destination that has the ability and capacity to host other major events was also viewed as an important legacy outcome.[57] From a social cohesion perspective, the Ministry of Business, Innovation and Employment acknowledges that social cohesion is difficult to quantify but claims that anecdotal evidence suggests that the level of community engagement was a significant legacy,[58] although this aspect has been contested, as highlighted earlier. The volunteer programme, through which 5,564 volunteers received training, is cited as a key legacy in relation to recognition of volunteering activities and setting the standard for other volunteering programmes.[59] The forecasting report on the economic impact of the 2015 RWC underscores the belief that legacy will play a significant role in terms of attracting tourists and business investment, as was the case for the 2011 edition, building capacity, and driving participation in rugby.[60]

Conclusion

The RWC as a second-order mega-event is linked to global capital and has evolved to become an international media spectacle that is entrenched in the signalling and place promotions of host nations. Countries will continue to bid for them because of the range of purported benefits associated with their hosting; however, the costs and benefits will be debated continually. The success of the RWC and its ability to deliver positive legacies for a host nation are impacted by a range of factors such as the size and development level of the host country, the timing (seasonality) of the mega-event, and the location in relation to the countries participating in the event.

While the RWC generates a tremendous amount of 'feel-good' effects for the host nation during the tournament, it is also associated with controversy, especially in relation to stadium locations and costs, although it appears to be less risky than other mega-events. The illustrative cases of the RWC highlight that the various editions are also subject to raised expectations from communities, overestimation of costs, bypassing of planning processes to fast-track projects, and unequal distribution of benefits. The RWC is thus as contested as other mega-events, and therefore requires continual discussion and debate with respect to competing social and economic priorities and associated opportunity costs as well as limited financial resources.

Rugby's reintroduction, albeit the seven-a-side version, to the Olympic sport programme at Rio 2016 will contribute to positioning rugby in general and the RWC in particular as a global sporting attraction, despite it being dominated by a very small group of nations. Furthermore, the hosting of the event in Japan in 2019 should further add to making the RWC truly global and also lead to more nations hosting this spectacle in the future.

Notes

1 S.J. Jackson, 'The 2011 Rugby World Cup: The politics and economics of a sport mega-event', *Movement & Sport Science*, 79 (2013), 5–10.
2 D.R. Black, 'Megas for strivers: The politics of second-order events', in J. Grix, (ed.), *Leveraging Legacies from Sport Mega-Events: Concepts and Cases* (Basingstoke, UK: Palgrave Macmillan, 2014), 13–23.
3 W. Maennig and A. Zimbalist, 'What is a mega-sport event?', in W. Maennig and A. Zimbalist (eds), *International Handbook on the Economics of Mega Sporting Events* (London: Edward Elgar, 2012), 9–16.

4 M. Muller, 'What makes an event a mega-event?: Definitions and sizes', *Leisure Studies*, 34:6 (2015), 627–642.
5 Ibid.
6 A. Varrell and L. Kennedy, *Mega-events and Mega-projects* (Bonn: European Association of Development Research and Training Institutes (EADI), 2011).
7 S. Cornelissen, 'It's Africa's turn. The narratives and legitimations surrounding the Moroccan and South African bids for the 2006 and 2010 Finals', *Third World Quarterly*, 25:7 (2004), 1293–1309.
8 J. Van der Merwe, 'Political analysis of South Africa's hosting of the Rugby and Cricket World Cups: Lessons for the 2010 Football World Cup and beyond?' *Politikon*, 43:1 (2007), 67–81.
9 B. Hutchins and M. Phillips, 'The global union: Globalization and the Rugby World Cup', in T. Chandler and J. Nauright (eds), *Making the Rugby World Cup* (London: Frank Cass, 1999), 149–164.
10 J. Harris, 'Definitely maybe: continuity and change in the Rugby World Cup', *Sport in Society: Cultures, Commerce, Media, Politics*, 16:7 (2013), 853–862.
11 Ibid.
12 D. Black and J. Nauright, *Rugby and the South African Nation* (Manchester: Manchester University, 1998).
13 Harris, 'Definitely maybe'.
14 Ibid.
15 Ibid.
16 Ernst and Young, *The Economic Impact of Rugby World Cup 2015* (2014), www.ey.com/Publication/vwLUAssets/EY-rugby-world-cup-final-report/$FILE/EY-rugby-world-cup-final-report.pdf.
17 F. Fourie and M. Santana-Gallego, 'The impact of mega-events on tourist arrivals', Working Paper 171 (2010), University of Stellenbosch and Universidad Da Laguna.
18 Ibid.
19 Ibid.
20 Harris, 'Definitely maybe'.
21 Muller, 'What makes an event a mega-event?'
22 Ibid.
23 Ibid.
24 S.J. Jackson and J.J. Scherer, 'Rugby World Cup 2011: Sport mega-events and the contested terrain of space, bodies and commodities', *Sport in Society: Cultures, Commerce, Media, Politics*, 16:7 (2013), 883–898.
25 Van der Merwe, 'Political analysis of South Africa's hosting of the Rugby and Cricket World Cups'.
26 Ibid.
27 Black and Nauright, *Rugby and the South African Nation*.
28 A. Grundlingh, 'From redemption to recidivism? Rugby and change in South Africa during the 1995 Rugby World Cup and its aftermath', *Sporting Traditions*, 20:2 (1998), 67–86.
29 Fourie and Santana-Gallego, 'The impact of mega-events on tourist arrivals'.
30 *Guardian*, 3 July 2015, 'Ireland, France, Italy and South Africa pitch for 2023 Rugby World Cup', www.theguardian.com/sport/2015/jul/03/rugby-world-cup-2023-ireland-france-italy-south-africa.
31 C. Jones, 'Mega-event and host-region impacts: Determining the true worth of the 1999 Rugby World Cup', *International Journal of Tourism Research*, 3 (2001), 241–251.
32 Ibid.
33 Ibid.
34 Ibid.
35 Ibid.

36 Jackson, 'The 2011 Rugby World Cup'.
37 S.J. Jackson, 'Rugby World Cup 2011: Sport mega-events between the global and the local', *Sport in Society: Cultures, Commerce, Media, Politics*, 16:7 (2013), 847–852.
38 Ibid.
39 Ibid.
40 T. Bruce, '(Not) a stadium of four million: speaking back to dominant discourses of the Rugby World Cup in New Zealand', *Sport in Society: Cultures, Commerce, Media, Politics*, 16:7 (2013), 899–911.
41 Ibid.
42 M.P. Sam and J.J. Scherer, 'Stand up and be counted: Numerical storylines in a stadium debate', *International Review for the Sociology of Sport*, 43:1 (2008), 53–70.
43 Jackson and Scherer, 'Rugby World Cup 2011'.
44 T. Shahwe, K. Davies and S. Carson, 'The impact of mega events on construction planning, processes and performance – Auckland's experience of the Rugby World Cup 2011', in S. Kajewski and K. Hampson (eds), *Proceedings of the 19th International CIB World Building Congress* (Brisbane: University of Technology, 2013).
45 E. Kassens-Noor, M. Wilson, S. Muller, B. Maharaj and L. Huntoon, 'Towards a mega-event legacy framework', *Leisure Studies*, 34:6 (2015), 665–671.
46 H. Preuss, 'The conceptualization and measurement of mega sport event legacies', *Journal of Sport & Tourism*, 12:3–4 (2007), 207–227.
47 J. Chappelet and T. Junod, 'A tale of 3 Olympic Cities: What can Turin learn from the Olympic legacy of other Alpine cities?', in D. Torres (ed.), *Major sport events as opportunities for development* (Valencia: Noos Institute, 2006), 83–90.
48 K. Swart and U. Bob, 'Reflections on developing the 2010 FIFA World Cup research agenda', in W. Maennig and A. Zimbalist (eds), *International handbook on the economics of mega sporting events* (London: Edward Elgar, 2012), 434–448.
49 Weed, M.E., Coren, E., Fiore, J., Mansfield, L., Wellard, I., Chatziefstathiou, D. and Dowse, S., *A systematic review of the evidence base for developing a physical activity, sport and health legacy from the London 2012 Olympic and Paralympic Games: report to funders* (Canterbury, UK: Physical Activity Network West Midlands on behalf of Regional Physical Activity Teams in the West Midlands, the East Midlands, the East of England, London and the South East, 2008).
50 S. Frawley and A. Cush, 'Major sport events and participation legacy: the case of the 2003 Rugby World Cup', *Managing Leisure*, 16 (2011), 65–76.
51 Ibid.
52 Ibid.
53 New Zealand Ministry of Business, Innovation and Employment, *The Stadium of Four Million. Rugby World Cup 2011: The New Zealand Experience* (2012).
54 Ibid.
55 Ibid.
56 Ibid.
57 Ibid.
58 Ibid.
59 Ibid.
60 Ernst and Young, *The Economic Impact of Rugby World Cup 2015*.

Part II

Rugby cultures and representation in the professional era

9 Making men in the twenty-first century

Metrosexuality and bromance in contemporary rugby

Adam White and Eric Anderson

Warming up

The twenty-first century has seen a significant shift in how men construct and perform masculinities, both inside and outside of sport. Whereas historically, one, somewhat orthodox, code of masculinity had been culturally esteemed, today we have multiple equally valued gender performances available to men.[1] Thus, what it means to be a man in contemporary western society has changed, with young men now engaging in many of the behaviours previously only afforded to women and gay men, due to their association with femininity.

To understand this cultural shift and change to masculinities, we must first understand the transformation of homophobia and its ability to police masculinity.[2] Utilizing the concept of homohysteria, which examines men's fear of being socially perceived as homosexual, we can explain why men are now increasingly engaging in homosocial emotional and tactile behaviours.[3] This framework also explains why heterosexual men today have a broader range of style and tastes that are socially sanctioned. In short, the previously rigid boundaries of the male gender role have collapsed, shifted and been redefined by contemporary men.[4] Sport has been instrumental in this socio-positive change.[5]

The benefits of declining homohysteria have not only affected gender, but also the way young men consider sexuality.[6] For example, young men now appreciate that sexuality is more complex than a homosexual to heterosexual binary, often inferring bisexual (or same-sex) aspects within their holistic notions of heterosexuality. However, most significant to this generation is the increasing acceptance of homosexual peers – even in sport.[7]

Accordingly, we start this chapter by first offering a theory for the understanding of modern masculinities. Anderson's Inclusive Masculinity Theory explains how gender behaviours change when men no longer denounce homosexuality.[8] We then explain how masculinities have changed in sport and youth culture over the past thirty years, starting with the 1980s and moving through to 2015. We then examine both the impact that this has had on adolescent rugby players, and the positive effect that adolescent rugby players have had on inclusive masculinities.

Understanding contemporary masculinity: Inclusive Masculinity Theory

Traditionally, scholarly work on masculinities has been dominated by Connell's 1995 concept of Hegemonic Masculinity. Connell explains that masculinities are hierarchically stratified in something she terms the 'gender order'. Here, men who present in alignment to an orthodox standard of masculinity (based upon being stoic, and competitive, physical, heterosexual, misogynistic and homophobic attitudes). Likewise, those who are effeminate or homosexual are subordinated at the bottom of the intra-male stratification. Men in this gender system continually attempt to raise their masculine status, primarily through deploying misogynistic and homophobic discourses.

We describe this (now older) style of masculinity as a king-of-the-hill hierarchy, whereby men competed and struggled to hold position at the top of the hierarchy.[9] In times and places where homosexuality was stigmatized within Anglo-American cultures, homophobia played a key role in this process, as it is able to improve one man's masculine capital. Men could distance themselves from homosexuality, while reducing another man's masculine positioning through implying that they are gay. Recognizing homophobia as central to stratification of masculinities during this epoch, Michael Kimmel asserted that 'homophobia is the fear that other men will unmask us, emasculate us, reveal to us and the world that we do not measure up, that we are not real men'.[10]

Much of the research that has applied Hegemonic Masculinity, as a tool to understand gender, was a product of the 1980s. This temporal context is significant, as much of the western world was highly homophobic in this era. Exemplifying this, social attitudes data in both the United Kingdom and the United States show that the late 1980s saw a peak in homophobic attitudes, with most citizens in both countries (82 per cent in the U.S.) believing homosexuality to always be wrong. It is suggested this spike in cultural homophobia was a result of two socio-political influences: the HIV/AIDS outbreak and increasing religious fundamentalism.[11] In this zeitgeist, homosexuality was stigmatized and therefore men actively disassociated with anything considered either gay or effeminate. This results in men having to perform a narrow code of conservative, heterosexual, masculine behaviour; this is something Anderson termed 'orthodox masculinity'.

Anderson calls the 1980s in western society a 'homohysteric' culture. Here, men feared being socially perceived as homosexuals, and therefore had to distance themselves from anything considered gay. He describes three principles for a culture to be considered homohysteric: (1) widespread cultural homophobia, (2) an understanding that members of our social network may be gay, and (3) the conflation of homosexuality with femininity. By utilizing homohysteria as a vehicle for conceptualizing male gender, we can offer a nuanced position on why homophobia has been able to police the normative gendered behaviours of men in varying cultural contexts.[12]

Understanding the relationship between these variables is important because social attitudes towards homosexuality change over time. Considering western contexts, such as Britain and the United States, we can see that the 1980s were a highly homophobic zeitgeist, with attitudes rapidly progressing ever since.[13] With the decline in cultural homophobia, homosexuality was decreasingly stigmatized in western society. This decrease in cultural homophobia means that homosexual discourse was less powerful in the regulation of male gender. As such, men were decreasingly anxious about being socially perceived as homosexual, and therefore homohysteria has dissipated. In other words, men no longer feared being thought homosexual, meaning homophobia has lost its power in policing masculinity.

Anderson's Inclusive Masculinity Theory (IMT) therefore postulates that when homohysteria declines, men are afforded a wider range of esteemed masculine behaviours. As such, rather than only one style of masculinity being culturally exalted, IMT recognizes that multiple codes of masculinity can be simultaneously esteemed in a more egalitarian and lateral intra-male hierarchy. Simply put, rather than just one type of orthodox masculinity being valued, other masculine archetypes are also popular among men. This is not to suggest that we are now in a gender utopia: in fact, hierarchies still endure among men.[14] We are, however, suggesting that no single masculine archetype holds hegemonic positioning; rather, multiple, often paradoxical, masculine ideals are valued and the expression of femininity among heterosexual men is also valued.[15]

Inclusive masculinities: the data

Anderson's Inclusive Masculinity Theory was born from his earlier ethnographic data on U.S. collegiate male cheerleaders.[16] Although Anderson firmly believed sport to be highly homophobic, in his ethnographic study he found men being somewhat inclusive of gay teammates and even embracing feminine elements of the cheerleading subculture. The majority of men in his studies had participated in American football at high school, but, through lack of ability, had to select other athletic pursuits in university. Although some men still valued and presented an orthodox archetype of masculinity, others embraced a more inclusive and feminine presentation, with neither being more esteemed or valued than the other. A few years later, in researching U.S. fraternities in 2008, Anderson also found the valuing of inclusive ideals of masculinities.[17] This research showed there exists a more inclusive form of masculinity institutionalized in the U.S. fraternal system: one based on social equality for gay men, respect for women and racial parity, and one in which fraternity men bond over emotional intimacy.

Similarly, in the early twenty-first century, Anderson was also analysing the narratives of gay athletes who were out (that is, had publicly disclosed their sexual identity) among their teammates.[18] Previous studies ascertained that sport was a hostile and homophobic environment for homosexual athletes, with no research examining out gay male athletes, because there were none.[19] Anderson conducted the first-ever research on gay men playing in ostensibly heterosexual teams. He found that, although they viewed the sporting terrain to be hostile and dangerous before coming out of the closet to teammates, their actual narratives of coming out were somewhat positive. Only two of twenty-six had experienced any form of verbal victimization, with the remainder suggesting their experiences to be optimistic. However, they did discuss how they were expected to hide their sexuality, often self-policing to prevent 'forcing' their homosexuality onto others. Likewise, all of the openly gay athletes in Anderson's study were valuable players in their teams, often due to their high athletic ability. It was therefore thought that only the best athletes were able to disclose their homosexuality, as they were beneficial to the teams' success. As a result of the segmented identities and the need for athletic capital, Anderson calls this 'reverse relative deprivation'. This is where the athletes consider they will be treated with extreme hostility and physical violence, and therefore when they are not, they perceive this to be extremely positive, even though they are still subjected to discrimination.

Only a decade later, Anderson replicated his study of openly gay athletes in the U.S. (2011), finding a rapid improvement in their experiences in sport.[20] The athletes he interviewed were often not athletically gifted, and were less fearful that sport would be hostile; all had positive coming-out narratives. They were not required to bifurcate their identities, often having open and endearing conversations about their sexuality with predominantly heterosexual teammates. The stories offered showed no signs of homophobia, with gay athletes feeling and suggesting they are fully included in their mainstream sports teams. Therefore, it is suggested that athletes are no different to mainstream society when considering attitudes towards sexuality.

Anderson argues that heterosexual men also benefited from this cultural shift in masculinities. This is because, when homophobia declines, men are no longer policed by homohysteria and are therefore able to transgress into behaviours, styles and tastes that would have traditionally been coded feminine and consequently gay.[21] Being socially perceived as gay is no longer stigmatizing to today's youth because the boundaries of masculinity have shifted; consequently fewer behaviours are associated with homosexuality. Athletes today can be feminine in presentation, physically tactile, emotionally literate and sexually liberal. As a product, the relationships between young men are changing, with close friendships often being termed as a 'bromance'.

Historically, boys' style has been regulated by other men, requiring them to present as masculine too.[22] However, athletes today are not so concerned about transgressing into feminine behaviours of dress or style.[23] In research on university soccer players, Adams found athletes would wear styled and tightly fitting clothing, with one player being praised for his pink soccer boots.[24] Formerly, pink, being associated with girls and femininity, would have been an indicator of homosexuality, yet in Adams' research it was a symbol of fashion and contemporary masculinity.

In addition to a broader range of style and taste, male athletes today engage in same-sex physical tactility – something that would have aroused homosexual suspicion in previous times.[25] However, in the twenty-first century this is considered a normative behaviour, particularly among young men. Showing this cultural shift, in his historical analysis of photography, Ibson recognized that as homohysteria increased, the physical spaces between men in their pictures also expanded.[26] However, now that homohysteria has declined, current research is showing athletes to be increasingly physically intimate. Today's athletes greet one another with cuddles, they lean on and stroke one another, they sit on each other's laps, sleep on each other's shoulders, and they cuddle and spoon in bed. Athletes now engage in a wide range of soft, physically tactile behaviours as a demonstration of their affection for one another, an indication of close friendships and love.[27]

In addition to physical touch, men are now enjoying homosocial kissing. Previous literature has suggested that kissing for affection or greeting is only acceptable for women or gay men; as Fox notes, 'with the possible exception of a father and a young son, in England men do not embrace or kiss on another'.[28] Today in the UK, however, 89 per cent of heterosexual male university students have kissed another male on the lips, with 37 per cent having made out with (pulled) another male.[29] The meanings of these kisses are not sexual, giving no implication that those who engage in homosocial kissing are gay. Rather, these men suggested it was a way of expressing affection in a close friendship.

Being stoic is also no longer a requirement of masculinity. Today, adolescent males support one another with problems, worries, secrets and fears.[30] In research on fraternities, Anderson found men being emotionally supportive of one another, even when disclosing secrets that may have previously led to homophobic or effeminate discourses. For example, one participant discussed being raped by a woman when he was younger, while another discussed his sexual experiences with a man.[31] Teammates responded to these disclosures by listening attentively and offering support. Similarly, Adams found his participants engaging in what they termed 'pillow talk'. As the name may suggest, these emotional discussions happened in the confines of bedrooms at night, often while often cuddling one another.[32]

Combining emotionality and homosocial love with physical behaviours of tactility, adolescent males also engage in a great deal of bromantic love. Here, men have emotional relationships somewhat similar to a romance, with the exclusion of sex.[33] Indeed, these athletes proclaim their love for one another and often show this through Facebook posts and their relationship statuses. These flourishing behaviours have been widely invoked and understood by modern-day athletes to represent the most important aspects of their friendships and team camaraderie.

In recognition of the changing nature of masculinities, young men's hierarchies have also shifted.[34] Today, rather than men being exalted based upon their alignment to an orthodox ideal of masculinity, McCormack theorizes that boys' popularity is based upon four, somewhat democratic, characteristics.[35] He suggests popularity is based upon the ability to be emotionally supportive, socially fluid, charismatic and authentic, meaning men of all masculine archetypes are able to achieve esteemed status. Recognizing this, Morris and Anderson examined the rise in popularity of YouTubers, finding those with the most followers held the four tenets of popularity offered by McCormack.[36] These men could be seen as feminine and somewhat soft in their displays of masculinity. They aligned to pro-gay attitudes and were highly tactile, emotionally tuned and energetic in presentation. Thus, the meaning of being a man has changed dramatically, allowing adolescent males of all sexualities to cuddle, kiss and love one another, without stigmatization.[37]

Masculinities in rugby

Findings that men are presenting softer, more feminine and liberal archetypes are not germane to men outside of sport alone. On the contrary, they are both reflected in and produced by men who once used to represent orthodox forms of masculinity – including rugby players.[38] It has become evident that the highly physical and competitive 'organised mock battle' that is rugby has also become a space where inclusive masculinities have proliferated.[39]

As with other research into men and their masculinities, research on rugby players from the 1980s and 1990s described it as a 'male preserve', where 'players of this sport have gained a reputation for violence, physical contact, nakedness, obscenity, drunkenness, and the treatment of women as if they were property'. Unsurprisingly, rugby scholarship has often labelled participants as also being homophobic.[40] Consequently, it was distinctly clear that rugby was an effective tool for the development of orthodox masculinity among men.[41] Schacht commented, 'rugby, like other sporting events, is literally a practice field where the actors learn how to use force to ensure a dominant position relative to women, feminine men, and the planet itself'.[42]

All of this, however, has been set to an ironic backdrop. Rugby culture, particularly in initiations, frequently involved males' genitals and same-sex behaviours.[43] These acts were done in an absence of homohysteria, ostensibly because those playing the sport had extreme heterosexual capital. With this capital they bought themselves insurance against being thought gay. With such insurance, they were able to partake in a surprising variety of homoerotic/homosocial physical, semi-sexual behaviours.

Although it was not analysed through such a lens at the time, this highlights how heterosexual men desire to behave when they are culturally permitted to do so. Anderson argues that it was these very behaviours that rugby players engaged in outside of homosocial rugby spaces, that began to make it acceptable for non-rugby, or non-football, players to engage in them as cultural homohysteria began to decline.[44] He thus suggests that these types of behaviours not only produced inclusive versions of masculinity, but that they became cyclical as cultural homohysteria began to loosen for adolescents during the first decade of the new millennium.

Exemplifying this, a longitudinal ethnographic research project on team sport hazing activities between the years 2003 and 2009 initially found the use of same-sex acts as a way of punishing non-compliant recruits, with men fearing games such as 'gay-chicken' (an activity where two participants are summoned to kiss, with the winner being the one who does not disengage from the kiss first). Often in the early stages of research on rugby initiations, men would not even reach a kiss – they would opt to drink alcohol as a forfeit instead.[45]

However, in line with other Inclusive Masculinities research on contemporary gender performances, rugby players soon began to engage in the same-sex behaviours without fear or stigmatization. The use of same-sex punishments was therefore no longer practical for the formation of intra-male hierarchies and policing of subcultural masculine behaviours. In the later stages of Anderson, McCormack and Lee's ethnographic study, gay-chicken often resulted in the men kissing with no distinct winner.[46] Games would be stopped, as no participant would pull away. Subsequently, the use of same-sex activities, such as gay-chicken and mock sex, declined in initiation agendas. In fact, these later gave way to rugby players just kissing each other as part of their social engagements, apart from initiations.

Rugby players' attitudes to homosexuality have also shifted. Traditionally, scholars have documented rugby as a homophobic environment, yet in the team Anderson, McCormack and Lee studied, the most valued (and most valuable) player was openly bisexual. Other research on rugby teams shows that gay players are also accepted and embraced.[47] Rugby players offer verbal support for homosexual men, often already having gay friends and family members.[48] Some of the rugby players in Anderson and McGuire's 2010 research expressed no concern with having a gay rugby player as a teammate, and others have symbolically supported gay peers through acts of kindness and support.[49] Although there was still some use of homosexually themed language among rugby players, which some interpreted as being homophobic, this was infrequent and possibly with a more complex meaning than just a disdain of homosexuality.[50] Across both Anderson and McGuire's study and Murray and White's research, there was little data to suggest homophobia. In fact, today's rugby players stigmatize homophobia, rather than homosexuality.[51]

This is also the case at the professional level. For example, international rugby referee Nigel Owens disclosed he was gay in 2007, before releasing his autobiography expressing the widespread support he received from the professional game.[52] Welsh rugby captain Gareth Thomas came out in December 2009, too. He received widespread support from teammates, players in other teams, fans and the governing body. Guinness even capitalized on his coming-out narrative in their marketing throughout the 2015 Rugby World Cup. Most recently, international England sevens player Sam Stanley announced that he was gay. He too received strong support from teammates and fans.

Less research has been conducted on rugby players' attitudes to, and relationships with, women. While Sheard and Dunning described the rugby club and environment in 1973 as a male preserve where women were excluded and/ or subjugated, and whereas Schacht argued that women who attend rugby practices or events are subjected to sexual harassment, this may not necessarily be true any more.

These behaviours were not found in more recent research by Anderson and McGuire on university rugby players. At one British university, participants expressed how there was limited misogyny in the rugby environment, with no sexism being deployed from the players themselves. The female friends of the rugby players spoke about the lack of disparaging language and also of the close platonic friendships they have with the rugby players. In fact, many of the men in this study showed disgust towards their coach, who often used gendered language and misogynistic discourse.[53]

Athletes in rugby have also incorporated some gay aesthetics into their personal fashion. Harris and Clayton discuss Welsh fly half Gavin Henson and his rise to stardom as being partially attributed to this: his fake tan, shiny boots and styled hair attracted significant media attention. However, metrosexuality has also been recognized in the amateur game. In more recent research, Murray and White show rugby players discussing the acceptability of using cosmetic products, tight-fitting clothing and dancing in feminized ways. Many recognized that these benefits were not afforded to men only ten to fifteen years ago, with one participant commenting,

> if males and females dressed like they do today, ten years ago or when I was 18/19, I reckon males would be ridiculed, the way they wear skinny jeans and skinny tops and all those things would've been seen as feminine.[54]

The incorporation of feminine or gay male aesthetics suggests that whereas Whannel previously suggested masculinity is 'experienced by many [men] as a straitjacket; a set of conventions of behaviour, style, ritual and practice that limit and confine, and are subject to surveillance, informal policing and regulation', this is not true any more.[55] Today, men are not so restricted in their masculine performance, with access to an array of styles only previously acceptable for women and gay men.

Cooling down

The way heterosexual male athletes understand and perform masculinity has changed significantly over the previous two decades, with many men opting for gentler, softer and more expressive masculine ideals. Adolescent males, of all sexualities, now kiss, cuddle and love one another. They adorn their bodies in feminine styles, develop bromances and celebrate homosexuality.

Utilizing data from numerous quantitative and qualitative studies of rugby culture, we show that rugby players have helped cultivate this culture of inclusivity. Empirical research on rugby players has shown that they appropriate a softer masculine archetype, showing the increasingly endearing, inclusive and loving homosocial relationships they have with one another. Initiations no longer use same-sex activities as a mode for punishing new recruits, due to the lack of stigma attached to homoerotic acts, and rugby players are inclusive of both gay men and women. Rugby players are also developing increasingly egalitarian notions of being a man off the field of play.

Anderson's Inclusive Masculinity Theory is the only gender theory capable of capturing this transition. Premised in the fact that a reduction of homohysteria promotes the co-existence of multiple, esteemed, heterosexual masculine archetypes, the theory was based in rugby research.[56] Inclusive masculinity research does not preclude men from taking physical risks with their bodies, overly valuing competition, or engaging in drinking copious amounts of alcohol. But those traits are self-harming, whereas homophobia and misogyny were exclusive of others. It is for this reason – the incorporation of those who were once excluded in rugby culture – that Anderson named it Inclusive Masculinity Theory.

Finally, while a few toxic aspects of masculinity might still exist within rugby culture, it is worth noting that youth are dropping out of competitive, organized team sports at alarming rates. In their ethnographic research, Anderson and McGuire found athletes less willing to take extreme risks with their bodies. With the long-term problems of chronic traumatic encephalopathy on the rise, we may find that, eventually, adolescent players are more interested in protecting their health than in reproducing the history of the game.

Notes

1 For the orthodox code see R. W. Connell, *Masculinities* (Cambridge: Polity Press, 1995). For multiple gender performances see E. Anderson, *Inclusive Masculinity* (Abingdon, UK: Routledge, 2009).

2 M. Kimmel, 'Masculinity as homophobia: Fear, shame, and silence in the construction of gender identity', in H. Brod & M. Kaufman (eds), *Theorising Masculinities* (London: Sage, 1994), 119–142.

3 M. McCormack & E. Anderson, 'Homohysteria: Definitions, context and intersectionality', *Sex Roles*, 71, 3–4 (2014), 152–158.

4 A. Murray & A. White, 'Twelve not so angry men: Inclusive Masculinities in Australian contact sports', International Review for the Sociology of Sport (2015), doi:10.1177/1012690215609786.

5 E. Anderson, *21st Century Jocks: Sporting Men and Contemporary Heterosexuality* (Basingstoke, UK: Palgrave Macmillan, 2014).

6 E. Anderson & A. Adams (2011) ' "Aren't we all a little bisexual?": The recognition of bisexuality in an unlikely place', *Journal of Bisexuality*, 11 (2011), 3–22.

7 A. Adams & E. Anderson, 'Exploring the relationship between homosexuality and sport among the teammates of a small, Midwestern Catholic college soccer team', *Sport, Education and Society*, 17, 3 (2012), 347–363. E. Anderson, R. Magrath & R. Bullingham, *Out in Sport: The Experiences of Openly Gay and Lesbian Athletes in Competitive Sport* (Abingdon, UK: Routledge, 2016). E. Anderson & R. McGuire, 'Inclusive masculinity theory and the gendered politics of men's rugby', *Journal of Gender Studies*, 19, 3 (2010), 249–261.

8 E. Anderson, *Inclusive Masculinity* (Abingdon, UK: Routledge, 2009).

9 E. Anderson, *In the game: Gay athletes and the cult of masculinity* (Albany, NY: State University of New York Press, 2005).

10 Michael S. Kimmel, 'Masculinity as homophobia. Fear, shame and silence in the construction of gender identity', in Nancy Cook (ed.), *Gender Relations in Global Perspective: Essential Readings* (Toronto: Canadian Scholars' Press, 2005), 79.

11 J. Loftus, 'America's liberalization in attitudes toward homosexuality, 1973 to 1998', *American Sociological Review*, 66 (2001), 762–782.

12 McCormack & Anderson, 'Homohysteria'.

13 B. Clements & C. Field, 'Public opinion towards homosexual and gay rights in Great Britain', *Public Opinion Quarterly* (2014), doi:10.1093/poq/nfu018. A. Keleher & E. Smith, 'Growing support for gay and lesbian equality since 1990', *Journal of Homosexuality*, 59 (2012), 1307–1326.

14 See Clements & Field, 'Public opinion towards homosexual and gay rights'.
15 R. Scoats, 'Inclusive masculinity and Facebook photographs among early emerging adults at a British university', *Journal of Adolescent Research*, doi:0743558415607059 (2015).
16 E. Anderson, *Masculine identities of male nurses and cheerleaders: Declining homophobia and the emergence of inclusive masculinities* (unpublished PhD thesis, University of California Irvine, 2003).
17 E. Anderson, 'Inclusive masculinities in a fraternal setting', *Men and Masculinities*, 10, 5 (2008), 604–620.
18 E. Anderson, 'Openly gay athletes: Contesting hegemonic masculinity in a homophobic environment', *Gender & Society*, 16, 6 (2002), 860–877.
19 P. Griffin, *Strong women, deep closets: Lesbians and homophobia in sport* (Champaign, IL: Human Kinetics, 1998). B. Pronger, *The arena of masculinity: Sports, homosexuality, and the meaning of sex* (London: St. Martin's Press, 1990).
20 E. Anderson, 'Updating the Outcome: Gay Athletes, Straight Teams and Coming out at the End of the Decade', *Gender & Society*, 25, 2 (2011), 250–268.
21 McCormack & Anderson, 'Homohysteria'.
22 T. Curry, 'Fraternal bonding in the locker room: A pro-feminist analysis of talk about competition and women', *Sociology of Sport Journal*, 8 (1991), 119–135. D. Plummer, 'Sportphobia: Why do some men avoid sport?', *Journal of Sport and Social Issues*, 30, 2 (2006), 122–137.
23 Murray & White, 'Twelve not so angry men'.
24 A. Adams, '"Josh wears pink cleats": Inclusive masculinity on the soccer field', *Journal of Homosexuality*, 58, 5 (2011), 579–596.
25 T. Field, 'American adolescents touch each other less and are more aggressive toward their peers as compared with French adolescents', *Adolescence*, 34, 136 (1999), 753–758.
26 J. Ibson, *A century of male relationships in everyday American photography*, (Washington, DC: Smithsonian Books, 2002).
27 For examples, see Scoats, 'Inclusive masculinity and Facebook photographs'; Adams, '"Josh wears pink cleats"'; and McCormack & Anderson, 'Homohysteria'.
28 K. Fox, *Watching the English: The Hidden Rules of English Behaviour* (London: Hodder & Stoughton, 2004), 191.
29 A. Bush, E. Anderson & S. Carr, 'The declining existence of men's homophobia in British sport', *Journal for the Study of Sports and Athletes in Education*, 6, 1 (2012), 107–120.
30 Adams, '"Josh wears pink cleats"'; Anderson & McGuire, 'Inclusive masculinity theory'; and Murray & White, 'Twelve not so angry men'.
31 Anderson, 'Inclusive masculinities in a fraternal setting'.
32 Adams, '"Josh wears pink cleats"'.
33 Anderson, *21st Century Jocks*.
34 McCormack 2012 – **NO DETAILS FOR THIS REFERENCE.**
35 See Connell, *Masculinities*; and M. Mac an Ghaill, *Making of men: masculinities, sexualities and schooling* (Buckingham, UK: McGraw-Hill International, 1994).
36 Morris & Anderson 2015 – **NO DETAILS FOR THIS REFERENCE.**
37 Anderson, *21st Century Jocks*.
38 Anderson & McGuire, 'Inclusive masculinity theory'.
39 K. G. Sheard & Eric G. Dunning, 'The rugby football club as a type of "male preserve"', *International Review of the Sociology of Sport*, 8, 3–4 (1973), 6. E. Anderson & R. McGuire, 'Inclusive masculinity theory'. Murray & White, 'Twelve not so angry men'.
40 Sheard & Dunning, 'The rugby football club as a type of "male preserve"', 5. K. B. Muir & T. Seitz, 'Machismo, misogyny, and homophobia in a male athletic subculture: A participant-observation study of deviant rituals in collegiate rugby', *Deviant Behavior*, 25, 4 (2004), 303–327.

41 P. Donnelly & K. Young, 'The construction and confirmation of identity in sport sub-cultures', *Sociology of Sport Journal*, 5 (1998), 223–240. P. G. White & A. B. Vagi, 'Rugby in the 19th-century British boarding-school system: A feminist psychoana-lytic perspective', in M. A. Messner & D. F. Sabo (eds), *Sport, Men, and the Gender Order* (Champaign, IL: Human Kinetics Books, 1990), 67–78.

42 S. P. Schacht, 'Misogyny on and off the "pitch": The gendered world of male rugby players', *Gender & Society*, 10 (1996), 562.

43 Sheard & Dunning, 'The rugby football club as a type of "male preserve"'.

44 Anderson, *21st Century Jocks.*

45 E. Anderson, M. McCormack & H. Lee, 'Male team sport hazing initiations in a culture of decreasing homohysteria', *Journal of Adolescent Research,* 20, 10 (2011), 1–22.

46 L. Lee, 'Religion: Losing faith?', in A. Park, E. Cleary, J. Curtice, M. Phillips & D. Utting, *British Social Attitudes Survey*, Volume 28 (London: Sage, 2012).

47 R. Pringle & P. Markula, 'No pain is sane after all: A Foucauldian analysis of mascu-linities and men's experiences in rugby', *Sociology of Sport Journal*, 22, 4 (2005), 472–497.

48 Anderson & McGuire, 'Inclusive masculinity theory'.

49 Murray & White, 'Twelve not so angry men'.

50 Anderson & McGuire, 'Inclusive masculinity theory'. McCormack 2012 – **NO DETAILS FOR THIS REFERENCE.**

51 Murray & White, 'Twelve not so angry men'.

52 Nigel Owens, *Half Time: My Autobiography* (Cardiff: Y Lolfa, 2009).

53 Anderson & McGuire, 'Inclusive masculinity theory'.

54 Murray & White, 'Twelve not so angry men', 10.

55 G. Whannel, 'Mediating masculinities: The production of media representations in sport', in C. Aitchison (ed.), Sport and gender identities: Masculinities, femininities and sexualities (Abingdon, UK: Routledge, 2007), 11.

56 E. Anderson, Sport, Theory and Social Problems (Abingdon, UK: Routledge, 2010).

10 The road from Wigan Pier

Professional rugby and the changing dynamics between Wales and England

John Harris

As he steadied the case, he looked at the rail-map, with its familiar network of arteries, held in the shape of Wales, and to the east the lines running out and elongating, into England. The shape of Wales: pig-headed Wales you say to remember to draw it. And no returns.[1]

I was a professional rugby footballer long before I moved to rugby league.[2]

If you were a rugby union player who made the move from this amateur sport to the paid ranks of rugby league before 1995, you would be banned from the union game for life – there really were no returns. Jonathan Davies, a highly skilled player in the prestigious number ten jersey of the Welsh rugby union team, 'went North' in 1989. For Davies, like many who had trodden the same path before him, this decision effectively ended any hope of involvement with the union game thereafter, but the open professionalization of rugby union six years later meant that Davies could return to Wales and the fifteen-man code. This change in 1995 meant that for recent converts to league, what had hitherto been a one-way journey to the north of England now became a two-way street and not all roads necessarily led to Wigan Pier. Welsh league players who had represented their country in the union game at the first Rugby World Cup (RWC), such as Davies, John Devereux, Dai Young, Paul Moriarty and Adrian Hadley, now had a number of different options to consider as the broader landscape of inter-national rugby changed.

The first RWC took place in New Zealand and Australia in 1987. Many north-ern hemisphere players were surprised by what they perceived as the open flout-ing of amateurism in New Zealand, where players from the All Blacks were quite prominent in advertising campaigns. The All Blacks won the inaugural competition and the difference in playing standards was markedly shown by their comprehensive victory over Wales in the semi-final. This tournament marked a significant moment in the eventual open professionalization of rugby union and was an important move to develop the international profile of the sport.[3] The one-sided nature of this match between Wales and New Zealand, along with two more heavy defeats for Wales when they toured New Zealand the following summer, was certainly a factor in influencing the movement of some players to league. Others remained in Wales by virtue of the somewhat loose interpretation of amateurism whereby many rugby union players were afforded special social status in a country where it is the national sport.[4]

The contested nature of amateurism in rugby union was not a new subject, and Wales had been accused of professionalizing the game many years before. Between January 1897 and March 1898 Wales played no international fixtures, as the country was ostracized by the other home unions (England, Ireland and Scotland) over the purchase of a house for the first superstar of Welsh rugby, Arthur 'Monkey' Gould. Funded by supporters and a regional newspaper, and endorsed by those governing the game, Gould was presented with a house in Newport, the town where he had played his rugby for a number of years. Despite the many protests, Wales refused to give in to the other home unions and withdrew from the International Board. Sean Smith described the controversy as 'a uniquely Welsh brand of amateurism', and (sh)amateurism was to remain a contested topic in Welsh rugby for almost a century after the Gould affair.[5]

Holt describes how rugby served an important function in the creation of a Welsh identity in the early industrialization of the south Wales valleys, providing both a way for outsiders to define the Welsh and a way for the Welsh to define themselves.[6] Tuck and Maguire have suggested that in more modern times 'the health of Wales as a nation is perceived as inseparable from the success/failure of the national rugby team'.[7] Periods of economic prosperity and economic decline in Wales have often mirrored the position of the national rugby team. It was not just during such periods that players took the road to Wigan, for many Welshmen had left their homes in Wales to seek a better life in the north of England. This chapter analyses the changes in rugby union since 1995 and looks at some of the main issues relating to player migration since the open professionalization of the sport. It focuses specifically on the movement of Welsh players from England to Wales in the period immediately after the change and looks also at some significant figures in the subsequent years who have also moved between the two rugby codes. It also briefly touches upon the migration of coaches between the sports and across the border between Wales and England. Some attention is also afforded to the odd case of players who have since 'gone North', and to considering what the professionalization of rugby union has meant to the wider international rugby landscape, and in particular the continued development of France and England as the economic core of the professional game.

The road to Wigan Pier

In his history of rugby league, Tony Collins noted that:

> Rugby league's appeal to Welsh rugby union players was simple. It offered them the opportunity to benefit financially from their footballing skills. Many were given jobs on a club's ground staff or with companies connected to club directors. For others, clubs guaranteed to make up a minimum wage

if the job that was found for the player did not pay an adequate sum. Some were given the tenancy of a pub.[8]

In what was a key marker in developing the academic focus on the topic of labour migration in sport, John Bale and Joseph Maguire's edited collection on *The Global Sports Arena* provided an array of examples detailing the movement of athletes across national borders.[9] Within this, Gareth Williams presented a historical account of the migration of Welsh union players to rugby league under the title of 'The road to Wigan Pier revisited'.[10] As Williams outlined, 'Since its formation in 1895 the Rugby League (RL), or the Northern Union as it was called until it changed its name in 1922, has been a source of magnetic attraction to Welsh rugby union players.'[11] The title of the chapter was taken from a famous novel by George Orwell, and I have adapted this title once more here to focus on the movement of players back to union and to explore aspects of the changing relationship between Wales and England in the international rugby world.[12]

Williams analysed the movement of players from Wales within and around an examination of the changing social and economic landscape of the country and noted how in the period from 1895 to 1990, of the 227 international rugby union players from the home unions who changed codes, 156 were from Wales.[13] Williams argues that this highlights how rugby union in Wales was more affected by the movement of its players to rugby league than in any of the other home unions.[14] It is also important to note that this figure refers only to those who had already been capped at the full international level, and many more players took the same road northwards before they had the chance to represent the national team. These included Jim Sullivan, who moved to the Wigan rugby league club from Cardiff RFC while still a teenager and later went on to represent Great Britain during a lengthy career in rugby league. Williams estimated that in total some 2,000 Welsh rugby players 'went North' in the period, with close to 900 moving between 1919 and 1939, although Collins suggests that this figure is an over-estimation and that less than half of that number actually went North.[15]

The landscape of the rugby world changed markedly through the open professionalization of rugby union in 1995. This gave those playing the game in Wales the chance to finally (openly) earn money from playing the sport and afforded the opportunity for some Welshmen who had changed codes to return home. Williams argues that Wales was far more susceptible to losing its players to the league game because of the social positioning of the union game in Wales.[16] In England, the sport had been built around a code of amateurism nurtured by a social elite, but in Wales it grew alongside an industrialization of the southern valleys, where mass immigration and economic growth were defining features.[17] The massive influx of migrants to the south Wales coalfields during the industrial revolution saw the population of the country increase markedly, and this dramatically changed the social and cultural landscape. Rugby union became the national game of Wales not because of any particular cultural affinity but because of the close geographical proximity of south Wales to the west of

England.[18] If it was the industrial revolution and the rapid urbanization of the southern valleys that partly explains why the sport became an integral part of the sporting landscape in Wales, then the open professionalization and increased internationalization of the game needs to be considered in terms of how it both challenged and reinforced the place of rugby union in contemporary Wales.

Of particular importance here, and a key focus of this chapter, is what this meant to the relationship between Wales and England. Wales sits in the shadow of its bigger and more powerful neighbour. Despite the creation of an Assembly government in 1999, for some it has moved little beyond the encyclopaedia entry for the country that simply said 'see England'. When discussing the two nations together, the combination is often presented as *EnglandandWales* as if this were one place. On the other hand, the difference between the nations within the context of rugby was coded in something of a dichotomy between amateur and professional, or centred around class-based ideologies that emphasize a particular type of Englishness based on the public schools and an 'old boys' network. Both of these were easy to caricature and proved useful in outlining the differences between rugby union in Wales and the respective rugby codes in the north and south of England. As Welsh rugby experienced something of a golden age in the 1970s, Max Boyce (an ex-miner from Glyneath) entered the public consciousness with his songs and poems about the game, which included commentary on the predatory scouts from rugby league and the well-spoken English union fans at 'Twickers, HQ'.

There are multiple layers and competing discourses within all national identities. Even in a small country of three million people, there is not just one Wales and one singular Welsh identity. In a similar vein, this bigger configuration of England is also much more multi-dimensional and complex than often presented. An essentialized representation of England and Englishness ignores the multiple tensions and divisions within the nation. The cultural studies scholar Raymond Williams, who grew up in a small village in Wales not far from the English border, has written cogently on the lived experiences of life on the border. For Williams it was the local that really mattered, and for the villagers of Pandy both the Welsh and the English were referred to as 'them'.[19] As evidenced in the quote from one of his novels at the beginning of this chapter, it was his own movement between Wales and England that framed much of his academic and popular writing. The work of Williams was shaped by a strong class-consciousness and it is clear that he was not that enamoured with some of the work of Orwell.[20] The work of Williams transcended so many disciplinary boundaries and subjects that it is tricky to capture his significance 'in the round'. It is perhaps sometimes easier to demarcate between the academic and the novelist. Some analysis of his work glosses over the subject of national identity and the ways in which Williams critically reflected upon his understanding of Wales and Welshness. Yet I believe that this is a very important part of understanding the contribution of Williams to the study of the nation and the wider ways in which he highlighted some of the tensions and complexities that shaped the Anglo-Welsh border region. While it is recognized that the use of perceived differences and national characteristics may be powerful tools in this 'othering' of neighbouring nations, we need to move beyond the somewhat simplistic delineations that may be used to characterize sameness and difference between the two nations.

Wales and England: the roads across the borders

In the lead-up to the Six Nations tournament in 1999, BBC Wales (the British Broadcasting Corporation's television service for Wales) featured the Stereophonics singing that 'as long as we beat the English, we don't care'. Although presented as fierce enemies on the rugby pitch, Wales and England are close bedfellows in rugby governance and have supported each other in various bids for hosting international tournaments.[21] Approximately one-fifth of the population of Wales were born in England and a similar number of Welsh-born people reside over the border.[22] Wales has a Prince who was born and raised in England, but the investiture of Charles in 1969 was in some ways a strategy aimed at blunting the appeal of Welsh nationalism.[23] His two sons were both strong supporters of the England rugby team (although William has since transferred allegiance to Wales), and a niece is married to a former England rugby captain. In wider popular culture, many Welsh people support football teams from England, watch English soap operas on television and read English newspapers.[24] Rugby sometimes serves as politics with a small 'p', but in many respects Wales and England are far more similar than they are different. Raymond Williams recognized the overly simplistic ways in which these national differences were often portrayed in various discourse. He appreciated the fact that there were multiple identities at play, and, as someone who had lived much of his adult life in England, was aware that the English 'are much more various than the myths allow'.[25]

While the Romford-born Tony Copsey may not be the only Essex man with 'Made in England' tattooed on his buttocks, this is probably something of a rarity amongst Welsh rugby internationals. Copsey, alongside his friend and Llanelli team-mate Rupert Henry St. John Barker Moon, won a number of caps for Wales in the 1990s. Moon was from Walsall in the English Midlands and once lined up against the son of a farmer from Powys during a Wales versus England match. Dewi Morris, born and raised in the small Welsh market town of Crickhowell, represented England 26 times and once sang both national anthems ahead of a match between the two nations. Williams made reference to the Welsh rugby team 'outrucking Chamberlain and Hoare and Halifax and the young toffs they'd persuaded to stand in for them' to demonstrate the ways in which rugby was often used as something more than just a game in the promotion and celebration of national difference.[26] The names referred to in this quote were not rugby players but members of the English bourgeoisie. As Collins has noted, class was a central part of the relationship between the two rugby codes for 100 years, but the significant events of 1995 were to change this landscape considerably.[27]

Opening the road from Wigan Pier

Rugby union's open professionalization in 1995 represented a seismic shift in the rugby world. Although the issue had been the subject of various workshops/ committees in the rugby world for some time, the sport in the northern hemisphere was ill prepared to cope with the change to professionalism.[28] It is important to remember that professionalism was forced upon those who governed the game in the northern hemisphere, and that many of those who were in positions of power saw it as a real threat to their hegemony and status.

As soon as the decision to make the sport openly professional was made, much speculation focused on what this would mean for the relationship between the two rugby codes. In Wales talk centred on the potential return of recent league converts such as Scott Quinnell, Dai Young and Scott Gibbs, who had all been big losses to the union team. The biggest star of all, though, in Wales, and the man who was the focus of most newspaper stories, was Jonathan Davies. His decision to 'go North' was influenced in large part by his frustration at what he saw as the incompetence and petty bureaucracy of those involved in the governance of the game. His request to address the Annual General Meeting of the Welsh Rugby Union (WRU), not long before he finally decided to leave for rugby league, was dismissed and he noted, 'I couldn't have been treated with more contempt if I'd suggested digging up the National Stadium and planting potatoes.'[29]

Despite the many predictions that he would fail, Davies proved a big success in the thirteen-man code, where he won team and individual trophies, captained a resurgent Welsh team to a European title and represented Great Britain. If there was one player who could symbolically highlight the shift in the relationship between union and league then Davies was the biggest catch of all. In November 1995, he moved from the Warrington rugby league club to Cardiff RFC in a deal aided by the WRU. There was some resentment from other clubs that the WRU had helped Cardiff with the transfer, and this theme would recur in both Welsh and English rugby when a player was signed from rugby league. Many of his new team-mates at Cardiff also seemed less than pleased with the return of the player, and it appeared in some matches as if Davies was being deliberately ignored and starved of the ball.[30] Yet despite being past his best, having returned home after reaching his peak in the thirteen-man code, Davies found himself recalled by the Welsh selectors after an eight-year absence.

While at Warrington, Davies had played alongside a teenager born in Oldham, Lancashire, who himself one day would also make the journey to play in Wales. Iestyn Harris developed into one of the top rugby league players in the country and in 1998 was awarded the 'Man of Steel' trophy, the highest individual honour in the game in England. His grandfather, Norman Harris, had played rugby union for Newbridge but was one of the many players tempted to rugby league in the 1940s. Like many other Welshmen who had made the move to the league game, he settled in the north of England after his playing career had finished.

Cardiff RFC and the WRU secured the services of Harris against stiff competition from the Rugby Football Union (RFU) in England, who wanted Harris to wear the red rose and represent the English national team. Harris, who is proud of his Welsh roots, had captained the Wales rugby league team, and noted in his autobiography that 'my father and grandfather ensured the young Iestyn Harris had the three feathers in his heart from day one'.[31] His was a particularly significant signing, not just because of his exceptional skills and status as one of the biggest talents in rugby league but also because this was the first signing made by Wales in this new professional era of someone born and raised in the heartlands of rugby league. This transfer symbolized something of a power shift in the relationship between rugby union and rugby league. Some ten years after the momentous events of 1995, Dunning and Sheard noted that since rugby union went openly professional no high-profile union player had made the switch to the thirteen-man code.[32] Later, the former Wales national team captain Gareth Thomas left Cardiff Blues to play for the Celtic Crusaders rugby league side towards the end of his career. At the end of the 2012–13 rugby union season, the Wales back-row forward Andy Powell made the move from the Sale Sharks rugby union team to the Wigan Warriors rugby league side.

At the beginning of the professional age of union, some players had experimented with 'dual contracts' that allowed them to play both codes, although the differences in the two games and the physical demands of year-round rugby meant that such experiments were short-lived. Although rugby league was often positioned negatively within south Wales, and all Welsh union players who made the move were viewed as mercenaries, the reality was that many of the players who 'went North' had to supplement their income from playing the game through other work.[33] It is also important to note that throughout the history of the amateur game many rugby union players remained in Wales because they were given jobs to enable them to stay.[34]

Ironically, in light of the 'Grannygate' affair, where some New Zealand-born members of the Welsh national team were found not to have Welsh grandparentage as originally claimed, it was the nationality of his grandfather (Norman) that was highlighted in many newspapers as the reason for Iestyn Harris's eligibility to represent Wales. Shortly after his transfer to Cardiff, and despite never having played the union game before, Harris scored 31 points in his first full match, against Glasgow. This created significant hype and celebration in Wales, with newspaper headlines such as 'Iestyn fever hits home' and 'Harris soaring to his destiny' proclaiming the arrival of 'The Great Redeemer (Mark II)'.[35] The symbolic importance attached to this one player was also framed in a discourse that hinted at how this was something of a payback to rugby league (and the English) for all of the players it had tempted out of Wales over more than 100 years. As an article in the *Observer* newspaper noted:

> Not so long ago Welsh rugby would lose their favourite sons to rugby
> league and weep. Now a one-man mission from Leeds has reversed the

trend and put a smile back on the face of the land of his forefathers. Iestyn Harris has arrived big time.[36]

While Davies and Harris had chosen to move to the capital city club, the road from the north of England did not only lead to Cardiff. The open professionalization of the sport meant that players now had a wide range of options to consider and could ply their trade as a professional rugby player in either code and in a number of different countries. Scott Quinnell left Wigan to join Richmond RFC on the outskirts of London, and Adrian Hadley moved from the Widnes rugby league club to join Sale RFC. just outside Manchester. So, although for a century the rugby league clubs were blamed for many of the problems besetting rugby union in Wales, now many different roads in and out of Wales presented new challenges to those involved in the governance of the game.

The road across the River Severn

The Severn Bridge was opened in 1966 to replace the ferry crossing between Aust and Beechley. This structure (symbolically) connects Wales to England even though both sides of the bridge are actually located in England. Due to the massive increase in traffic, and the fact that significant delays became commonplace in the summer months, a new crossing was proposed and, after much debate, was finally created. Thirty years after the first bridge became operational, a new one was opened where the movement of traffic was much quicker and also where travellers only pay to get into Wales: there is no charge for crossing from the Welsh side into England. The journey from Cardiff to Wigan takes almost three-and-a-half hours by car, yet it takes less than three hours to get from the capital of Wales to London, and there is also a good rail link between the two cities.

On the way down the M4 motorway, within a short distance of the Severn crossing, signposts for cities such as Bristol and Bath come into view. These are places where rugby union has always been popular and presented some Welsh players with significant financial opportunities without them even having to move home. For it was often the thought of leaving home that prevented many Welsh players from seriously considering the large sums of money they were offered to turn professional and move to the north of England. Llanelli players, and members of the great Welsh teams of the 1970s, Phil Bennett and Ray Gravell, were both too attached to their home to consider moving away despite the approaches made by league clubs.[37] The chance to play club rugby and earn decent money just across the water was something a number of Welshmen immediately took advantage of, and some continue to do so today. International players such as Arwel Thomas and Robert Jones played for Bristol in the mid-1990s, while former Wales captain Ieuan Evans finished his illustrious career at Bath. In more recent years a number of Welsh players have joined Bristol Rugby, and many of these players continue to live in Wales and make the trip across the Severn Bridge on a daily basis.

Here, then, it is the geographical positioning that is particularly important to acknowledge when looking at the migration of players between these two nations. As Gareth Williams has noted, it is the geographical proximity of south Wales to the west of England that partly explains how and why the sport came to occupy the position it now does in Wales.[38] Numerous workers move between England and Wales every day, with no restrictions and little comment about this frequent border crossing (save for complaints about the cost of entering Wales across the bridge). Ian Woosnam, the 2006 Ryder Cup captain and 1991 US Masters champion, learned the game of golf on a course where you crossed the border to England and came back into Wales during the round.

As highly skilled workers, professional rugby players are no different to professionals in a range of other occupations who move between nations in an increasingly global (or at least international) employment market. The financial rewards on offer with some of the English clubs in the early days of professionalism were hard to turn down despite pressure from the administrators of the game in Wales for Welsh players to remain in, or in some cases return to, the country. Joining Scott Quinnell in the leafy London suburbs of Richmond were his brother Craig, front-row forwards John Davies and Barry Williams, half-backs Adrian Davies and Andy Moore, and another returnee from rugby league, Allan Bateman. It was not just the financial rewards that tempted players to England. Many were also motivated by the chance to play at a higher level and by what they perceived as a lack of any clear vision or direction from those governing the game in Wales.

Large sums of money were paid to some players in Wales, yet the English game was richer and able to offer far more lucrative contracts. As dual international Allan Bateman noted:

> Professionalism in union seemed to revolve around pay rather than attitude. I was surprised at the high rates of pay: six-figure contracts were offered with abandon, virtually double the wages of established rugby league players. It reflected the involvement of benefactors in union, but it meant that salary levels, which were not weighted towards bonuses, were unrealistic.[39]

When Graham Henry first arrived in Wales from New Zealand to take up the position of coach of the Welsh national team, he was amazed that players in some of the lower divisions were being paid to play. Many of the early forays into professional rugby ended abruptly as some realized that there was little money to be made from the sport, and so many of these wealthy benefactors quickly disappeared from the game. The move to a regional rugby structure in 2003 also limited the number of professional players and coaches in Wales. Yet what we did begin to see in the openly professional era of rugby union was the increased movement of professional coaches across codes and between the two nations. It is to this subject that I now turn.

Coaches on the road

In the winter of 2007 the Welsh Rugby Union appointed Warren Gatland as national team coach, as he became the third New Zealander to lead the Welsh national team in less than a decade. Gatland had previously coached the Irish national team and English club side London Wasps. Assisted by Englishman, the former Great Britain rugby league international Shaun Edwards, Gatland led Wales to the Grand Slam in his first season in charge and followed this with another four years later. Despite this success, Gatland had also voiced his concern about the number of foreign players playing in the country, and within one hour of being officially unveiled as the new coach of Wales he expressed his disquiet over the number of overseas imports and how they were preventing home-grown players from playing top-level rugby. There is some irony in a New Zealander coaching Wales expressing such a view, and this points to some of the tensions inherent in discussions of migration in sport.

Edwards had played for Wigan when they were by far the dominant force in the English game, during the period immediately prior to the professionalization of rugby union. This team transcended the sport and were admired by players of the union game for their exciting play and professional approach.[40] So although for 100 years rugby league had been positioned as the scourge of rugby union, particularly in Wales, the open professionalization of the game was to lead to many changes. One of the biggest impacts upon the thirteen-man code was its loss to union of players and coaches who were tempted by the better financial packages and opportunities to develop their careers and compete on a more international stage. Jason Robinson, a team-mate of Shaun Edwards at Wigan, was one of the most successful converts and was England's try scorer in the 2003 World Cup final. Other cross-code converts made less of an impact, and some expensive signings failed to live up to the large sums of money invested in them. This, of course, was a repeat of what had often happened with players leaving union for league. Although they may share the same shaped ball, the two codes are very different and not all players were able to successfully make the transition from one code to the other. It is beyond the scope and focus of this chapter to discuss the case of Sam Burgess here, but his brief move into union and then back to league continues to be analysed and discussed.

In addition to Edwards, many other coaches who had originally trained and worked in rugby league have made a significant impact on the fifteen-man code. Dave Ellis worked with the French national team for many years, and Phil Larder was a part of the coaching set-up for the England World Cup-winning team of 2003. The prevalence of former league men, often labelled as 'defence gurus', led to an expressed concern that the professional union game was focusing too much on not allowing the opposition to score, and neglecting to afford time to develop the creative and attacking aspects. The converts from league were credited with bringing a newfound professionalism to union. Another former playing colleague of Edwards, Andy Farrell, made the journey south as a player when he moved from Wigan to join Saracens. Farrell's son, Owen, is a key member of the England squad. The wider reach of player migration is also shown by the presence of the Vunipola brothers in the England team and their cousin Taulupe Faletau in the Welsh team. These men are the sons of Tongans who had moved to Wales to play rugby in the 1990s.

The Welsh national team was led by Gatland for a decade, but there are numerous opportunities for Welshmen to develop professional coaching careers outside of Wales. For the 2012–13 rugby season three of the twelve leading English clubs had a Welshman at the helm, with former internationals Nigel Davies (Gloucester), Lyn Jones (London Welsh) and Dai Young (London Wasps) leading operations. Other Welsh internationals such as Mark Ring, Adrian Hadley, Paul Turner and Kingsley Jones have also coached in England. The development of coaching and coach education in England at the RFU has been directed under the tutelage of former Wales national coach Kevin Bowring for some time. This 'brain drain' is not a one-way street, though, for England's World Cup-winning player Josh Lewsey and former England and Great Britain rugby league legend Joe Lydon have both held senior positions within the WRU in recent years.

A whole host of players born in England have represented the Welsh national team. In the Wales 2015 RWC squad there were eleven men who were born outside of Wales (of whom nine were born in England). This is not just a recent development, for the team who defeated New Zealand in the famous match of 1905 was captained by a man born in Gloucestershire. The roads between Wales and England have facilitated the continued movement of people for centuries, and so it is no surprise that the make-up of the national rugby teams has reflected this.[41] A more recent development that affects the sport of rugby in both nations concerns the increased movement of players from both England and Wales to France.

The road to Provence

While the road to Wigan Pier had provided a well-trodden path for the migration of many Welsh rugby players over the previous century, in the period since 1995 we have witnessed an increased internationalization of both rugby codes and the movement of rugby players across numerous national boundaries. This change saw a rise in the number of different nationalities playing the game in Wales, with men from (for example) Fiji, Tonga, Canada, the USA and South Africa regularly playing alongside those born and/or raised in Wales.

Members of Grand Slam-winning squads such as Mike Phillips, Gethin Jenkins, Lee Byrne and James Hook all plied their trade in France during the 2012–13 season. The talismanic centre Jamie Roberts moved from Cardiff Blues to Racing Club Metro in the summer of 2013, where he was also joined by his Wales and British and Irish Lions team-mate Dan Lydiate. Roberts returned from France in 2015, but, despite speculation that he would once again play in Wales, he signed a contract with Harlequins in England. Leigh Halfpenny won the European Champions Cup with Toulon in 2015 and is one of the best-paid union players in the world. The national press regularly features articles centred on fears of a mass exodus of the top players from Wales and the often turbulent governance of the game in Wales. France and England increasingly represent the dominant economic core of the sport, and all other nations are at risk of losing their leading players to the richest clubs in these two countries, even though there is an increased pressure on them to stay in Wales if they wish to be considered for the national team.[42]

At the end of 2012, the WRU announced the creation of a new Regional and Professional Game Board to oversee professional rugby in the nation. Amongst its main objectives was a stated aim to keep senior Welsh international players in the country. Sam Warburton and Alun Wyn Jones are amongst the most high-profile players to have signed central contracts, whereby the WRU pays over half of the player's wages and sets a limit on the number of matches these players can take part in for their regions. Other players such as Taulupe Faletau and Rhys Priestland have signed lucrative contracts with Bath Rugby, as the financial rewards on offer elsewhere sometimes surpass what the Welsh regions and/or WRU can offer. While visits from rugby league scouts with 'briefcases full of banknotes' are less commonplace for top-level union players, the lure of the euro and the financial power of England's leading clubs have emerged as a major challenge for those involved in the governance of the game in Wales as they try to best manage these new border crossings.

Concluding comments: the road forward

This chapter is intended as a point of departure for discussing some of the key issues surrounding professional rugby union within, and between Wales and England. Future research may investigate some of the topics touched on in this overview, and there is certainly scope for greater attention to be afforded to the narratives of coaches and administrators in better understanding aspects of the border crossings. The border between Wales and England has always been a porous one, and people will continue to move between the two nations. George North, one of the most highly rated wingers in the world, took the road to England, moving from Llanelli to Northampton in 2013, and signed a contract extension with the club in 2015.

It is clear, when we look back at the history of migration in the two rugby codes, that financial factors have always been a prime motivation for the movement of rugby players over the years. It is also important to note here, though, that in this respect these men are no different to the numerous other highly skilled workers across the world who change jobs and move between nations to make the most of their talents.[43] In a hard, physical game like rugby, the playing careers of most players are relatively short, and even the vast majority of the elite players will have to find alternative employment when they retire from the sport. England presents more elite-level coaching opportunities for Welshmen who embark upon such a career pathway than Wales does, and it is likely that the best coaches will continue to seek opportunities across the border in England or further afield.

It is clear that the changes in rugby union not only impacted on the relationship between Wales and England in that sport but also had a significant impact on rugby league. The Welsh national rugby league team often features individuals with somewhat tenuous Welsh links or calls upon players playing at a far lower level than the opponents they encounter at the top level of international competition. A match against England in 2012 resulted in an 80–12 reversal that clearly demonstrated the gulf in playing standards.

The quest to develop rugby league in Wales and cement a foothold for the thirteen-man code there continues. Wales was awarded a franchise in rugby league's Super League in 2009, but the Celtic Crusaders finished bottom of the league and the franchise moved north (within Wales) to Wrexham from Bridgend. The organization ran into financial difficulties and entered administration in 2011. Andy Powell's move from Sale to Wigan should also be noted here, although Powell had been out of favour with the Welsh selectors for some time and switched to league towards the end of his playing career. His move did not really work out, and he returned to rugby union, signing for the Newport Gwent Dragons before joining Merthyr RFC in 2015.

The 2013 Rugby League World Cup was hosted by England and Wales, but the hyperbole that suggests this is a major international event must be tempered by an honest appraisal of its limited reach. If rugby union has a very narrow core and struggles to develop beyond particular geographical regions, then rugby league is even more limited in terms of its geographic reach and profile as an international sport.[44] In union, the 2015 RWC was the biggest and most economically successful tournament to date. In addition to matches being staged at twelve stadia across nine English towns and cities, eight matches also took place in Cardiff. The inclusion of the Welsh capital in this tournament further evidences the close relationship between the two nations in international rugby governance. Quite what including Cardiff in an event marketed and promoted as 'England 2015' does for the brand identity of Wales is open to debate.

Despite the Grand Slam triumphs of 2005, 2008 and 2012, no Welsh club side or region has ever won the premier European trophy in the club/regional game up to the time of writing, whereas English sides have won it six times, although the last of these was ten years ago. As concerns are raised about the financial stability of the four professional rugby regions in Wales, there has been an upturn in the fortunes of the two leading Welsh football clubs and the national football team. Swansea City gained promotion to England's Premier League in 2011 and Cardiff City joined them in the top flight for the 2013–14 season. In the summer of 2016 Wales played in the UEFA European Championship finals for the first time, featuring Gareth Bale, who at the time was the most expensive footballer in the world based on his transfer value.

Wales defeated England in the group stages of RWC 2015, to reclaim the bragging rights for the time being at least. This was front-page news in Wales, with a *Wales on Sunday* headline proclaiming it to be 'Our greatest win ever!'[45] This victory was achieved with a squad including nine players born in England, and a number of the players were employees of English clubs. Raymond

Williams suggested that the relationship between Wales and England is 'hard and complex'.[46] The militaristic language used in various media ahead of rugby matches between the two nations is not quite 'war minus the shooting' but serves as an important site for the recognition and celebration of difference within and between the two neighbours.[47] Beck notes how George Orwell viewed international sport as 'one of the most visible peacetime manifestations of nationalism'.[48] It will be interesting to observe the ways in which professional rugby union moves forward from here and whether Wales and/or England are finally able to consistently compete with the leading southern hemisphere nations in future World Cup competitions. The road to Wigan Pier may be a thing of the past for the best Welsh rugby union players, but it is likely that migration out of the country on other roads, to seek playing opportunities and greater financial rewards, will continue to be a contentious topic for many years to come.

Notes

1 R. Williams, *Border Country* (London: Chatto & Windus, 1960), 8.
2 J. Davies with P. Corrigan, *Jonathan: An Autobiography* (London: Stanley Paul, 1989), 136.
3 See J. Harris, *Rugby Union and Globalization: An Odd-shaped World* (Basingstoke, UK: Palgrave Macmillan, 2010); H. Richards, *A Game for Hooligans: The History of Rugby Union* (Edinburgh: Mainstream, 2007).
4 See N. Jenkins with P. Rees, *Life at Number 10* (Edinburgh: Mainstream, 1998); B. Windsor with P. Jackson, *The Iron Duke* (Edinburgh: Mainstream, 2010).
5 S. Smith, *The Union Game* (London: BBC Worldwide, 1999), 6.
6 R. Holt, *Sport and the British* (Oxford: Oxford University Press, 1989); see also M. Johnes, *A History of Sport in Wales* (Cardiff: University of Wales Press, 2005).
7 J. Tuck and J. Maguire, 'Making sense of global patriot games: Rugby players' perceptions of national identity politics', *Football Studies*, 2, (1999), 30.
8 T. Collins, *Rugby League in Twentieth Century Britain* (London: Routledge, 2006), 54.
9 J. Bale and J. Maguire (eds), *The Global Sports Arena: Athletic Talent Migration in an Interdependent World* (London: Frank Cass, 1994).
10 G. Williams, 'The road to Wigan Pier revisited: The migration of Welsh rugby talent since 1918', in Bale and Maguire (eds), *The Global Sports Arena*, 25–37.
11 Ibid., p. 26.
12 G. Orwell, *The Road to Wigan Pier* (London: Victor Gollancz, 1937).
13 Williams, 'The road to Wigan Pier revisited', 26.
14 Ibid., 26–28.
15 Ibid., 26; Collins, *Rugby League in Twentieth Century Britain*.
16 Williams, 'The road to Wigan Pier revisited', 27.
17 See T. Collins, *A Social History of English Rugby Union* (London: Routledge, 2009); Johnes, *A History of Sport in Wales*; D. Smith and G. Williams, *Fields of Praise: The Official History of the Welsh Rugby Union, 1881–1981* (Cardiff: University of Wales Press, 1980).
18 Smith and Williams, *Fields of Praise*; G. Williams, *1905 and All That* (Llandysul, UK: Gomer, 1991).
19 R. Williams, *Politics and Letters: Interviews with New Left Review* (London: Verso, 1979).
20 R. Williams, *George Orwell* (London: Fontana, 1971).
21 See H. Richards, *The Red and the White: The Story of England v Wales Rugby* (London: Aurum Press, 2009).

22 Office for National Statistics, *Census: Key Statistics for Wales, March 2011* (2012).

23 See J. Ellis, *Investiture: Royal Ceremony and National Identity in Wales, 1911–1969* (Cardiff: University of Wales Press, 2008); R. Weight, *Patriots: National Identity in Britain 1940–2000* (London: Pan Books, 2002).

24 M. Johnes, *Wales Since 1939* (Manchester: Manchester University Press, 2012).

25 R. Williams, 'Welsh culture', in D. Williams (ed.), *Who Speaks for Wales? Nation, Culture, Identity: Raymond Williams* (Cardiff: University of Wales Press, 1975/2003), 10.

26 R. Williams, 'Wales and England', in D. Williams (ed.), *Who Speaks for Wales? Nation, Culture, Identity: Raymond Williams* (Cardiff: University of Wales Press, 1983/2003), 17.

27 See Collins, *Rugby League in Twentieth Century Britain*; Collins, *A Social History of English Rugby Union*.

28 E. Dunning and K. Sheard, *Barbarians, Gentlemen and Players* (Oxford: Martin Robertson, 1979); T.J.L. Chandler and J. Nauright (eds), *Making the Rugby World: Race, Gender, Commerce* (London: Routledge, 1999); also see S. Jones, *Midnight Rugby* (London: Headline, 2000).

29 Davies with Corrigan, *Jonathan*, 136.

30 See J. Davies with P. Corrigan, *Code Breaker* (London: Bloomsbury, 1996).

31 I. Harris, *There and Back: My Journey from League to Union and Back Again* (Edinburgh: Mainstream, 2005), 35.

32 E. Dunning and K. Sheard, *Barbarians, Gentlemen and Players* (2nd edn), (London: Routledge, 2005).

33 Collins, *Rugby League in Twentieth Century Britain*.

34 See for example Jenkins, *Life at Number 10*.

35 See J. Harris, '(Re)Presenting Wales: National identity and celebrity in the postmodern rugby world', *North American Journal of Welsh Studies*, 6, (2006), 1–12; J. Harris, 'Tales from the outside half factory: From (sh)amateurism to professionalism in the autobiographies of Welsh rugby's number tens', in G. Ryan (ed.), *The Changing Face of Rugby* (Newcastle: Cambridge Scholars Publishing, 2008); J. Harris, 'A new Prince of Wales? Long live the King!', in C. Sandvoss, M. Real and A. Bernstein (eds), *Bodies of Discourse* (Frankfurt: Peter Lang, 2012), 165–184.

36 *The Observer*, 28 October 2001.

37 P. Bennett with M. Williams, *Everywhere for Wales* (London: Arrow Books, 1981); A.W. Bevan, *Grav: In his Own Words* (Llandysul, UK: Gomer, 2008).

38 Williams, *1905 and All That*.

39 A. Bateman with P. Rees, *There and Back Again* (Edinburgh: Mainstream, 2001), 90.

40 Jenkins, *Life at Number 10*.

41 See Richards, *The Red and the White*.

42 See Harris, *Rugby Union and Globalization*; J. Harris and N. Wise, 'Geographies of scale in international rugby union', *Geographical Research*, 43, (2011), 375–383.

43 See J. Beaverstock, 'Rethinking skilled international labour migration: World cities and banking organisations', *Geoforum*, 25, (1994), 323–338.

44 Chandler and Nauright, *Making the Rugby World*; Harris, *Rugby Union and Globalization;* Harris and Wise, 'Geographies of scale'; J. Nauright and T.J.L. Chandler (eds), *Making Men: Rugby and Masculine Identity* (London: Frank Cass, 1996).

45 *Wales on Sunday*, 27 September 2015.

46 Williams, 'Wales and England', 26.

47 See Richards, *The Red and the White*.

48 P. Beck, 'War minus the shooting: George Orwell on international sport and the Olympics', *Sport in History*, 33, 1 (2013), 80.

11 'When jerseys speak'

Contested heritage and South African rugby

Marizanne Grundlingh

Introduction

This chapter is concerned with how sport museums, and in particular rugby museums, in South Africa tell the story of South Africa's rich rugby heritage. Using the author's observations at the opening of the Springbok Experience rugby museum, several visits made by the author to the museum, the sourcing of hitherto untapped archival sources from the South African Rugby Board archives, and the conducting of in-depth interviews with curators of private and commercial rugby museums in South Africa, this chapter unpacks the sports heritage within broader heritage debates. It draws attention to the commercial nature of sports heritage initiatives, such as the Springbok Experience museum. It is proposed that the professional turn in rugby in South Africa since the mid-1990s has made rugby heritage a viable commercial proposition, used not only to tell the story of the country's rugby past, but also to solidify the Springbok brand through the use of sports heritage modalities. More specifically, the aim of this chapter is to probe the politics of South African rugby heritage with reference to the complexity of representing black and 'coloured' heritage at the Springbok Experience. I show how, despite the best attempts of the South African Rugby Union (SARU) to depict an inclusive rugby heritage in the country, the politics of how 'to make jerseys speak' is a complex practice.

The interpretive and experiential qualities of heritage have increasingly become the focus of contemporary studies on heritage production.[1] Sport as a form of heritage has been considered as an especially relevant social setting where the experiential qualities associated with heritage can manifest, whether through intangible means (for example, songs, rituals or superstitions associated with a sports team or venue), or more tangible means (by visiting sport stadiums, sport museums and sport Halls of Fame). This chapter is concerned with the tangible aspects of South Africa's rugby heritage as they are portrayed in community and corporate rugby museums. SARU has made a significant contribution to the preservation of South Africa's rich rugby heritage by opening a modern interactive rugby museum at the Victoria and Alfred Waterfront in Cape Town on Heritage Day, 24 September 2013.

The Springbok Experience serves as a case study to explore the commercial nature of sports heritage preservation and production in the country. The Springbok brand has historically been associated with white national identity.[2] This chapter shows how, through SARU's active marketing campaign, the association with that particular group has been strategically diminished and the brand is now projected as a symbol of a highly successful sports team recognised nationally and globally.

This chapter deals with the complexities of how the representation of South Africa's rugby heritage has changed. It considers the ramifications of the professionalization of rugby in South Africa, with a specific focus on how the rugby heritage has become commercialized and strategically used by SARU to solidify the Springbok brand through sports heritage. Considering that heritage initiatives are closely aligned with economic and commercial objectives, this chapter shows that South Africa's rugby heritage has not always been preserved with a commercial goal in mind. Rather, in the amateur era of the game, rugby museums espoused an intimate, personal association with rugby memorabilia, mostly in community or private rugby museums. With the inevitable tide of professionalism sweeping through South African rugby, SARU has been able to market South Africa's rugby heritage as a commodity which showcases the Springbok brand in a very competitive sports market. The museum as an expression of heritage is analysed, with specific reference to the changing nature of museums and what they 'do'.

Heritage and museums in motion

Most heritage initiatives in post-apartheid South Africa tend to memorialize and commemorate leaders or events of the country's political past. Heritage initiatives in South Africa have also been important for economic reasons, attracting tourists to destinations that showcase its unique social and political heritage.

Heritage is a fluid concept that is continually being socially constructed.[3] An argument in scholarship on heritage studies is that heritage is an active process of making memory and meaning. In other words, it is something we do and experience, and can be understood as 'the practice that occurs at places rather than just the place itself'.[4] It has also been proposed that heritage is not 'an object or a site but ... a process and an outcome; it uses objects and sites as vehicles for the transmission of ideas in the service of a wide range of values and understandings'.[5] In other words, heritage and the consumption of heritage is an active process. Lowenthal, quoting a British custodian, notes: 'It is not that the public should learn something but they should *become* something.'[6] It is also not necessarily the behavioural aspect that enables visitors to feel connected to a heritage site, but rather the emotional aspect of performance.[7] Heritage is a product of the present, which uses the past – whether relics, history or memory – and constructs it for the requirements of an imagined future.[8]

Museums are one expression of heritage. They are physical places for the display of material artefacts, but their roles and functions have changed – from offering static representations of 'how life once was' to becoming a form of entertainment, with interaction becoming a key element of the museum experience.

Kirshenblatt-Gimblett highlights this shift by noting that 'museums were once defined by their relationship to objects: curators were "keepers" and their greatest asset was their collections. Today, they are defined more than ever by their relationship to visitors.'[9] Museums have become part of an 'experience economy', and their dual role has become both to entertain and to engage visitors.[10]

The experience economy relies on four features: education, entertainment, escapism and aestheticism. The Springbok Experience adheres to all the elements of the 'experiential economy', as it is designed to teach/educate visitors about South Africa's history through rugby as well as entertain through active displays and individual involvement in the 'Springbok Trials Rugby Skills Zone'. It also offers a form of escapism from everyday life for the visitor. This is done by drawing on a strong narrative of the successes of the Springbok team: the successes, albeit fleeting, allow the visitor to be distracted from the turmoil of everyday life. Portswood House, the Victorian-style building that houses the Springbok Experience, has Table Mountain looming in the background with the harbour below, and the displays themselves are designed for a pleasurable aesthetic experience. Elaborating on the pitfalls of the 'experience economy', one scholar writes:

> The key danger in the experience economy is the 'commodification trap' – the disillusionment of customers because things stay the same. In sharp contrast with service economies, the drive in the experience economy is toward customization, creating the impression that every experience is unique and has been developed for the individual alone.[11]

This is particularly apparent in the entrance foyer to the Springbok Experience, where visitors can take individual photos of themselves that are then superimposed onto a Springbok team photo. This attraction gives the visitor a unique opportunity to feel that he/she as an individual is symbolically part of the display.

This chapter shows how the Springbok Experience slots into the 'experience economy'. Through this, the nature of rugby heritage collection and preservation has changed, from small, intimate collections to large, public, commercial collections. This shift has occurred within global changes in museum practices, a trend that scholars have termed 'New Museology'. New Museology emphasizes the political, ideological and aesthetic aspects of museums and 'intensifies the subtexts and the present-centred nature of showcasing objects of the past'.[12] Sharon Macdonald analyses three salient aspects of the New Museology. First, museums and their objects are not fixed, but rather shift with changing contexts. In other words, they are 'situational and contextual, rather than inherent'. Second, visitor and public perceptions of museums and their contents are also changeable, with multiple meanings that are often independent of curatorial intent. Third, New Museology considers museums as going beyond their educative and instructive role to 'include mundane or market concerns' such as entertainment and commercialism.[13]

The Springbok Experience evinced all these trends in New Museology. The words of SARU's CEO, Jurie Roux, at the opening of the Springbok Experience echoed this view: 'People can forget their traditional ideas of what museums are like – the Springbok Experience will be completely different. It will be interactive, digital and immersive as well as displaying some incredible artefacts in telling rugby's South African story.'[14] The change in museum practice allows for reflection on how the politics of representation manifest within these trends of New Museology.

Several scholars have contributed to understanding the growth and consequences of heritage initiatives in South Africa, but the study of sport as a form of heritage has yet to be explored academically in the South African context.[15] Recently studies on sports heritages have increased in Europe and the United States.[16] There is considerable scope for studying the way in which sports heritage has been preserved and commodified in South African sports culture.

The Springbok brand as national heritage

It is not coincidental that one of South Africa's national days, Heritage Day, was selected by SARU as the day that would mark the opening of the Springbok Experience in Cape Town. Sport, in particular rugby, has long been promoted as a form of South African heritage, most recently by SARU's 2012 brand and marketing campaign 'Our Honour, Our Heritage'.

Since South Africa is a diverse nation stratified along cultural, social, political, racial and economic lines, this initiative is aimed at homogenizing rugby as a form of heritage that many South Africans could associate with. Of course, this is a simplistic approach and in reality the spectatorship and following of the national team varies, but the 'Our Honour, Our Heritage' campaign does allow one to unpack the intricacies of considering sport as a form of cultural heritage. Accordingly, it provides a vantage point from where to make sense of sports heritage, and in particular the heritage that rugby sought to convey with the opening of the Springbok Experience.

Jurie Roux hinted at the commercial and marketable value of the Springbok brand when he addressed the crowd at the official opening of the Springbok Experience: 'People talk about a museum; this is not a museum, this is an experience of the most powerful rugby brand in the world, this is the Springboks.' SARU's initiative to preserve and display South Africa's rugby heritage is therefore linked to sports heritage and the Springbok brand's popularity worldwide and seen as an opportunity to lure tourists to the venue to get a glimpse of South Africa's rich rugby heritage.

Professionalization and the establishment of a corporate rugby museum

Professionalism has radically changed the face of South African rugby. During its amateur era, funding ensured the financial wellbeing of provinces and clubs, but the most important commodity, the player, was bypassed.[17] The administrator and president of the South African Rugby Board (SARB), Dr Danie Craven, was strongly opposed to players being compensated financially for their services. He considered professionalism in rugby union to be the 'cancer that will kill it' and was quoted as saying that 'when the actual thrill of winning is not enough, and you must have cash incentives, then it is time for me to move out of rugby'.[18] Although rugby was played under amateur rules, this does not mean that players were not compensated in other ways. Amateurism in rugby was therefore not applied in the strict sense of the word, as players were often compensated in less overt ways. Before the formalization of professional rugby in South Africa, players had been remunerated behind the scenes and 'match fees' were often paid under the table by the unions.[19]

The mid-1990s saw rugby become fully professional at the elite level, and this development was fuelled by the interest Rupert Murdoch's News Corporation (News Corp) showed in acquiring sole television rights for screening the southern hemisphere competition between provincial franchises in South Africa, New Zealand and Australia (today the competition is known as Super Rugby) as well as international matches between these countries. South African rugby had now been catapulted into the global sporting economy, which meant that the players themselves became commercially viable and marketable products for global sports brands. The consequence of this development is that in the era of professional rugby both players and South Africa's rugby heritage have become overtly commercial.

It is worth considering the different manifestations of sport museums when looking at how the representation of the South African rugby heritage has changed. A leading sports heritage scholar has developed a typology that lists four exhibition types of sport museums. These include academic, corporate, community and vernacular sport museums.[20]

South African rugby heritage was memorialized mostly in community sport museums and on a private level during the amateur era of rugby. Prominent rugby schools, such as Paul Roos (Stellenbosch), Paarl Gymnasium (Paarl) and Grey College (Bloemfontein) have school museums or archives in which rugby features prominently. This form of memorialization, albeit on a small scale and developed in accordance with an identification with a specific institution, speaks to the value of a rugby heritage for rugby-playing students, but more importantly alludes to the fact that these forms of 'informal' sports heritage collections form the backbone of South Africa's rugby heritage collections.

Another example of a local sports heritage initiative is the Choet Visser Rugby Museum in Bloemfontein. This museum boasts of having the largest private rugby collection in South Africa.[21] It hosts a collection of rugby memorabilia that was donated to Visser, a former Springbok manager, by friends, players and administrators in rugby. At the entrance to the museum is a sign quoting Visser that reads: 'I am not a collector. Every piece in my museum is a personal keepsake. Friends have to give it to me with a personal message. Only then does a rugby souvenir qualify for the museum.'

The intention and rationale of the museum was never commercial, but depended on the willingness of rugby players and administrators to give him their rugby gear as gifts to be displayed in the museum. Visser's son-in-law, who showed me through the museum, elaborated on the difficulty he had in obtaining memorabilia relating to rugby players in the professional era:

> The museum is getting less and less *[sic]* gifts, Why, because the guys are keeping their jerseys, pants and boots, and what do they do then? Their benefit year, they sell it. Everything revolves around money, there you have it.[22]

The Choet Visser Rugby Museum was able to thrive in the amateur era in the sport, when the value of rugby jerseys and memorabilia was associated with a sense of loyalty and association with a person, in this case Visser. The memorabilia donated to him by players was a personal gift. The idea that a sporting artefact needs to have a personal connotation associated with it to make it truly authentic was a trend in community rugby museums of the amateur era in South African rugby.

The practice of writing letters to influential players and administrators requesting rugby memorabilia from them also serves as an example of the intimacy associated with rugby memorabilia during the amateur era. The SARU rugby archives, housed at Stellenbosch University, have many letters addressed to Craven. Several letters from avid rugby supporters and players request him to send them signed rugby memorabilia, including ties, jerseys, socks and photos. One such letter from a young fan reads:

> Dear Dr. Craven. I am a great rugby lover and am obsessed with rugby. I collect all rugby memorabilia that I can get hold of. I have written to you before to ask if you could send me memorabilia, like rugby emblems, rugby jerseys, rugby photos and rugby books. I play for our school's under 15 team and we have not lost a match this season.[23]

Craven responded to all these letters meticulously. There is a sense of intimacy associated with such requests and many of the letters reflect the personal affiliation his supporters felt with Craven, although they never met him. In the amateur era rugby memorabilia was donated, by either the players themselves or administrators, while in the professional era rugby memorabilia has become commodified and as such consists of consumable products for those who can purchase them.

On a bright spring day in September 2013, the Victoria and Alfred Waterfront in Cape Town saw the launch of one of the latest tourist attractions in the city. The twenty-three million visitors who annually pass through the Waterfront now had the opportunity to delve into South Africa's rich rugby heritage.[24] SARU spent two years building up to this day, which saw the opening of South Africa's most expensive sport museum. The Springbok Experience, as noted on its advertising pamphlet, is dedicated to 'telling South Africa's story through the eyes of its most powerful sport'. By September 2015, 80,000 people had visited the museum.[25] SARU's strategic communications manager and project director for the Springbok Experience, Andy Colquhoun, explained that the rationale for the Waterfront as a location for the Springbok Experience was both a practical and an operational decision, in that the old museum had to be refurbished and the Waterfront was considered to be a place where a large spectrum of people could get the chance to appreciate South Africa's rugby heritage.[26]

The opening of the Springbok Experience was marked with the current Springbok team in attendance and autograph hunters, young and old, queuing to get a glimpse of (and perhaps an autograph from) their rugby heroes. The current team, management and coaching staff were neatly dressed in suits and ties, representing a clean-cut professional image of the team, which was to face Australia that coming Saturday in a Tri-Nations clash. The excitement was palpable as young fans almost flattened the railings where the team had congregated before they entered the new museum. But the day was more than just a chance for rugby fans to get a glimpse of the current Springboks. Behind the current players were former Springbok captains, representing the historically white, 'coloured' and black South African rugby federations.

The museum itself is impressive, with the 800 m^2, double-storey venue catering for both rugby fanatics and those with a general interest in the sport. It has various features from an interactive 'Springbok Trials Rugby Skills Zone', where one can mimic the movement of players on the field and 'try out' the physical skills that the Springboks themselves master on the field, to a digital and interactive retelling of South Africa's rugby past on the second floor. One is taken on a journey ranging from rugby's arrival in South Africa during the colonial era in the late nineteenth century, to the Springbok tours in the early twentieth century, to the political turmoil of playing rugby during the apartheid years. A concerted effort is made to represent South African rugby's fractured history by commemorating and venerating all players who excelled in rugby, as well as by including the previously overlooked histories of the black and the 'coloured' rugby leagues. As SARU president Oregan Hoskins put it: 'Our new rugby museum will embrace the past. We want to celebrate South African rugby in all its diverse histories, as well as shine a spotlight on its troubles and turmoil and its growing pains.'[27] But the museum experience is also a celebration of the successes that South African rugby enjoyed on the field over a period of 100 years. The 1995 and 2007 Rugby World Cup victories stand out as memorable achievements that venerate the players, captains and coaches who contributed to those victories.

The 'rhythm' of the museum tour is designed to allow the visitor to experience a complete narrative, spanning from rugby's origins in the country up to the present day. A chronicle is recounted from separation to integration, from colonialism to apartheid and to post-apartheid, culminating with Mandela's involvement in the 1995 Rugby World Cup. The museum tour concludes with a short film entitled *Match Day in South Africa*, depicting rugby as a game ostensibly played and appreciated by all. This romantic narrative resonates with what Kirshenblatt-Gimblett has termed the 'museum effect ... where not only ordinary things become special ... but the museum experience itself becomes a model for experiencing life outside its walls'.[28] The grandeur of the museum was recognized internationally, when it was shortlisted for an international museum award at the annual Museum and Heritage Awards in the United Kingdom in May 2014.

Furthermore, SARU's decision to look at international best practice in sport museums and its choice of UK-based company Mather & Co as design partner indicate the importance it placed on representing South Africa's rugby heritage as a professional product. Evidently the conceptualization of the museum from the beginning was to use it and South Africa's rugby heritage to further the interests of SARU as a business and the Springboks as its brand. According to SARU's museum and heritage manager, Dr Hendrik Snyders, promoting the Springbok brand was one of SARU's main objectives. He explained:

> The Springbok emblem is one of the most marketable emblems in the world. It is regarded as one of the most successful brands too. The Springbok Experience Museum gives us an opportunity to showcase the Springboks in a different way and by doing this we keep it [the Springbok brand] in the public eye.[29]

'When jerseys speak': contested heritage at the Springbok Experience museum

Sport museums are heavily nostalgic, on both a personal and a collective level. An argument in heritage studies is that 'nostalgic sporting exhibitions that market specific sports as corporate brands often minimize or ignore controversial, contested and potentially divisive issues as well as marginalize a great deal of cultural, gendered and political social context'.[30] The way in which the silences, discrepancies and divisive issues are dealt with in sport museums has been a topic of concern among sport historians, and the exhibitions of the 'coloured' and black rugby boards at the Springbok Experience prove no different.[31]

South Africa's racially segregated past has made the politics of representation of South Africa's rugby history an especially delicate matter. Although SARU made a concerted effort to commemorate the marginalized and neglected heritage of black and 'coloured' rugby players, there are still those who feel that their rugby heritage is not truly represented in the Springbok Experience. This was particularly apparent when the former team captains of the white, black and 'coloured' rugby unions were invited to attend the opening of the museum. Each captain's name was called out, and somewhat embarrassingly to the organizers, when the names of the 'coloured' and black captains were called out, there was hardly any acknowledgement from the crowd. I could not help hear a middle-aged Afrikaner man murmur, 'These players were not Springboks.' Former SARU team captain Salie Fredericks, who attended the event, relayed his discontent to a journalist:

I was very disappointed to find that none of those guys [the Springboks] knew of me. I had a feeling that I never really existed, yet rugby was my life for many years. It is not the first time that I've been invited to an event for past and present players, and it is not the first time that we've players that I have played with felt like total strangers. I had hoped that by going along with projects such as these it would be unifying.... I still hear that players who played for their national teams were not good enough to be Springboks and that is why we had no media, like radio and television, or why records were not kept.[32]

This development was not a vindictive act on the part of the crowd, but rather shows how packaging heritage in broad brush strokes under the historically white symbol of the Springboks is problematic. Despite SARU's best intentions to represent South African rugby heritage in its entirety, the politics of representation proved more complex. This shows the difficulty of packaging heritage as 'show business'. One of the intentions of the Springbok Experience was to tell the untold story of black and 'coloured' rugby in South Africa, yet the material culture to tell the story with proved difficult to find. According to Snyders, many of their documents had been discarded or destroyed in an attempt to prevent government officials from following a paper trail regarding their anti-apartheid activities.[33]

The artefacts in the Springbok Experience that represent the history of the South African African Rugby Football Board (SAARFB), the South African Rugby Union (SARU) (affiliated to SACOS, the South African Council on Sports) and the South African Rugby Football Federation (SARFF) (aligned with the South African Rugby Board) are minimal. Dr Snyders hinted at the 'over representation' of the South African Rugby Board's memorabilia. According to him:

> The South African Rugby Board of Danie Craven and the Springboks associated with that board had the opportunity to play tests against New Zealand, England, France and so on. So it is assumed and it is true that there is a lot more memorabilia associated with the Springbok jersey. To tell you the truth, that memorabilia is more than 80% that we have in the museum collection. There are trophies, badges, jerseys, and ceramic plates, anything under the sun. While for the South African African Football Union, the South African Rugby Union and the South African Rugby Football Federation that is not the case. So when trying to conceptualise the Springbok Experience Museum we were confronted with a critical gap in the record. This is the difficulty in trying to make jerseys speak, when you simply don't have as many jerseys to tell stories with.[34]

It is not that remembrances of these rugby boards do not exist, but rather that the memorabilia is not readily available. A leading sports heritage scholar argues that 'sport heritage is a globally disseminated and consumed commodity, and the values and objectives can change depending on who is consuming the heritage'.[35] In this instance, SARU was an architect in determining the heritage to be consumed in the museum. In an attempt to fill this crucial gap in the record (in terms of the material culture of the black and 'coloured' rugby boards that is available to display at the Springbok Experience), SARU had to manufacture displayable heritage of these rugby bodies.

Prior to the opening of the museum, 40 former captains from the former white, 'coloured' and black rugby boards were invited to a ceremony at the Waterfront. The captain's handprints were captured in special moulds to be displayed later at the museum as a permanent exhibition. SARU president Oregan Hoskins said the ceremonial capturing of the handprints of living national rugby union captains – pre- and post-unity – was a symbolic unifying of those traditions. According to him:

> There is no better way to link the past with the present than take a piece of the past – in the shape of the captains' hand prints – and place them into our present and future by capturing them for posterity and installing them as part of our *Springbok Experience*.[36]

Among those casting their handprints were Des van Jaarsveldt, the oldest living captain of the old South African Rugby Board Springboks; Austen van Heerden, the oldest living captain of the former South African Coloured Rugby Football Board; and Bomza Nkhola, the oldest surviving captain of the South African African Rugby Board.[37] A critical analysis of this initiative shows how divisive issues related to the heritage of 'coloured' rugby in South Africa were overlooked. The Springbok Experience, one can argue, has tried to show the inequities of the apartheid side of rugby through various displays, including frank accounts of overseas boycotts of Springbok tours. But the issue of historical representation is more complicated than this. Despite its valiant attempts to be even-handed, lurking behind its overarching message of a superior brand is the primary, if unspoken, premise of the historical achievements of rugby as a pre-eminently Afrikaner game. Using the past for present-day purposes is complicated and not as simple as SARU management would propose.

At the back of this is the fragmented past of 'coloured' rugby, divided along political lines of its own. SARFF, established in 1959 in the Western Cape district, aligned itself with the white South African Rugby Board. Its apathetic position to politics in sport was criticized by the more politically driven SARU (not to be confused with post-democratic SARU), which in 1973 was one of the founding members of the anti-apartheid sports body SACOS. SARU organized its own competitions and refused to be associated with the South African Rugby Board of Dr Craven. SARU's main objective was to boycott Springbok rugby in an attempt to show that its players were not willing to be used as political tokens on the rugby field, and would only compete internationally once all South Africans, irrespective of race, had the vote. It considered 'coloured' players who operated outside of SARU as 'sell-outs' and 'tokens'. Its slogan was 'no normal

Figure 11.1 The handprints of the former white, coloured and black rugby captains displayed on the grass outside the Springbok Experience Museum (Photograph taken by author).

sport in an abnormal society' and it was adamant that sport could be used to showcase the racial inequality brought forth by apartheid. SARFF, on the other hand, was less politically driven and its slogan was 'Where rugby is, we play.' The SARFF-aligned Errol Tobias, notably known as the first 'coloured' rugby player to play for the Springboks in a test match, against Ireland at Newlands in 1981, writes in his autobiography about the friction between SARFF and SARU:

> The SARU supporters would remind me that I am good enough to play for the white people, but not good enough that they would go to the extent to give me the vote. I would always encourage them to continue with their cause and wished them well. We all knew that the vote and equal rights was the only way forward in South Africa, but just as their approach wasn't wrong, so too what I did wasn't wrong.... Till this day I have no regrets. I feel exactly the same as I did then. I was a sportsman, not a politician.[38]

The symbolic display of the handprints of former captains of both SARFF and SARU was perhaps relevant for representing a 'unified' heritage for present-day purposes, but it opportunely overlooked the very different political agendas of these two groups. The heritage motive, in this instance as in so much else in the country, sugar-coated history with a thin commercial veneer designed to make it palatable to an increasingly consumerist-oriented society.

An exhibition dedicated to Errol Tobias in the Springbok Experience show-cases his role in shaping rugby history in the country. Sporting heroes can be considered a form of living heritage, and this idea became especially prevalent at the opening of the Springbok Experience.[39] Tobias was clearly proud of his achievements, as he hovered around the exhibition, giving autographs and taking photos with visitors to the museum. I asked Tobias about how he felt about the recognition he now receives almost three decades after his playing days. He explained that it is the first time that he has been able to bring his children to a place where they can see and learn who their father was. Tobias is proud that his role in breaking down racial barriers in sport had become immortalized in a museum. This points to how heritage and the material culture used to promote the sporting past is a powerful medium through which nostalgic recollections of a bygone era can be relived, not only on a national or international level, but also on a very intimate personal level. This nuanced personal form of nostalgia and heritage is, however, problematic to exhibit and often overshadowed by broad brush strokes of politically persuaded heritage.

Conclusion

This chapter has shown how the preservation of South African rugby has changed from small-scale, intimate collections of rugby memorabilia to com-mercialized forms of preservation in the professional era. The politics of repres-entation in museum exhibitions were probed with specific reference to the 'manufactured' heritage of the black and 'coloured' rugby boards. Ultimately, in the professional era of South African rugby, both rugby's heritage and the story of South African rugby are closely aligned with one of the biggest rugby brands in the world, the Springboks. This points to the delicate and complex relation-ship between rugby, heritage, identity and commercialization in an era of profes-sional sports in South Africa. Moreover, in South Africa a recalcitrant past is always likely to brush against the neat folds and contours required in the manu-facturing of heritage.

Notes

1 For examples, see S. Gammon, 'Sporting New Attractions? The Commodification of the Sleeping Stadium', in S. Gammon and J. Kurtzman (eds), *Sport Experiences: Contemporary Perspectives* (London: Routledge, 2010), 115–112; S. Gammon, 'Heroes as Heritage: The Commoditization of Sporting Achievement', *Journal of Heritage Tourism* 9, 3 (2014), 1–11; G. Ramshaw, 'Living Heritage and the Sport Museum: Athletes, Legacy and the Olympic Hall of Fame and Museum, Canada Olympic Park*', Journal of Sport and Tourism* 15, 1 (2010), 45–70; G. Ramshaw, 'The Construction of Sport Heritage Attractions', *Journal of Tourism Consumption and Practice* 3, 1 (2011), 1–25; L. Smith, *The Uses of Heritage* (London: Routledge, 2006); H.Y. Park, *Heritage Tourism* (London: Routledge, 2014).
2 J. Nauright, 'Sustaining Masculine Hegemony: Rugby and the Nostalgia of Masculin-ity' in J. Nauright and T.J.L. Chandler (eds), *Making Men: Rugby and Masculine Identity* (London: Frank Cass, 1996), 227–244.

3 See Gammon, 'Heroes as Heritage', 1–11; G. Ramshaw, S. Gammon and E. Waterton, *Heritage and the Olympics: People, Place and Performance* (London: Routledge, 2014); G.J. Ashworth, 'Paradigms and Paradoxes in Planning the Past', in M. Smith and L. Onderwater (eds), *Selling or Telling? Paradoxes in Tourism, Culture and Heritage* (Arnhem: ATLAS, 2008), 23–24; J. Hill, K. Moore and J. Wood, *Sport, History and Heritage: Studies in Public Representation* (Woodbridge: The Boydell Press, 2012).

4 G. Ramshaw, S. Gammon and W.J. Huang, 'Acquired Pasts and Commodification of Borrowed Heritage: The Case of the Bank of America Stadium Tour', *Journal of Sport and Tourism* 18, 1 (2013), 17–31.

5 Ashworth, 'Paradigms and Paradoxes', 11.

6 D. Lowenthal, *The Heritage Crusade and the Spoils of History* (Cambridge: Cambridge University Press, 1998), 23.

7 G. Bagnall, 'Performance and Performativity at Heritage Sites', *Museum and Society* 1, 2 (2003), 87–103.

8 B. Graham, G.J. Ashworth and J.E. Tunbridge, *A Geography of Heritage: Power, Culture and Economy* (London: Arnold, 2000).

9 B. Kirshenblatt-Gimblett, *Destination Culture: Tourism, Museums, and Heritage* (Berkeley: University of California Press, 1998), 138.

10 B.J. Pine and J.H. Gilmore, *The Experience Economy: Work is Theatre and Every Business a Stage* (Boston: Harvard Business School Press, 1999); M. Hall, 'The Reappearance of the Authentic', in I. Karp, C.A. Kratz, L. Szwaja and T. Ybarra-Frausto (eds), *Museum Frictions: Public Cultures/Global Transformations* (Durham, NC: Duke University Press, 2006), 70-101.

11 Hall, 'The Reappearance of the Authentic', 78.

12 M. O'Neill and G. Osmond, 'A Racehorse in the Museum: Phar Lap and the New Museology', in M.G. Phillips (ed.), *Representing the Sporting Past in Museums and Halls of Fame* (London: Routledge, 2012).

13 S. Macdonald (ed.), *A Companion to Museum Studies* (Malden, MA: Blackwell, 2006), see in particular the introduction by Macdonald.

14 C. Dolley, 'Design Companies Give SARU Red Card', *Cape Times*, 8 May 2013, 6.

15 For examples see L. Witz, C. Rassool and G. Minkley, 'Repackaging the Past for South African Tourism', *Deadalus* 130, 1 (2001), 277–296; L. Meskell, *The Nature of Heritage: The New South Africa* (Oxford: Wiley-Blackwell, 2012); A.E. Coombes, *History After Apartheid: Visual Culture and Public Memory in a Democratic South Africa* (Durham, NC: Duke University Press, 2003).

16 For examples see S. Gammon and G. Ramshaw, *Heritage, Sport and Tourism: Sporting Pasts – Tourist Futures* (London: Routledge, 2007); Hill *et al.*, *Sport, History and Heritage*; Herzog, *MemorialkulturimFußballsport: Medien, Rituale und Praktiken des Erinnerns, Gedenkens und Vergessens* (Stuttgart: Kohlhammer, 2013); M.G. Phillips, 'Introduction: Historians in Sport Museums', in Phillips (ed.). *Representing the Sporting Past*; J. Reilly, 'The Development of Sport in Museums', *The International Journal of the History of Sport* (2015), available at http://dx.doi.org/10.1080/09523367.2015.11083 06 (accessed 17 December 2015); Ramshaw *et al.*, *Heritage and the Olympics*.

17 A. Grundlingh, *Potent Pastimes: Sport and Leisure Practices in Modern Afrikaner History* (Pretoria: Protea Book House, 2013).

18 T. Partridge, *A Life in Rugby* (Halfway House, South Africa: Southern Book Publishers, 1991), 108.

19 C. Schoeman, *Player Power: A History of the South African Rugby Players Association* (Cape Town: SARPA, 2009).

20 Phillips, 'Introduction: Historians in Sport Museums', 6.

21 N. Du Plessis, *Choet Visser Rugby Museum: The World's Biggest Private Rugby Museum* (Bloemfontein: Dreyer Publishers, 1994).

22 N. Du Plessis, Choet Visser Rugby Museum, Bloemfontein, 1 October 2013, interview with author.

23 SARU rugby archives, Box 1, 9 Butler to Craven, 11 July 1977.
24 Dolley, 'Design Companies Give SARU Red Card', 6.
25 G. Germishuys, 'Springbok – rugbymuseum kry groot eerbewys' (2015), available at www.netwerk24.com/nuus/2015-09-18-wb-springbok-rugbymuseum-kry-groot-eerbewys (accessed 20 October 2015).
26 A. Colquhoun, SARU Strategic Communications Manager, interview with author, coffee shop at Victoria and Alfred Waterfront, Cape Town, 12 November 2013.
27 Dolley, 'Design Companies Give SARU Red Card', 6.
28 Kirshenblatt-Gimblett, *Destination Culture*, 51.
29 Dr H. Snyders, SARU Museum and Heritage Manager, interview with author, SARU Offices, Cape Town, 14 August 2013.
30 M.G. Phillips, 'Introduction: Historians in Sport Museums', 11.
31 For examples see W. Vamplew, 'Facts and Artifacts: Sports Historians and Sports Museums', *Journal of Sport History* 25, 2 (1998), 268–282; K. Moore, 'Sport in Museums and Museums of Sport: An Overview', in Hill *et al.*, *Sport, History and Heritage*; D. Adair, 'Le Musée Olympique: Epicentre of Olympic Evangelism', in Hill *et al.*, *Sport, History and Heritage*.
32 H. Gibbs, 'Kicked into Touch Again: While Lager Mentality Exists in Rugby, Transformation Won't Go Full Circle Says ex-SARU Captain', *The New Age*, 4 April 2013, 1.
33 Snyders, interview.
34 Ibid.
35 Ramshaw, 'The Construction of Sport Heritage Attractions', 5.
36 'SARU Launches Springbok Experience Museum' (2013), available at www.rugby15.co.za/2013/03/saru-launches-springbok-experience-rugby-museum/ (accessed 14 October 2015).
37 Ibid.
38 E. Tobias, *Errol Tobias: Pure Gold* (Cape Town: Tafelberg, 2015), 28, 48.
39 Gammon, 'Heroes as Heritage', 1–11.

12 Performativity, identities and rugby from field to stage in the new South Africa

Carla Lever

When victorious Springbok captain François Pienaar was asked after the 1995 World Cup final how it felt to have the support of the 65,000 South Africans in the stadium, his response has become the stuff of legend. 'David, we didn't have 65,000 South Africans,' he replied to deafening cheers. 'We had 43 million South Africans.'[1]

Pienaar's comment crystalized a sense of the potential for the reach of the game to expand ever outwards into a broader cultural sphere, in this case creating a very specific 'national' moment for a racially divided, newly democratic country. Too often, when not reminded by such overt socio-political context, we forget that sport does not operate in a social vacuum: it is spectated and played, consumed and con-textualized by countless small habits and happenings, not all of which may be visible from the stands. From the mega-event of a World Cup to the social custom of a beer and braai (barbecue), South African rugby culture is sustained through a myriad of seemingly peripheral, often under-considered cultural habits, from the corporeal minutiae of the group chant to coy product advertising references or, as in the case study in this chapter, creative re-presentation.

In this chapter, written two decades after Pienaar's comments quoted above, I consider this reach of sporting culture – specifically rugby culture – into the ongoing negotiation of South African national identity. I will specifically be focus-ing on one example of a way that the game has been taken out of the stadium and into a very different set of public discourses and practices: those of the arts scene.

I will be suggesting some very simple things over the course of this chapter. First, that sport occupies an interesting place in what I will call, for the sake of convenience, a South African national sensibility. Specifically, I will tease out rugby's relationship to what we might term 'contemporary South Africanness': not South Africanness as experienced in the fraught Apartheid-era or during the World Cup-winning Madiba magic years, but as it plays out under the compli-cated, contested reign of Jacob Zuma – this dystopian time when citizens can lose both 250 million taxpayer Rand to presidential housing upgrades … and a Rugby World Cup match to Japan.

If sport can both reflect and create a sense of national identity, in many ways this chapter is about how *doing* impacts upon *being*. I explore how intangible concepts like national identity find the conditions of their possibility in the materiality of tangible, repeated actions, about what the supporter's shouts, the group gatherings, the team identification – and, importantly, the silences from those sidelined and marginalized – might be making of South Africans today.

With this in mind, I finally suggest that sometimes we can better understand or unpack this dynamic relationship by framing it in a different way, by skewing the picture. After all, that is what academia does – re-frame *doing* in order to see the *being* it is creating. With this in mind, I will be referring to an award-winning 2013 avant-garde Afrikaans performance work called *Balbesit* (or 'Ball Possession') that aims to do exactly that: to re-frame a sporting *doing* so unquestioningly South African that it often escapes critical scrutiny. This re-doing before our eyes (and ears) enables us to see (and hear) it more clearly.

Of course, before approaching this chapter on the broader implications and resonances of a sporting culture, we may do well to recall that Pienaar himself was immortalized in the film *Invictus*, itself partly a story about how the Springboks galvanized their own team fortitude through the inspiration of a Victorian poem. As scholars of sport, we ignore these broader cultural resonances at our peril.

Let us start with understanding 'national doing' in South Africa. Where better to begin than with the words of a man who, in many ways, sparked the ideal of a new 'rainbow' nation itself: Nelson Mandela? At his inaugural presidential address on 10 May 1994, Mandela said: 'Our daily deeds as ordinary South Africans must produce an actual South African reality. [...] We must therefore act together as a united people, for national reconciliation, for nation building, for the birth of a new world.'[2] Since rainbows – much like rhetoric – are famously elusive, Mandela used his first presidential speech to clarify that this new nation's identity was one that would be crafted through 'daily deeds': everyday acts of individuals coming together. In urging South Africans to 'act together', his call for a series of performances that would make a 'new world' showed an understanding of the repeated, embodied, enacted nature of identity. Performance, after all, stands bodily at the interface between words and worlds. At the same time, he was at pains to convey that national identity is not a top-down phenomenon created through constitutions or charters. 'South Africanness', he seems to suggest, is lived: it happens in everyday acts.

Paul Connerton's 1989 work *How Societies Remember* explores this very concept. Connerton contends that there are two fundamental ways in which social memory (a fundamental basis for group identity) is forged and maintained. The first way involves inscription practices: intentional acts of commemoration – we see their narrative laid before us in everything from the museum to the photo album. He suggests that these methods, being so overtly curated, are particularly adept at fostering critical engagement over cultural narrative formation: their very externality allows for perspective.

Yet, Connerton argues that such inscription methods are not ultimately the most successful in terms of prolonging (and, in South Africa's case, forging) social memory. He suggests that a far more powerful method lies in incorporation practices – intrinsic ways of embodying memories through repetitive actions, words or social habits. While these practices tend to leave no textual trace, meaning their significance is often dismissed in societies that privilege written texts, Connerton argues that they often seep into a subject's – and, consequently, what Clifford Geertz would understand as a culture's – sensibility. The very habitual nature of these practices may not allow for the critical scrutiny of, say, a monument, yet they are deeply inscribed on the far more dynamic surface of the body-mind. People often claim to 'live and breathe' rugby – and Connerton would suggest that is exactly how its 'culture' is experienced.

Of course, at the time of Mandela's inaugural speech, South Africans had precious few shared social memories on which to hang a national identity. In fact, Apartheid had perfectly combined inscription and incorporation practices to divide rather than unite – segregation meant there was no shared experience of space; legislation meant there was no shared experience of civic duty. Through enforcing separate education, work and leisure areas, sports, amenities and even suitable partners, the state exercised its systemic aim of controlling and minimizing collective experience at a physical as much as an ideological level. As Connerton explains:

> To the extent that their memories of a society's past diverge, to that extent its members can share neither experiences nor assumptions ... we will experience our present differently in accordance with the different pasts to which we are able to connect that present.[3]

As Homi Bhabha notes, 'Liberation is ... a time of cultural uncertainty, and, most crucially, of significatory or representational undecidability.'[4] Rather than wiping the slate clean, then, democratic change in South Africa may merely have rendered the script indecipherable. In representational terms, there was everything to play for.

At the time of the 1994 democratic transition, efforts at drafting a shared social narrative were clearly beginning. Overwhelmingly, these fell into the category of inscription practices – the Constitution and Bill of Rights were forged, history syllabi and street names had begun to be changed, new memorials erected. Enacting change around how people *felt*, however, was proving much harder. As Mandela knew, complete identity would be found in the gathering of action – action individually perfected, collectively repeated.

When it comes to embodied habits, where else do South Africans gather more regularly, with more ritual-like fixation and fervour, than at stadia, in front of televisions, at braais and bars, shebeens (African township bars) and sports fields across the country for the rugby, the football, the cricket ... the *game*? What more everyday repeated action than the tackle, the group chant, the cheer? As John Nauright has pointed out, historically rugby was always seen as a pathway to group solidarity – building physical and mental toughness.[5] It makes sense: if Judith Butler speaks of the power of repeated actions to create identity – how we fundamentally are what we do – then there is something larger to be said for the strict repetition of set plays, the line outs and scrums, the embodied understanding of a way of engaging in the world that sport both creates and reflects.

I started this chapter by referencing a culture of sport in South Africa – in this case, a particular rugby culture. Of course, for rugby to be something of a national obsession is hardly unique. Its general vocabulary of attack and defence, territorial gains and physical confrontation reflects a broader concern with the politics of ownership, of chance, of (often violent) strategic attack on the body of the other. In our complicated, quasi-postcolonial, competitively capitalist world, these are relatively universal preoccupations. And yet, I'd like to suggest more: that there's something about performing through the body, the spectacle of contested physicality, that resonates particularly strongly with South Africans.

'Sport', Nelson Mandela famously proclaimed, 'has the power to change the world.'[6] Historically, sport has certainly played its role in changing South Africans' worlds. For all the organized political responses to the Apartheid system, sports sanctions played a remarkable role in uniting international condemnation and – finally – mobilizing white national frustration. An oft-tapped resource for post-Apartheid nation building, sport's contribution to national identity is difficult to quantify but unquestioningly accepted. Connerton may well explain Mandela's claim through theories of incorporated practices building powerful social memory, Butler through the idea of identity sedimenting at an embodied level through repeated action. Yet one only has to feel the buzz on game day to appreciate the fact that it simply makes sense.

However you approach the matter, sport has proven time and again to combine a heady mix of high emotion, aggressive competition and contained, resolvable conflict. At base, though, it offers embodied spectacle. If contemporary South Africans can unite around any one collective social experience some twenty-one years into democracy, it surely must be anxiety about and obsession with the spectacle of the body. Of course, the reasons for this corporeal fixation draw on both historical fact and current experience. Under a repressive Apartheid government (1948 to early 1990s), people's capacity for direct expression was limited while their awareness of bodily signifiers was deliberately – forcibly – heightened. Bodies – both ideologically central and physically dispersed – were obsessively fetishized by a government intent on controlling every aspect of performance. Surely it is not too much to suggest that this combination of bodily fetishization and suppression encouraged a culture of keen atunement towards performativity – towards the (transgressively) seen, felt, lived and living body.[7]

The body was at the heart of anti-Apartheid protest, from the symbolic gesture of a single raised fist or *toyi-toyi* protest dance to the more literal expression in confrontation or incarceration.[8] Yet even post-democracy, the inherent communication difficulty with having eleven official languages means that it remains the logical site of connection. South Africans are then, for reasons both political and practical, attuned towards bodies – their skins, their gender, their class – but also their movements. That we fused a political resistance song into our new anthem, that even our whitest sporting events resound with the call-and-response strains of a mining worker's song, speaks to the calling to – and feel for – an embodied sense of nation.[9] From metaphor to movement, creative expression – often embodied, always imaginative – has been the marker of our national mood. Where better to celebrate this than on that most direct engagement of the rugby field, where bodies perform anxious corporeal contests?

And so I would suggest that contemporary South Africa has a very particular relationship to rugby – one importantly, perhaps uniquely, rooted in anxiety; in a national obsession with embodied identity, with skin-on-skin contact, with aggressive gains in territory, with the moving, acting, challenging body.

No coincidence, then, that local journalist Stephen Grootes was drawn into invoking a sports scenario while trying to articulate an elusive sense of national identity:

> ... it surely must be true that South Africans can be defined. During the ... World Cup, you could spot a South African in a stadium, not because of how they looked, but because of how they acted, and how they interacted with each other.[10]

What Grootes – and Mandela before him – has picked up is that national identity in the new South Africa cannot easily be spoken but can be felt; that it is, essentially, an act rather than an account. Where it has most clearly been felt – easily been enacted – seems so far to have been on the sports field. Rugby, particularly, has proven to be the game with which South Africans have had the most international success. So, in a nation obsessed with the centrality of the body, sports figures have occupied a position of anxious hope. Many nations build mythologies on the backs of their sports heroes; South Africa's are all the more high stakes for being set against a painful past and a desperate hope for the present. Tracing a history of the country's obsession between the surface of the skin and, paradoxically, the hidden depths of the land, we can map a peculiarly South African sportscape – that place in the popular imagination that is as real, as contested and as politically volatile as the ground on which it is played.

While it is important not to give the Hollywood-style impression that sport has simplistically united South Africans – support for the three major national games of cricket, football and rugby remains blatantly, often embarrassingly, racially divided – we should not overlook the fact that the stadium has, with historical regularity, been the setting for far more than merely a sports game. Whether a focus for unity or conflict, sport has proved a potent space for re-enacting these national negotiations of place as well as a repeated communal act fostering the ongoing (re)creation of social memory.

Crucially, despite this position of deep social relevancy, sport itself occupies a curiously hybrid space, being at once light personal entertainment and serious national engagement. Important enough to have its own Ministry, to contribute almost 2 per cent towards the GDP (1998), to make news headlines alongside political happenings, it is still, when it comes down to it, 'just a game'. Like a good piece of satire or a well-placed jibe, sport can hold multitudes ... but crucially, it also doesn't have to. This fluid position allows it to be taken as seriously – or as lightly – as one wishes, enabling it to offer a uniquely flexible space for social engagement, something that more traditional attempts at socio-political mobilization often struggle with.

Previously, I referred to Connerton's argument that incorporation practices tend to be dismissed for this very reason: they are considered too ephemeral, too frivolous to be taken seriously. Yet Bhabha suggests that it is the tensions inherent in the performative, hybrid jumble of the everyday that are how 'newness' enters the world: new systems, understanding, perspectives.

Democratic South Africa – just two decades old – is still new. It is unavoidably complex, intrinsically hybrid, anxiously performative. Its shining mid-1990s rainbow rhetoric has seemingly given way to a stormier narrative. A person who is interested in exploring this weather-change – in the links between the doing of sport and the being of nation – is South African theatre director Jaco Bouwer (2008 Most Promising Young Director, 2008 Standard Bank Young Artist of the Year), best known for his cutting-edge, experimental work in Afrikaans physical theatre.

Bouwer teamed up with award-winning local playwright Saartjie Botha in 2013 to create *Balbesit* – a multi-disciplinary performance work staged at various South African theatres and subsequently commissioned to be adapted into a film by the country's primary pay television channel, MNET.

While the text and basic narrative structure of the two works remain virtually identical, it is important to note that the visual perspectives offered by cinematography are very different to those experienced live in the theatre (and Bouwer certainly makes the most of the creative freedom of the film genre, with ample use of split screen, slow-motion choreography, subtitles and splice editing). Likewise, the mediated experience of a work is profoundly different to the immersive, often volatile live experience, where the visceral thrill of breaking the fourth wall cannot somehow translate on screen.

We might be tempted to suggest that the difference between genres is one of experiencing inscription versus incorporation practice, but Connerton argues this would be an error:

> [T]he cinema inscribes; but it could not be a practice of inscription if it were not also in a specific sense, an incorporating practice. What is incorporated is an ocular convention: the identification of the object with the camera. During the cinema performance spectators duplicate the action of the projector, their eyes behaving as it were like searchlights. Without this identification with the camera, certain facts would remain unintelligible: for example, the fact that spectators are not puzzled when the images on screen 'rotate' in a panning movement, yet the spectators know that they have not turned their heads ... they have turned their heads in so far as they have identified as all-seeing subjects with the movements of the camera.... In cinema, I am simultaneously in this action and outside of it, in this space and outside of this space; have the power of ubiquity, I am everywhere and nowhere. The inscriptional practice of cinema makes possible, and is in turn made possible by, the incorporating practice of the cinema spectator.[11]

For the sake of accurate quotation from a stable text, this analysis, while referring to the critical success of the theatrical production, will take textual references from the film version only.

Balbesit is an Afrikaans pun on the term 'ball possession', with strong
implications of power, in a stroke broadening the work's application from sport
into the realms of both politics and gender. Dubbing itself a *Studie in Stemme*
('Study in Voices') and sporting a fifteen-man cast in full rugby gear, *Balbesit* is
part choreographed movement piece, part choral onslaught. With scenes built
around players' set pieces – the scrum, the line out, the half-time break – the cast
clash voices and bodies to challenge what it ultimately may mean to be young,
male and South African.

The disjointed script, delivered in short bursts of dialogue that imitate the
rapid-fire style of web forum article comments, delivers searing sociological
commentary, aggressively tackling issues of contested identities in the new
South Africa head on. 'In a country that's eighty per cent black, it should take a
real effort not to have any black friends,'[12] says a sideline pundit to the audience,
matter-of-factly. His friend chimes in, 'I get really uncomfortable hearing about
you growing up with your black nanny. Who was raising *her* children?' As the
game carries on unfolding comfortably, predictably in front of us, the sudden
raw challenge on our own blind side is as effective as a tackle at the knees.

Bouwer and Botha deliberately designed the work to be fragmentary, mirror-
ing an actual rugby match in its ticking clock counting down exactly eighty
minutes of the play. During this time, fifteen actors dressed in unbranded white
kits engage with a referee who continually loses control of the spiralling action.
The team itself is full of characters: the overly-optimistic mascot who spouts
teeth-gratingly trite lines about the power of sport to unite, the drunken, hysterical bearded Boer who loves talking about death metal almost as much as he does
about emigrating, the elite schoolboy who is terribly earnest about what the
country should do better, the world-weary white realist who has cynically calculated his playing odds, the slick-talking black pundit who gets his kicks with
well-placed sideline commentary. For all these men, all these voices, we never
once see whom they are playing. What, after all, we might ponder, is the opposition South Africans are really up against?

We may meet all of these well-worn characters ... but where we start – and
where else could we start? – is with one old white man. In an opening segment
called 'Dreams of Tries', this old man, dressed in a well-worn suit and tie, takes
us down memory lane – about his childhood, the centrality of sport to family,
community belonging, national and personal pride, all inextricably linked in
eighty minutes of Saturday contestation. '*Rugby maak my bly*' (rugby makes me
happy), he states simply and, in the space that lingers after that, we too are
carried on a wave of nostalgia – the sounds of Hugh Bladen commentary filter-
ing through whistle blasts, the indistinguishable shouts from crowds and clear
line out calls; the unmistakable sounds of winter weekends in the heartland.

Yet, of course, these are very white sounds. Over the course of the next eighty
minutes we are forced into an unflinching consideration of this nostalgic rush,

this gut feeling. Nostalgia for whom? Nostalgia for what? 'We don't understand space – we just don't understand space,' the beleaguered referee laments after a poor example of territorial possession. And what could be truer, in a nation marked by goldfields and bantustans,[13] where stadia are built even as townships sprawl? We don't understand space.

It is important, of course, to consider that the space of South African theatre – mainstream or avant-garde – is just as white-dominated an industry as rugby has traditionally been. Perhaps it has been interrogated and challenged even less, since it is correspondingly less commercially successful. Bouwer's work, then, is particularly aimed at a specific South African demographic – a mirror, mirror on the fourth wall.

As the pace of the action quickens, phrases are tossed around, meeting and melding until the chaos reaches fever pitch. Some words hit home harder than others. 'It's like this country keeps knocking out my WIND,'[14] cries a player, at breaking point, face right up in the camera lens. His anguished expression is replaced by a sequence of men hoisted one by one by their teammates high up into the air, hoisted in their whites against a pitch-black background – an expectant line out into the void. Instead of receiving a ball, each elevated man completes the set play by delivering an individual, iconic gesture – in this surreal suspension sequence, we see everything from Caster Semenya's characteristic shoulder brush morphing into cupid's arrow pull, to a crucified Christ's widespread arms segueing into parting an invisible pair of legs. Suddenly, the screen is alive with moving, anxious bodies – bodies suffused with meanings, a physical palimpsest of cultural layering. What are we to make of this stylized disarray, the jolt of these overwhelming juxtapositions?

'No wonder it's a fuck up,' wails the referee suddenly, poignantly echoing our own disorientation. 'No-one communicates in their first language and people simply don't have the vocabulary. What does it help if I say something and no-one hears me? What does it help if someone speaks and I can't understand them?'[15]

As if to combat this frenzy of miscommunication, the players' twitches begin to synch into recognizable, repeatable movements. We soon realize that these are riffs on the stylised regulation hand gestures of the rugby referee, only here the field signals are refigured as nervous tics – are sped up, hysterical and insistent; a physical chorus of semiotics, a group united in a form of repetitive remedial action for traumas that would otherwise divide them.

The point is powerful: that the language of sport both masks our own social failings and proffers a tenuous bridge across the communication abyss – an apt metaphor for a country with eleven different languages and no common experience. We are playing witness to the breakdown of the semantics of rugby: the 100 symbolisms, inner logic and psychological tensions that communicate a communal experience of power and place. Here, of course, Bouwer masterfully offers us the very embodied habits, cultural ties, chants, practices that most jolt collective social memory. As Connerton notes:

It is through the essentially embodied nature of our social existence, and through the incorporated practices based upon these embodyings, that [we are provided] with metaphors by which we think and live. Culturally specific postural performances provide us with a mnemonics of the body.[16]

In the manic juxtaposition of these body habits, though, they become estranged and problematic – they are offered for critical examination. They become what Bhabha would term the 'unhomely'. Yet, it is the unhomely that might, ironically, provide the only authentic sense of place for South Africans:

> To live in the unhomely world, to find its ambivalences and ambiguities enacted in the house of fiction or its sundering and splitting performed in the world of art, is also to affirm a profound desire for social solidarity: 'I am looking for the join ... I want to join ... I want to join.'[17]

Balbesit certainly enjoins its audience to both think and feel about what it means to be part of a complicated, contested country. Bhabha reminds us that the '[t]erms of cultural engagement are produced performatively',[18] but also that it is only in the complex representation of the postcolonial struggle for identity that ideas attain depth and weight, that we are given self-reflexive space to take 'a measure of the "me"'.[19] Perhaps, then, Bouwer's work should be seen not merely as a social critique complete in itself, but also as a collective critical opportunity.

In addressing new frontiers, one suspects radical new forms are needed. 'In this encounter with the global dialectic of the unrepresentable, there is an underlying, prosthetic injunction,' Bhabha suggests. 'Something like an imperative to grow new organs, to expand our sensorium and our body to some new, yet unimaginable, perhaps impossible, dimensions. What might this cyborg be?'[20]

Perhaps what might be is revealed to us in a section called 'Strapping', where a heart – a real heart – is thrown in the middle of a huddle. With the spotless white uniforms against the clinical white stage floor, the effect is medical, incongruent. Blood spatters, the men stare down. 'The heart is a muscle,' we are told. 'Big as a fist. Divided into four chambers. Automatic. Removed from the body it can keep on beating for hours without nerve stimulation.'[21]

South Africans, they suggest, have been playing their hearts out ... literally. The automatic muscle twitch, disconnected from a functioning, healthy vascular system, blood isn't flowing to all parts equally. What happens with a disconnection from the centre, when you are a national body missing a central co-ordinating muscle? If the country is disheartened, is a win ever truly possible? More positively, if the heart is a muscle, is love trainable? If love is trainable, what flexing and repeating, what set plays and resistant force strengthen it?

Of course, all of these similes, all of these scenes and sounds, are deeply familiar to the (urban, predominantly white) South African theatre crowd. Yet when these practices are framed as art, framed by the raise of a stage or the filter of film effects, this familiarity is estranged.

So how did audiences see the production? While *Balbesit* occasionally uses English, isiXhosa and isiZulu as well as providing constant English subtitles in the film version, the production is overwhelmingly in Afrikaans. This language is a loaded one in contemporary South Africa. While it is a second language for a majority of the country and a first for a growing group of mixed race communities, overwhelmingly it is associated with white decedents of the Dutch – the so-called Boers. For these previously culturally dominant white Afrikaner communities, coming to terms with their own identity – and specifically their language's overt Apartheid association – has been a problematic process. Novelist Andre Brink points out that, while Afrikaans was utilized as both identifier and tool of Apartheid, an 'alternative', resistant white Afrikaans was always in existence in the field of the arts. Struggle poetry, novels and theatre created a site of mainstream disruption during Apartheid and have proved a site of mainstream redemption after the transition, with Afrikaans language theatre being particularly well supported.

With Afrikaners facing a need to both reaffirm and redefine a cultural identity, it should be no surprise that a significant number of new Afrikaans arts festivals[22] came into existence after 1994.[23] While support for the arts, particularly English-language theatre, is generally very poor, the Klein Karoo Nationale Kunsfees (Little Karoo National Arts Festival or KKNK) is the largest arts festival in South Africa, despite the existence of the predominantly – some would say quintessentially – English National Arts Festival, which has been held since 1973.

That the experimental and boundary-pushing *Balbesit* sat well within the confines of its commissioning patron, the KKNK, then, should not surprise. That it did similarly well in its run in art-friendly Cape Town is similarly foreseeable. However, the decision to take the production to Pretoria – heart of Blue Bulls rugby territory, but hardly of the cultural scene – was a significant break with established knowledge.[24]

The deeply unusual programming decision to mount a full run at the Pretoria State Theatre indicates that Bouwer may well have been looking to do more with his production than merely court traditionally receptive audiences. Certainly, weighing the logistics of a full set transfer and payments for a crew of nearly thirty actors, operators and stage managers against almost guaranteed small houses, it could hardly have been motivated by financial concerns.

Yet, the move paid off handsomely in critical appreciation, if not financial returns. As might have been expected, *Balbesit* swept nominations for the Kanna awards at the 2013 KKNK festival, nominated for Best New Script, Best Production, Best Mind-blowing Work, Best Actor and Best Direction. Playwright Saartjie Botha won the *Onbeperk* award for innovative thinking for her script and, in an unprecedented move, the festival award for the Best Actor went collectively to the entire cast of the production.

Cape Town's own annual theatre awards – the Fleur du Caps – nominated Braam du Toit for Best Sound Design and awarded Bouwer the Best Director award, as well as Best Lighting for designer Wolf Britz after their 2014 run. Yet Pretoria expressed its own critical appreciation by awarding *Balbesit* Best

Cutting Edge Production at the 2013 Naledi theatre awards, an annual ceremony that celebrates theatrical excellence in the cities of Johannesburg and Pretoria. The awards were not restricted to the theatre production, with Albert Pretorius being awarded Best Actor for his role in the production at the Silverskermfees Afrikaans film festival in Cape Town.

Cape theatre critic Theresa Smith described the action as 'Pina Bausch-meets-calisthenics, but with more grace', saying the overall effect was 'haunting and powerful'.[25]

Independent critic Marilu Snyders felt the production was '[t]hought-provoking... unsettling... show-stopping... brilliant', also saying: 'Through the masterpiece that is *Balbesit*, playwright Saartjie Botha and director Jaco Bouwer have taken that uncertainty of the national identity crisis and created something that has never been seen before.'[26] In Pretoria, Adrienne Sichel gushed for IOL news:

> It lies in the performance, the execution, the physicality of the performance, the humming energy or a moment of quiet melancholy [....] The rhythmic movement, sometimes explanatory but often eliciting an emotional response, sets the pace [....] The enchantment of the experience – even when harried and horrifically confrontational at times – is because of the way they have broken away from the norm as if setting new rules for a traditional game. They want you to engage, to take the ball and run.[27]

Reaction seemed overwhelmingly positive among younger audiences too. Erene Oberholzer, for the University of Pretoria student paper, said:

> Deur die musiek, choreografie en die maatskaplike kwessies wat deur rugby uitgebeeld word, is hierdie produksie 'n ervaring wat mense nog lank gaan onthou.[28]
>
> [Because of the music, choreography and the social issues that are played out through rugby, this production is an experience that people will remember for a long time.]

Overwhelmingly, critics cited the 'physicality'[29] as being both confrontational and also intimate – something that meant the piece operated on both an intellectual and a strangely visceral level. Snyders, for instance, simultaneously spoke of the work 'blowing away the audience' and making them 'think about how to change things, how to change [themselves]'.[30]

Perhaps this appeal to both the critical and the emotional is best summed up by Botha and Bouwer in the production itself. In an amusingly articulate moment of sportsman's philosophizing, the intellectual of the team tells us matter-of-factly, 'Our inner worlds can't be fathomed by intellectual discourse alone.'[31]

> .... And no, they can't. We are thinking bodies, experiencing minds, feeling, acting, moving creatures. We experience the world first and foremost by being in it bodily – an experience from which everything else follows. Perhaps sport

in general, and rugby in this particular case, can be thought of as a type of national proprioception – a learning to walk together, play together, learning to *be* together. Again, national identity is more act than account. Perhaps sport has the power to change the world because it lets us play with beingness. Its symbolism and space, its psychology and signs are there, but they need to be played out in the drama of the world. This is as old as philosophy itself; the need for catharsis through seeing – the *theatron*, the seeing – of drama.

Back, though, to *Balbesit*, where, when our insightful player laments 'people simply don't have the vocabulary', he may not be far off the mark. I often wonder whether academia sometimes lacks the vocabulary to fully articulate everyday experience.

Academia can often be criticized for creating elite, insular knowledge communities, though there are plenty of movements (particularly within approaches influenced by phenomenology) that specifically attempt to find a way of accessing and articulating everyday experience. Theatre, of course, is no different. There is powerful insight – an authenticity of experience – that can come from critically bringing the doing and the being back together again: an insight that must surely add to the academic vocabulary.

South African rugby culture as it is lived can be considered an example of Connerton's incorporated social memory – embodied actions, habits and gestures that, together, help forge complex sites of social memory. As Connerton cautions, however, incorporation methods, though the most powerful and deeply embedded, are also the most unconscious and, therefore, the least critically examined.[32] As a narrative performed bodily before us, Bouwer's work occupies a hybrid space between inscription – between narrative memory – and incorporation or embodied experience. The confrontational physicality of its staging/ cinematography hits us viscerally, jogging an embodied, responsive sympathy in us as viewer. Similarly, the fractured narrative at once allows and escapes the confines of inscription. 'Solidarity', Richard Rorty has claimed, 'has to be constructed out of little pieces,'[33] and, certainly in *Balbesit*, we are always given only glimpses, never a narrative whole. I would suggest this simultaneous offering and denial of text allows for a critical third space – an incorporated inscription, if you will. As Bhabha again comments: '[I]t is only through a structure of splitting and displacement – "the fragmented and schizophrenic decentering of the self" – that the architecture of the new historical subject emerges at the limits of representation itself.'[34] In Bouwer's bizarre and bold artistic disruption of the national sporting set play, then, I think that possibilities are opened up for a more nuanced engagement with the culture of the South African game and, importantly, the contested idea of South Africanness itself.

Yet this hybrid approach to narrative – both invoking the doing and critiquing the being – might well hold lessons for academics, too. Performance returns the critical enquiry to the anxious, living, moving body. In considering the cathartic power of an embodied, creative perspective on our topics of academic pursuits, who knows? We might even return to our own words with more to say.

Notes

1 B. Gallagher in *Telegraph*. 29 January 2010.
2 African National Congress, http://web.archive.org/web/20160308212930/http://anc.org.za/show.php?id=3132. Site accessed 10 November 2015.
3 P. Connerton, *How Societies Remember* (Cambridge: Cambridge University Press, 1989), 2–3.
4 H. Bhabha, *The Location of Culture* (New York: Routledge, 1994*)*, 51.
5 J. Nauright, *Long Run to Freedom: Sport, Cultures and Identities in South Africa* (Morgantown, WV: Fitness Information Technology, 2010), 50.
6 D. Bond on the BBC, 6 December 2013.
7 For a discussion of bodies and race in South Africa, see D. Booth and J. Nauright, 'Embodied Identities: Sport and Race', in J. Nauright, A. Cobley and D. Wiggins (eds), *Beyond C.L.R. James: Race and Ethnicity in Sport* (Fayetteville: University of Arkansas Press, 2014), 41–62.
8 See, for example, O. Jolaosho (2013), ' "You Can't Go to War Without Song": Performance and Community Mobilization in Post-apartheid South Africa' and (2015) 'Political Aesthetics and Embodiment: Sung Protest in Post-apartheid South Africa', *Journal of Material Culture*, 20, 4 (December 2015), 443–458, first published on 26 August 2015.
9 'Shosholoza'.
10 S. Grootes in the *Daily Maverick.* 18 February 2015.
11 Connerton, *How Societies Remember*, 78.
12 J. Bouwer and S. Botha, *Balbesit* (MNET production, 2013).
13 Bantustans were the 'homelands' invented by the Apartheid government during its multi-nationalism strategy phase. It was claimed under this policy that Africans originated in 'homelands' which should be partially self-governing in spaces where only black South Africans from a particular 'tribe' or ethnic group should live. These were viewed with disdain globally as they were never legitimate, and in one case consisted of thirteen unique parcels of unconnected land meant to operate as if it were an autonomous state.
14 Bouwer and Botha, *Balbesit*.
15 Ibid.
16 Connerton, *How Societies Remember*, 74.
17 Bhabha, *The Location of Culture*, 26–27.
18 Ibid., 3.
19 Ibid., 68–69.
20 Ibid., 211–212.
21 Bouwer and Botha, *Balbesit*.
22 Among these are the Klein Karoo Nationale Kunsfees (est. 1994), Aardklop (est. 1998 but discontinued as of 2016), Inniebos (est. 2004), Voorkamerfees (est. 2003) and the Suidoosterfees (est. 2003).
23 T. Hauptfleisch, 'Eventifying Identity: Festivals in South Africa and the Search for Cultural Identity', *New Theatre Quarterly*, 22, 2 (2006), 181–198.
24 The Blue Bulls are a Super Rugby and South African provincial team, known during the segregation and apartheid eras as Northern Transvaal – a provincial team which was supported by a hard-core Afrikaner fan base who were loyal defenders of Apartheid and notoriously conservative in nature. In 2009, the Blue Bulls created a sensation in the rugby world by playing their finals matches in the then Super 12 competition in Soweto, the heart of black urban South Africa.
25 T. Smith in *IOL*. 19 June 2014.
26 M. Snyders in *Artlink*. 27 June 2014.
27 A. Sichel in *IOL*. 28 May 2013.
28 E. Oberholzer in *Perdeby*. 27 May 2013.

29 A. Sichel in *IOL*. 28 May 2013.
30 M. Snyders in *Artlink*. 27 June 2014.
31 Bouwer and Botha, *Balbesit.*
32 Connerton, *How Societies Remember*, 28.
33 Bhabha, *The Location of Culture*, 336.
34 Ibid., 310.

13 Dressed for success

Historicizing Nelson Mandela's involvement in the 1995 Rugby World Cup

Albert Grundlingh

South Africa's famous rugby victory over the All Blacks on 24 June 1995 at Ellis Park Stadium in Johannesburg to become world champions has received considerable academic attention and filmic interest.[1] Even scholars, who in the normal course of research would not care to dwell on sport history, have made contributions. In a way this is understandable, as the effects of the victory reverberated well beyond the stadium in Johannesburg and alerted academics of all stripes that quite an unusual phenomenon had occurred. The merriment of the crowd and the chimera of "nation-building" between white and black constituted enchantment at its best. Following on the heels of the official demise of apartheid and the tense build-up to the historic election of 1994, which saw the African National Congress (ANC) with Nelson Mandela as president sweep to power, the crowning of the rugby Springboks as world champions in their first tournament, and its seemingly positive social effects further afield, created the impression that more than just the sporting gods were smiling on South Africa. For once, however fleetingly, the fractious South African society seemed to have found a healthy if somewhat unexpected antidote to its major ills.

The existing historiography does well in explaining the general context and dynamics of the extraordinary event. Similarly, on one level Nelson Mandela's "super reconciliatory role" – as he appeared in almost messianic fashion on the field after the Springbok victory, decked out in a replica of captain Francois Pienaar's number 6 jersey – has been dealt with adequately as far as the immediate ramifications of the event are concerned. On another level, though, the specifics of Mandela's involvement, and in particular its historical dimensions, have not been scrutinized in sufficient depth.

This is all the more intriguing, as in the intervening years Mandela has become a symbolic synecdoche for the Springbok victory and the memorable occasion has become ever more closely aligned with him. The players, with the exception of Francois Pienaar, have all virtually disappeared from public view, but Mandela's rugby persona lives on as the embodiment of that moment. Probably the fullest recent public expression of this was that at the time of the 2015 Rugby World Cup in the United Kingdom, Mandela was posthumously inducted into the World Rugby Hall Of Fame. The chairman of World Rugby, Bernard Lapasset, described the honour as "a fitting tribute to a man who did so much for his country and for rugby union".[2] As the event has now almost indissolubly been linked to Mandela, it prompts one to ask: how has this alliance between Mandela and the number 6 jersey come about?

A spontaneous act from a rugby enthusiast?

As far as Mandela's interest in sport is concerned, he was keen on boxing while in Johannesburg in the 1950s and at times during his gaol term he kept to a strict fitness routine. He never showed enthusiasm for rugby, though, a game described by some in the ANC as the "opium of the Boer".[3] But Mandela realized that through rugby he could engage with some Afrikaner warders. He even went so far as to study reports on rugby in the newspapers, enabling him to talk knowledgeably about the game to a specific warder intent on vindictive discipline. In trying to foster a common interest, Mandela hoped that he would be able to extract some concessions from the warder. He succeeded.[4] In the light of what happened in 1995, one cannot but surmise that Mandela's performance at Ellis Park had its roots while he was in gaol. Rugby, it appears, was twice used as an instrument: first, to obtain better conditions in gaol, and second, to demonstrate a form of identification with Afrikaners. This is not to imply that he deliberately strategized along these lines, but at the back of his mind in 1995 he could almost instinctively have drawn on past experiences of dealing with Afrikaners and their favourite interest.

The euphoria in the wake of the Springbok victory has not only created the impression that it was a spontaneous outburst of emotion, but also that Mandela's involvement was on the spur of the moment. Morné du Plessis, the former Springbok captain, who was deemed politically enlightened at the time and was drafted in as manager on that basis, gave voice to the idea of an impromptu appearance of the prisoner-turned-president:

> What Madiba [Mandela's clan name] did was an absolute masterstroke. It was not a calculated or premeditated gesture – purely his feeling at the time. To see him coming into our dressing room radiating brightness, enthusiasm and humility into what was a very sombre atmosphere, will remain with me forever.[5]

Du Plessis' fond remembrances, laced with some nostalgia, can be well understood, but they do not necessarily accurately reflect the background to Mandela's dramatic involvement. There is evidence to suggest at least a degree of planning took place: one of Mandela's bodyguards, Linga Moonsamy, after chatting to some of his colleagues about the forthcoming match against the All Blacks, apparently came up with the idea that Mandela should wear a Springbok jersey on match day. Mandela immediately warmed to the suggestion and without further ado Louis Luyt, president of the South African Rugby Union, was contacted to provide a jersey to Mandela's residence.[6] When Mandela appeared in the VIP box with his rugby outfit, Luyt was struck by the president's appearance and "envied this unusual man his effortless ability to cut such a regal figure in just about anything he chose to wear".[7] Unwittingly, Luyt has put his finger on one of the political nerve ends of Mandela's public persona.

Dress and symbolism

In order to provide greater historical depth to Mandela's celebrated appearance at Ellis Park, it needs to be seen as part of a wider and well-established pattern of public performances that marked him as a politician. Central to this is the issue of dress, deportment and political projection.

As a young lawyer in Johannesburg and as a member of the ANC Youth League, Mandela had developed a reputation as a suave and debonair man-about-town. Ellen Kuzwayo of the ANC Women's League remembered in 1985 that in the 1940s and 1950s he stood out from fellow activists. He was described as the "glamorous one", with Oliver Tambo second in tow and Walter Sisulu a distant third.[8]

Mandela was particularly keen on suits and, at 1.90 metres tall, his frame displayed his clothes to best advantage.[9] His wardrobe included clothes made by Alfred Kahn, a Jewish tailor who plied his trade opposite the prestigious Rand Club in the centre of Johannesburg. These outfits, which included a brass-buttoned, double-breasted jacket, did not come cheap: none other than the Oppenheimer tycoons had their suits made by Kahn.[10] Although he might have bought his clothes in the centre of the city, it was in the vibrant, predominantly African, parts of Johannesburg, such as Sophiatown and certain streets in Orlando (part of modern-day Soweto), that Mandela made his playground. Here he could display himself as a street-smart African gentleman attired in the finest cloth, his suits impressively tailored and neatly pressed. It was also this image that he wished to convey when he appeared at the 1958 Treason Trials dressed in an elegant double-breasted suit, white shirt and matching pocket handkerchief.[11]

Mandela, the sophisticated urbanite, could, however – almost chameleon-like in his public demeanour – revert to his rural Transkeian roots and adopt the identity of an abaThembu. Charged with incitement in 1961 after being underground for nearly a year, he appeared in court in a tribal "kaross" blanket with beads around his neck. Through his attire he wished to signal to a white court that he came from a long lineage of warrior leaders and that the court in which he found himself was alien to his cultural and historical background. In doing so he demonstrated that he was a man of several identities, and for each of these there was a distinct way to be dressed.[12] Clothes were essential elements of his political armour and served a specific purpose. "He worked the vocabulary of dress to assert his control over situations and to encapsulate the values he espoused," one scholar observed.[13]

In prison Mandela initially had to wear the regulation short trousers issued to all African prisoners. Predictably he objected to this and considered it demeaning, as short trousers were associated with children and not grown men. He would not allow his stature as a political leader of men to be infantilized and his sense of dignity to be impaired. When his lawyer, George Bizo, was interviewed on the issue, Bizo responded: "Nothing is going to deprive Mandela of his evaluation of himself."[14]

The matter of dress once again emerged near the end of his gaol term, although that was not known at the time, when he was set to meet President P.W. Botha in the presidential residence in Cape Town in July 1989. Although the meeting was only to be of an exploratory nature, it was historic in the sense that it was the first occasion for Mandela to meet a South African head of state. For such a significant encounter, he had to have the right attire; he was intent on meeting Botha as an equal and his outfit had to reflect that understanding. Appearing in a prisoner's garb before the president was out of the question. The prison authorities duly took Mandela's measurements and a neat dark suit, white shirt and paisley tie embroidered with flowers were delivered to him. When he was ready to leave the gaol precinct, he was an epitome of elegance. Dr Niël Barnard, Head of National Intelligence, who accompanied him on the trip, later recalled that Mandela was one of the few people who could in an instant change from a drab prisoner's outfit to a stylish three-piece suit and appear dignified in both.[15]

Once released from prison, Mandela created his own sartorial style. Although he still appeared in public in the regulation suit, in more informal contexts he now often took to wearing high-quality, colourful, silk shirts. These shirts became very popular amongst the wider public, especially tourists, and acquired a distinct brand identity as Madiba shirts. They appeared African in design and pattern but were actually of Indonesian origin, and Mandela was introduced to them in 1990 while on an Asian tour. Mandela's appearance in these casually elegant garments was a break from the more staid and formal dress code of politicians of the former dispensation. In these more loose-fitting outfits, he explained, he wanted to "feel freedom".[16]

Mandela's concern about symbolism and image at times assumed greater importance than actual political substance.[17] During the early phase of apartheid, as an historian has observed, "Mandela was one of the first media politicians, "showboy" as one of his contemporaries nicknamed him, embodying a glamour and a style that projected *visually* a brave new African world of modernity and freedom."[18] In prison he remained aware of his symbolic image as the jailed leader of a mass movement during the 1980s. Not without vanity, he reportedly told a foreign visitor before his release: "I am not God or a prophet, but I have to act like one."[19] Emblematic politics clearly ranked high in Mandela's world view. His "public political life", it has been explicitly stated, "can be viewed as an on-going publicity event in which he was both the centrepiece and the most relentless of managers".[20]

Viewed from this perspective, it is not all that surprising that Mandela's sensibilities alerted him to the symbolic potential of the Springbok rugby badge. For many black people who had an interest in sport, the Springbok was closely associated with the apartheid regime, while for Afrikaner rugby enthusiasts the badge had a long and revered tradition and assumed pride of place in Afrikaner cultural imaginary. Before the Rugby World Cup, Mandela had to oppose those in the National Sport Council who were intent on "killing the animal". Mandela, with his knowledge of Afrikaner cultural concerns, managed to persuade them otherwise, arguing that, if dealt with circumspectly, the badge could be used as a symbol of nation-building.[21]

Mandela, then, had much to do with the survival of the Springbok badge, but at the same time his investment in its continued use also made him a shareholder in a rugby culture, and he could reasonably expect some future dividends. Admittedly this was not necessarily a cold and clinical calculation on his part, but, with Mandela's penchant for understanding the power of symbolism, it was at the time a wise decision which ultimately was to pay off handsomely.

In reviewing Mandela's ingrained sense of the connection between dress and power as expressed at various points during his career, his appearance at Ellis Park slots perfectly into the well-developed pattern as evident from the tailor-made suits of the 1950s through to the Madiba shirts of the 1990s. His use of dress to project himself was, as noted, not incidental, but an essential part of his political being. In this sense the relationship with the number 6 jersey had its own antecedents in a different guise and cannot be seen as an impromptu once-off event.

Politics of the spectacle

The World Cup tournament coincided with a groundswell of buoyant public opinion in 1995: "If ever a country was in need of a party, a good time … it was South Africa."[22] It was indeed a rare historical moment. Public spaces for interaction at a different level than what had been possible under apartheid had opened up; black and white could, in a relatively harmless way, express a common sentiment without either side sacrificing or risking too much.[23]

Most Afrikaners, excluding those on the right, adapted much more quickly to the new dispensation than many observers had anticipated. In part this was because they still had representatives at the highest level in the Government of National Unity. They also believed, given the assurances of Vice-president F.W. de Klerk of weights and counterweights, that the transformation process was well under control. As such, the new dispensation was not too threatening yet. On the contrary, as sociologist Heribert Adam explained at the time:

> By endorsing the ANC rule in a negotiated settlement, and in turn being praised for pragmatic foresight, Afrikaner nationalists wallow in a self-congratulatory mood of having achieved the ultimate triumph of survival as a recognised minority in a hostile environment. In their self-perception, Afrikaners have not handed over power, as it appears to the outside observer, but … secured a much more stable and amiable environment for future greatness.[24]

The perception that political negotiations had worked to the benefit of Afrikaners had its parallel in the connections between sport and society. There was more than an element of truth in the observation of one journalist that "Afrikaners had swapped apartheid for rugby, and there was every sign they thought it a fair deal".[25]

A central figure in the new government's blessing of the World Cup tournament was, of course, Nelson Mandela. It is common practice, as the American academic Allen Guttmann has noted, for governments to "collect political prestige by staging extravagant sports spectacles and democratic leaders seldom miss an opportunity to throw out the first ball, to telephone congratulations to the winners, and generally to bask in the reflected glory of athletic achievement".[26] However, in the case of the South African rugby team, the Springboks stood more to gain by the association with Mandela than the other way around. Mandela already had a long-established international reputation as an anti-apartheid icon, while the Springboks still had to prove their international credibility. Mandela's strategic appearances and his identification with the team helped elevate them, a virtually all-white team, to a symbol of nationhood.

It turned out to be a marketing masterstroke. One media specialist commented that Mandela – "he of the perpetual smile and the studied stoop of humility" – has "instilled and enthused the brand image of South Africa with his personality". What was particularly striking was the rupture from the past. Gone was "the hateful image created over decades by the amorphous polymer of bald, grumpy old men pointing fingers and frowning under their black trilbies". Now a new perception was about to take root:

> Instead of that dull country with its dour leaders and bloody conflicts, the world sees Nelson Mandela adorned with the inevitable shirt from a selection – it becomes apparent – of infinite colour and variety, making a speech at the opening game of the Rugby World Cup. They hear the mostly white South African crowd ... chanting Nel-son, Nel-son, praising him in their own boorish rugby manner. Later infinitely compassionate and forgiving, he calls to wish the team luck – a subtle reminder of why they are playing in the tournament at all. The jibe missed, they are duly impressed and they win.[27]

The closed cultural space occupied by rugby, hitherto a predominantly Afrikaner preserve, was sufficiently prised open to allow at least a partial reinscription of the game's narrow cultural identity. In addition, the public ownership of rugby was symbolically democratized and extended. Afrikaner claims of possession were compromised with Mandela's anointment of the game; the metaphorical message was that the game belonged to the new South Africa and the old order had passed. Perhaps with slight exaggeration, a British journalist nevertheless made the point well:

> Mandela had ... pulled the political magician's trick of all times; to have allowed his rivals the most precious of prizes they could ever wish for and – swish – with one sweep of the cloak represented the prize unchanged, yet suddenly belonging to not the minority but the majority.[28]

Mandela's performance also drew calculated praise from Frederik van Zyl Slab-bert, the former political leader of white opposition to apartheid:

> He [Mandela] was the master at exploiting the appropriate moment, making a conciliatory gesture, and persuading the international community that South Africa was "on its way".... Nobody must underestimate his perform-ance at the Rugby World Cup final in 1995. I was there that day, and saw pot-bellied right-wing fanatics from the deep rural areas weeping when Mandela came up to present the victory cup at the end of the game. This was one of the final blows to exclusive right-wing Afrikaner nationalism. I saw and heard one of the pot-bellied brigade whisper through his tears: "That is my president."[29]

Ultimately the Springboks, their management and die-hard rugby devotees will-ingly played along, not fully realizing that at a meta-level they were bit players in a far greater bigger political drama than the World Cup. Wrapped up in their limited sporting concerns, they were feted and momentarily ensnared by "Madiba magic".

The Springbok victory, Mandela's starring role and the crowd's reaction assumed transcendental proportions. "The rugby World Cup final", one author observed, "was a sporting contest, a political event, and a religious ceremony all thrown into one."[30] Indeed, even the uncompromising and flinty Springbok winger, James Small, framed his responses in religious terms: "It was like we were his [Mandela's] disciples. He had touched us with his hand and said: 'Come on, let's have a go now' ".[31]

In retrospect, the event almost appears tailor-made for Mandela to indulge in what has been called "politics as enchantment".[32] The very way in which politics of this kind play out presupposes an element of surprise. However, for it to gain legitimacy, it has to appear authentic; if it is mere showboating it is less likely to succeed. In this respect Mandela was able to carry it off because he actually did get caught up in the moment. One of his legal advisors in the presidency explained: "He saw the political opportunity, yes, but it was not something cold because he too, as an individual, got swept away by the fervour of it all and became just another mad-keen patriotic fan."[33]

Mandela's amalgam of heart and mind and keen sense of the dramatic, it can further be argued, is to be found in the deeper recesses of his past. His notion of performance politics and the potential impact of spectacular events had in itself a history.

In this respect it is necessary to turn the clock back to his high school years at Healdtown in the Eastern Cape, where he studied from 1937. On one occasion the renowned Xhosa praise poet (*imbongi*) SEK Mqhayi was invited to the school. As an *imbongi* Mqhayi had few peers. His oral poetry, an academic has noted, "was marked by the richness and depth of diction, and by his remarkable ability to inspire his audience". He produced poetry that "coursed through men like blood".[34] Initially, though, as Mqhayi entered the school hall, Mandela was not all that taken by the much-feted poet, as he looked rather ordinary. Yet when Mqhayi started his performance, waving his spear and dramatically varying his tone of voice from high to low, invoking what he considered the virtues of Xhosa society as opposed to those of the western world, Mandela was deeply impressed. He later recalled:

> When he [Mqhayi] spoke his last word, he dropped his head to his chest. We rose to our feet, clapping and cheering. I did not want ever to stop applauding. I felt such intense pride at that point, not as an African but as a Xhosa; I felt like one of the chosen people.[35]

It was an event that was destined to stay with Mandela. He later named his and Winnie's daughter, Zindziswa, after the poet laureate's own daughter.[36]

One does not wish to imply that Mandela on 24 June 1995 consciously harked back to the performative politics of Mqhayi 58 years before, but the incident and Mandela's remembrance of it emphasized that from a relatively young age Mandela was sensitive to, and susceptible to, the allure of the spectacle. Although it was in an obviously completely different setting from Healdtown all those years ago, in retrospect one can suggest that the kind of magic Mqhayi weaved in the school hall of Healdtown was replicated on a grander scale by Mandela at Ellis Park. While the context and intent differed vastly, the enduring awareness of the persuasive power of performance stayed intact.

Although political theatre has its place and can create historical memories that can serve as a benchmark in popular consciousness, it is often of a fleeting nature. The magical whitewash of the 1995 World Cup soon began to flake, and two years after the event, clashes between administrators and players and a rough transition from amateur to professional rugby undermined the unity that had been in evidence during the tournament. At the same time, the ANC government started to flex its muscles with greater intent, giving rise to increased alienation amongst Afrikaners. To top it all, Louis Luyt, in an ill-considered move, thought it wise to challenge Mandela in court in a matter pertaining to the way in which the Department of Sport conducted its business. Rugby in South Africa in 1997 was clearly not rugby in 1995. Perhaps the hubris of the victory of 1995 was just too much, engendering overconfidence in the rugby fraternity and allowing old traits to appear with a vengeance.

Conclusion

In dealing with Mandela's involvement in the rugby tournament, it was pointed out that it was not quite as spontaneous as often assumed, nor did he have a particular interest in rugby before the event. He was, however, alert to the possibilities of using rugby as a political instrument in order to relate to Afrikaners.

It has further been argued that there are certain benefits in viewing the remarkable event of 24 June 1995 in terms of a longer timeframe as far Mandela's public performance is concerned. The iconic photograph of an elated

Mandela with captain Francois Pienaar has created the impression that this was an unique occasion in South Africa's turbulent history. In many ways, this was indeed the case. However, one can be so taken by the moment that it obscures all else. This analysis has demonstrated that Mandela's appearance in a Springbok jersey can be viewed as the outcome of a particular trajectory in which he, at various junctures in his career, employed dress as a key element in projecting himself politically. The number 6 jersey episode was the most visible before a vast television audience, and came at a crucial point after the transition to majority rule in South Africa. It therefore attracted the most attention. It was, as one journalist accurately remarked, "the ultimate example of power dressing. Somehow, a man in his mid-70s made the wearing of a rugby shirt cool."[37] As valid as this may be, though, it would be misleading to view the performance in isolation; it had a much longer genealogy. Similarly, Mandela's penchant for political theatre and the way in which the Rugby World Cup tournament provided him with a platform to peddle his brand of politics, as one historian has observed, left Afrikaners for a while in a "state of charismatic bewilderment".[38]

Notes

1 For example GJ Botma, "Lightning strikes twice: The 2007 Rugby World Cup and memories of a South African rainbow nation", *Communicato: South African Journal for Communication Theory and Research*, 36, 1, 2010, pp. 1–19; D Booth, "Mandela and Amabokoboko: the political and linguistic nationalisation of South Africa?", *Journal of Modern African Studies*, September 1996, pp. 457–477; JM Coetzee, "The World Cup of Rugby", *Southern African Review of Books*, 1995; L Strelitz and L Steenveld, "Sport en Nasiebou in Suid-Afrika: Die betekenis van die 1995 Rugby Wêreldbeker", *Ecqui Novi*, 17, 2, 1996, pp. 137–152; J Maingard, "Imag(in)ing the South African nation: representations of identity in the Rugby World Cup 1995", *Theatre Journal*, 49, 1, 1997, pp. 15–28; S Crawford, "Nelson Mandela, the number 6 jersey and the 1995 Rugby World Cup: Sport as a transcendental unifying force, or a transparent illustration of bicultural opportunism" in RR Sands (ed.), *Anthropology, sport and culture*, London, 1999, p. 129; A Grundlingh, "From redemption to recidivism? Rugby and change in South Africa during the 1995 Rugby World Cup and its aftermath", *Sporting Traditions: Australian Journal of Sport History*, May 1998, pp. 1–19. For a roundtable discussion of the film "Invictus", dealing with the 1995 Rugby World Cup event, see *Safundi: The Journal of South African and American Studies*, 13, 1–2, January–April 2012, pp. 115–150.
2 SuperSport, "Madiba inducted to Rugby Hall of Fame", 3 October 2015, http://mobi. supersport.com/rugby/sa-rugby/news/151003/Madiba_inducted_to_Rugby_Hall_of_ Fame, accessed 7 October 2016.
3 J Carlin, *Playing the enemy: Nelson Mandela and the game that made a nation*, London, 2008, p. 65. For rugby on Robben Island, see C Korr and M Close, *More than just a game: Soccer vs apartheid*, London, 2008, pp. 167–181, and for sport in general, F Buntman, *Robben Island and prisoner resistance to apartheid*, Cambridge, 2003, pp. 70–71.
4 Carlin, *Playing the enemy*, pp. 34–36.
5 D Cruywagen, P Dobson, H Wilson, P van der Schyff, D Retief, V Qunta and A Mackaiser., *The badge: A century of the Springbok emblem*, Johannesburg, 2006, p. 204.

6 Carlin, *Playing the enemy*, p. 205; L Luyt, *Walking proud: The Louis Luyt autobiography*, Cape Town, 2004, p. 257.
7 L Luyt, *Walking proud*, p. 257.
8 Boehmer, *Nelson Mandela: A very short introduction*, Oxford, 2008, p. 116.
9 Boehmer, *Mandela*, p. 116.
10 DJ Smith, *Young Mandela*, London, 2010, p. 106.
11 Boehmer, *Mandela*, p. 111.
12 R Suttner, "Periodisation, cultural construction and representation of ANC masculinities through dress, gesture and nationalist influence" *Historia*, 54, 1, May 2009, pp. 80–81.
13 Boehmer, *Mandela*, p. 128.
14 Smith, *Young Mandela*, p. 111. See also Boehmer, *Mandela*, p. 132.
15 A Sampson, *Mandela: The authorised biography*, London, 1999, p. 391; T Lodge, *Mandela: A critical life*, Oxford, 2006, p. 162; N Barnard, *Geheime revolusie: memoires van 'n spioenbaas*, Cape Town, 2015, p. 214.
16 Boehmer, *Mandela*, p. 133; S Klopper, "Redressing the past: the Africanisation of sartorial style in contemporary South Africa" in A Brah and A Coombes (eds), *Hybridity and its discontents*, London, 2010, p. 228.
17 C Bundy, *Nelson Mandela*, Johannesburg, 2015, p. 17. See also TF Scheckles, "The rhetoric of Nelson Mandela: a qualified success", *Howard Journal of Communications*, 12, 2, 2002, pp. 85–99.
18 Lodge, *Mandela*, p. ix.
19 D Posel, "'Madiba magic': Politics as enchantment" in R Barnard (ed.), *Cambridge companion to Nelson Mandela*, Cambridge, 2014, p. 74.
20 Boehmer, Mandela, p. 133.
21 Cruywagen *et al.*, *The badge*, pp. 199–200.
22 E Griffiths, *One team, one country: The greatest year of Springbok rugby*, Johannesburg, 1996, p. 51.
23 Compare Griffiths, *One team*, p. 113.
24 H Adam, "Ethnic versus civic nationalism: South Africa's non-racialism in comparative perspective", *SA Sociological Review*, 7, 1 (1994), p. 26.
25 P Waldmeir, *Anatomy of a miracle: The end of apartheid and the birth of the new South Africa*, Middlesex, 1997, p. 269.
26 A Guttmann, *Sports spectators*, New York, 1986, p. 179.
27 *Living*, December 1995.
28 Quoted in *Cape Times*, 27 June 1996.
29 F van Zyl Slabbert, *The other side of history: An anecdotal reflection on the political transition in South Africa*, Johannesburg, 2006, p. 61.
30 J Carlin, *Knowing Mandela*, London, 2013, p. 121.
31 Carlin, *Knowing Mandela*, p. 118.
32 Posel, "Politics as enchantment", p. 70.
33 Quoted by Carlin, *Playing the enemy*, p. 194.
34 J Opland, "Introduction" in J Opland and A Nyamende (eds), *Isaac Wauchope, selected writings, 1874–1916*, Cape Town, 2008, p. 8.
35 N Mandela, *Long walk to freedom*, London, 2000, p. 49.
36 Mandela, *Long walk to freedom*, p. 302.
37 *Telegraph*, "Nelson Mandela seized the opportunity of the Rugby World Cup 1995", 6 December 2013, www.telegraph.co.uk/news/worldnews/nelson-mandela/10140763/Nelson-Mandela-seized-the-opportunity-of-the-Rugby-World-Cup-1995.html, accessed 7 October 2016.
38 H Giliomee, *The Afrikaners: biography of a people*, London, 2003, p. 648.

Index

Adidas 20, 63, 65, 69; 'Adidasification' of
    the All Blacks 64
advertisements 27, 31, 65, 109
African Games 108, 172
African National Congress (ANC) 175–6
Algeria conflict (1954–1962) 43
amateur rugby 30, 38
amateurism: Amateurism Committee 100;
    code of 134; ethos of 97
Aotearoa Fisheries Ltd 64
Arnold, Thomas 94
Arsenal Football Club 28
Asian Games 108
Australian rugby: Collective Bargaining
    Agreement (CBA) 55; cultural diversity,
    need for 53–4; diversity management 53;
    National Rugby League (NRL) 54, 85;
    Pacific concepts related to 57; Pacific
    Cultural Awareness workshop 59; Pacific
    cultural inclusion in 54–5; Pacific
    leadership, development of 52; PATHE@
    RUPA programme 52, 55–9; Rugby
    Union Players Association (RUPA) 52;
    Super Rugby club 56–7; vocational
    planning for Pacific players 58; Western
    Sydney University (WSU) 52
Australian Rugby League 84
Australian Rugby Union (ARU) 2, 52,
    58–9, 101, 114

Balbesit (Afrikaans play) 2, 162, 166–72
Bank of New Zealand (BNZ) 64
Baravilala, Manasa 87
Benazzi, Abdelatif 48–9
Beneath the Māori Moon 66
Best Cutting Edge Production 170–1
Bhabha, Homi 163, 166, 169, 172
Biarritz Olympique Pays Basque club
    (France) 44

'Black Saturday' of the XV de France
    38–40
black-blanc-beur (black-white-Arab)
    French team 40
Blanco, Serge 44
Boer War (1899–1902) 97
boot camp 30
Borthwick, Ian 49
Botha, P.W. 166–7, 170–1, 178
Bourdieu, Pierre 54
Bowring, Kevin 142
Boyce, Max 135
brain drain 142
BRICS (Brazil, Russia, India, China and
    South Africa) countries 109
British football, commercialization of 28
British masculinity 97
Britz, Wolf 170
broadcast rights, monopolization of 113
Burke, Dave 69

Cardiff RFC 134, 137–8
Carter, Dan 78
Catholic Church 13–14
Celtic Tiger Ireland 13, 19–21
Charlie Hebdo shootings 49
child sex abuse scandals 14
Choet Visser Rugby Museum (South
    Africa) 151–2
class hierarchy, impact on development of
    rugby 96
club membership 32–3
coaches 141–2; coaching and coach
    education, development of 142
code-swapping 84–5
codified laws, of Rugby School football
    94–5
Collective Bargaining Agreement (CBA)
    55

Colquhoun, Andy 153
commodification of the haka, in Māori
    rugby 64
Commonwealth Games 93, 108
Commonwealth Games Federation 102
Connell, R.W. 122; hegemonic
    masculinity, concept of 122
Connerton, Paul 162–4, 166, 168, 172
Copsey, Tony 136
Craven, Danie 151–2, 155–6
Crawford, Luke 69, 71–2
Cricket World Cup 108, 112
Croke Park, Ireland 14–15
Crowley, Chris 11
Cullen, Christian 67
Cultural Diversity Development Manager
    (CDDM) 56
cultural homophobia 122–3; socio-political
    influences of 122
cultural identity 59, 70–1, 170, 180
cultural workshop, development of 59

Dakuidreketi, Keni 87
Davies, Jonathan 132, 137, 139–40
Dawai, Orisi 84
Dawson, Ronnie 11
de Gaulle, Charles 42
de Villiers, Peter 65
defence gurus 141
Dewey, Robert 3
Dine, Philip 22
Durie, Mason 69, 74

Edinburgh Academy 94
Edwards, Shaun 141
Edwards, Tiki 69
Ellis, William Webb 40
Empowering Act (2010), New Zealand
    113
Essentially Group (NZ) 86
European Rugby Champions Cup 17, 39,
    44–5
European Union (EU) 13
experience economy 149

Farrell, Andy 141
Fay, Michael 83
Federation of Oceania Rugby Unions
    (FORU) 83
FIFA World Cup 3, 108–10, 112
fifteen-a-side format, Scottish rugby 97,
    103
Fiji Rugby Union (FRU) 84
Fiji Sport 82

Fiji Times 86
Five Nations Championship (1996) 12, 42
Fleur du Caps (Cape Town's annual
    theatre award) 170
Fleuriel, Sébastien 38
Fredericks, Salie 154
French rugby: association with sub-
    Saharan Africa 39–40; 'Black Saturday'
    of the *XV de France* 38–40; challenges
    and opportunities of 43; competitiveness
    of 42; consciousness-raising, through
    participation 47; exclusion from the
    Five Nations tournament (1931) 42;
    Fédération Française de Rugby (FFR)
    40, 42–3; 'French Flair' 42; history of
    42–3; home-grown talent 47; inaugural
    overseas tour 42; international 'Masters'
    tournaments 43; *Les 30 Glorieuses*
    (1945–1975), restructuring of 42; media
    coverage of 43, 45; origin of players of
    43; performance at 2015 Rugby World
    Cup (RWC) 39; poaching of players 42;
    political mobilization of 40; in
    professional era 43–8; *rugby-*
    champagne of the 1950s and 1960s 42;
    self-confidence of 42; sociocultural
    factors influencing 41; Third Republic
    (1870–1940) 41; Union Française de
    Rugby Amateur (UFRA) 42; victory in
    European Rugby Champions 44; victory
    in Five Nations tournament (1954) 42;
    violence, level of 42; from William
    Webb Ellis to the Webb Ellis Cup 40–3;
    XV de France (2015) 48–50

Gaelic Athletic Association (GAA) 10, 14,
    19; ban on 'foreign' games, removal of
    14
Gatland, Warren 141–2
Gavoka, Bill 88
gay athletes, study of 124; pro-gay
    attitudes 126
Geertz, Clifford 163
Geraldine Rugby Club, New Zealand 31
Ghiringhelli, Bruno 46
Glenmark club, New Zealand 29
global sports industry 100
globalization of rugby game: process of
    94; World Rugby 104
Godignon, Nicholas 86
Gow, Ian 99
The Great Redeemer (Mark II) 138
Grootes, Stephen 165
Guttmann, Allen 180

Habitus, concept of 54
Harris, Greg 55
Harris, Iestyn 137
Hayes, John 17–18
Heartland Championship (New Zealand) 30–1
hegemonic masculinity, concept of 122
Heineken Cup (Ireland rugby) 12–13, 17, 19, 21–2, 44
heterosexuality, notion of 121
Hill, Roland 98
HIV/AIDS outbreak 122
Hokowhitu, B. 62–8, 75
homohysteria, concept of 121, 124–6, 128
'homohysteric' culture 122; principles for 122
homophobia 121–4, 127, 129
homosexuality, rugby players' attitudes to 127
Hong Kong Football Club 99
Hong Kong Rugby Football Union (HKRFU) 99
Hong Kong Sevens 94, 98–100; formation of 103; growth of 100
Hoskins, Oregan 153, 156
How Societies Remember (1989) 162
Huddersfield Cricket and Athletic Club, in Yorkshire 96
Hughes, Thomas 94

Inclusive Masculinity Theory (Anderson) 121, 122–6; data on 123–6
Indian Premier League 104
Indo-China conflict (1946–1954) 43
industrial revolution 134–5
Interdepartmental Committee on Physical Deterioration 97
International Olympic Committee (IOC) 93
International Rugby Board (IRB) *see* World Rugby
International Rugby Football Board (IRFB) 93, 98–100; Amateurism Committee 100; Rugby World Cup Limited 100
interpersonal communication skills, for Pacific players 58
Invictus (film) 162
Irish Gross National Product 13–14
Irish rugby 9; class profile 18; domestic professional game 10; economic crisis, implication of 21; Five Nations Championship (1996) 12; Heineken Cup 17; ingredient for success of 17;

Leinster professional team 13; Munster professional team 12–13; period of success 10; professionalism 10; representation on British and Irish Lions tours 10; rugby players 16–18; rugby-playing school 19; status of 11; success at provincial level 21; team sports' training and match schedules 17; television audiences 19
Irish Rugby Football Union (IRFU) 10–11, 21; contracts to professional players 12; financial and public relations 21; recruitment policies 22
Irish sporting nationalism 15

Jones, Alun Wyn 143
Joseph, Jamie 68

Kamea, Culden 84, 87
kapa haka (Māori performing arts) 70, 72–3
Kimmel, Michael 122
'The Kings of Sevens' 96
Kirk, David 28
Kirshenblatt-Gimblett, B. 149, 154
Knell, Cris 64
Konno, Shiggy 100

labour migration, in sport 134, 142–3
Laidlaw, Chris 28
Lapasset, Bernard 175
Larkin, Michael 13
Le Figaro (French daily) 45
Le Monde (journal) 39; 'Black Saturday' headline 38–40; 'team of mercenaries' 45
leadership initiatives, in clubs 58
Les 30 Glorieuses (1945–1975) 42
Lesprit, Bruno 39, 46–7
Levula, Iosefa 84
Ligue Nationale de Rugby (LNR) 44
literature, on depiction of rugby 28, 94
logistics, of hosting rugby game 99

McCaw, Richie 78
McGee, Eugene 14, 22
McKenna, Ewan 9–10
MacRae, Ian 68
Male, Kevyn 26
Malielegaoi, Tuilaepa Sailele 88
Mandela, Nelson 48, 112, 162–4, 175; dress and symbolism 177–9; interest in sport 176; involvement in the 1995 Rugby World Cup 153, 182;

Mandela, Nelson *continued*
  penchant for political theatre 183;
  performance politics, notion of 181–2;
  politics as enchantment 181; politics of
  the spectacle 179–82; public political
  life 178; super reconciliatory role 175;
  Treason Trials (1958) 177
Manu Samoa Rugby Limited (MSRL)
  83–4, 87, 89
Māori rugby: 'Adidasification' of the All
  Blacks 64; Apartheid-era decisions 66;
  benefit to Māori players and society
  69–74; as brand to an international
  market 69; celebrating 65–6;
  development of 62; haka in 64–5;
  history of 65; *kapa haka* (Māori
  performing arts) sessions 72–3; in
  mega-sport events 66; Māori All Blacks
  63–4, 68–9; in Pacific Nations Cup 67;
  as political tool 66; post-tour survey 72;
  professional era of 63;
  professionalisation of 62; Rugby World
  Cup (RWC) campaign (1999) 65; as site
  for *tino rangatiratanga* and *mana* 66–9;
  sponsoring relationships 63–4; symbols
  and rituals 62; *tangata whenua* of
  Aotearoa (New Zealand) 62; Te Hoe
  Nuku Roa project 71; 'Te Pae Roa 2040:
  Pathways for Māori development into
  the future' conference 74; *tikanga Māori*
  (Māori culture) 65; *Timatanga haka,*
  performance of 65; tours 69, 71;
  Waitangi, Treaty of 74
Marshall Aid 42
masculinity in sports: codes of 123;
  concept of 121; gender order 122;
  hegemonic masculinity 122; Inclusive
  Masculinity Theory 122–6;
  incorporation of feminine or gay male
  aesthetics 127–8; intra-male
  stratification 122; in rugby 126–8; same-
  sex activities and 127
Massy club (France) 46–7
Match Day in South Africa (film) 153
Mather & Co 154
Meads, Colin 28–9
media coverage, of rugby: advertisements
  27, 31; in France 43, 45; in Ireland 19;
  Le Monde's 'Black Saturday' headline
  38–40; media-sport nexus 20, 28; in
  New Zealand 27; in television 19, 27
mega-events: global distribution of 108;
  infrastructure-related projects associated
  with 113; key features and attributes of

110; literature and media focus on 114;
  types of legacies of 114
Melrose Cup 101
Melrose Rugby Club 95–6
Melrose Sevens 96
memorabilia, rugby 152, 158
Merchiston School 94
middle-class game 18
Middlesex Sevens 97–8
Millennium Stadium 112
misogyny 127, 129
Moon, Rupert Henry St. John Barker 136
Morris, Dewi 136
Mortimer, Gavin 39, 47
Mulholland, Malcolm 66
Muller, M. 110
Munster rugby 18, 22; strategic plan for
  2014 to 2017 22
Murdoch, Rupert 84, 101; News
  Corporation (News Corp) 151; Super
  League 84
muscular Christian ideals, inherent in
  rugby 97

Nakazawa, Makoto 69
Naledi theatre awards (2013) 171
National Football League (NFL), USA
  108
National Sport Council, South Africa 179
New Zealand Herald 78
New Zealand rugby: All Black team 27,
  29; club closures and mergers 35;
  cultural globalization, impact of 32;
  documentaries on 29–30; economic and
  social transformation 32; as game for all
  New Zealanders 30; Glenmark club 29;
  Heartland Championship 30–1; history
  of 25, 27; literature on depiction of 28;
  media report on 28; Māori involvement
  in *see* Māori rugby; participation and
  club membership 32–3; perceived and
  actual nature of 27; portrayal of 28;
  primacy of rural rugby 31; renaissance
  of East Coast 26; rise and fall of clubs
  30; rural rugby supremacy 27; rural
  transformation, implication of 32–4;
  rural-urban divide 25; 'Southern Man/
  Pride of the South' Speights beer
  advertisements 27; strength and values
  of 25; success of 25–6; Super 12
  competition 28–9; television coverage
  of 27; urban-based franchises 25
New Zealand Rugby (NZR) *see* New
  Zealand Rugby Union (NZRU)

New Zealand Rugby Union (NZRU) 28, 30, 63; on number of loan players 31
Northern Ireland peace process 14
Northern Union 95, 134
Novès, Guy 44
NZ Māori Rugby Board (NZMRB) 65, 67

Official History of the Melrose Sevens, The 94
Olympic Games 93–4, 108–9, 112; Olympic rugby 103; Sydney Olympics (2000) 101
'one country for life rule' 87
Orwell, George 134, 145
Owens, Nigel 127

Pacific Cultural Awareness workshop 54, 57, 59
Pacific Islands Players Association 89
Pacific Islands rugby: code-swapping 84–5; expenditure on the All Blacks 79; Federation of Oceania Rugby Unions (FORU) 83; fortunes of 79; High Performance Units (HPU) 79; 'historic' match with New Zealand 78–80; local histories and regional connections 80–1; 'one country for life rule' 87; player-to-population ratios 79; 'poaching' allegations 85–6; professionalization of 79, 81–3, 84; recruitment and inclusion overseas 84–7; regional organization 83; SANZAR Super Rugby 82–3; structures of exclusion 81–3; Tonga's approach to 82; Tri-Nations (later Rugby Championship) competitions 83
Pacific Islands Rugby Alliance 88
Pacific Nations Cup 63, 67, 88
Pacific people, in rugby 52–3
Pacific Rugby Cup competition 88
Packer, Kerry 101
Pasifika Achievement To Higher Education (PATHE) 55–6
PATHE@RUPA programme 52, 55–9; development of model for 55–6; for enhancing social and cultural capital 60; outcomes of 58–9; outreach of 57; for player support 56; projects 57–8
Percy Park tournament 97
Perpignan club (France) 44
Perry, Nick 27
physical education 47
Pienaar, François 48, 161–2, 175, 183
Player Development Managers (PDMs) 55–6

players, rugby: attitudes to homosexuality 127; black and 'coloured' 154–5, 157; culture of inclusivity 128–9; exclusion and inclusion, dynamics of 88; in France 48–9; gay aesthetics of 128; graduating from the club system to the international team 17–18; in Ireland 16–18; masculinity, issue of 126–8; memorabilia relating to 152; migration of 87; in New Zealand 32–3; psychosocial wellbeing of 56; recruitment of 48; used as cheap labour 88
'Polynesianization' of clubs 84
Popplewell, Nick 10
Pretoria State Theatre 170
Process Rugby Foundation 86–7
Provale (French players' union) 44
Putnam, Robert D. 31–2
Putting Rugby First 83

Racing Club de France 41, 46
Racing Club Toulonnais 45
recruitment of players 48, 84–7
religious fundamentalism 122
Renan, Ernest 41
River Severn, road across 139–40
Robinson, Jason 141
Romanos, Joseph 28
Roux, Jurie 150
Royal Commission on Social Policy (1988) 74
Rugby Almanack 26
Rugby Club Massy Essonne (RCME) 46
rugby codes 101, 133, 135–7, 142–3
rugby documentaries: on effect of professional rugby on rural game 30; *Grapes of Wrath, The* 29; *Ground We Are Losing, The* 30; *Ground We Won, The* 29; *Whole New Ball Game, A* 30
Rugby Football Union (RFU) 29, 95, 99, 138
rugby governance 82–3, 98, 136, 144
Rugby League (RL) 22, 42, 133–4, 137–8, 141–4; code-swapping 84; history of 133; migration of Welsh union players to 134; National Rugby League (NRL), Australia 54, 85; Super League 144; World Cup 144
Rugby School football 94
rugby union 143; acceptance into Olympic movement 101; amateurism in 133; conflict with commercialization and globalization 100; professionalization of

rugby union *continued*
132, 134, 137, 141; social positioning of
134; sporting and structural
development 102
Rugby Union Players Association (RUPA)
52
Rugby World Cup (RWC) 1, 5, 26, 79,
108, 132, 179, 181; All Blacks
campaign 65; capital investments in
110; creation of 43; economic impact of
113; 'feel-good' effects of 112, 115;
fifteen-a-side 100, 102–3; French
performance at 39; global spectacle of
100–3; growth of *111*; hosting of 114;
image-boosting strategies 112;
inauguration of 11; Mandela's
involvement in 153; mega-events
108–10; as nation-building project 112;
objectives of hosting 114; planning
processes and grant approvals 113;
promotional campaign 113; 'Stadium of
Four Million' report 114; tourism,
impact on 110
Rugby World Cup Limited 100, 112
Rugby World Cup Sevens 93, 100–2
rugby-playing school 17; in Ireland 19
Rugger (book) 98
rural rugby 28, 33; 'backblocks' players
26; decline of 30; future of 35; in New
Zealand 34; primacy of 31; urban-based
franchises and 25

'Sacred Seven' English schools 94
Sakimi, Moera 56
same-sex physical tactility 124, 127
Samoa Rugby Union (SRU) 79, 98
Sanderson, David 96
SANZAR (South Africa, New Zealand and
Australia Rugby) competitions 82–3, 90
Saturday Review, The 98
Schuster, Harry 83, 86
Scottish Borders 95–6, 103
Scottish Football Union 95; alignment
with RFU governance 96; fifteen-a-side
format 94
Scottish Rugby Union (SRU) *see* Scottish
Football Union
Sealord 64
seven-a-side rugby: conflict with
commercialization and globalization
100; fifteen-minute matches, rules in 96;
game within a game 94–6; Hong Kong
Sevens 98–100; importance of 93, 94;
individual contests between teams 102;

influence and impact of 93; 'The Kings
of Sevens' 96; Middlesex Sevens 97–8;
nature of 102; popularity of 93; Rugby
World Cup Sevens 93; 'Sacred Seven'
English schools 94; sevens women's
game 102; Tier 1union 100, 102; Tier 2
and 3 unions 93–4, 100, 102
Severn Bridge 139–40
sexual harassment 127
Smith, Sean 133
Smith, Theresa 171
Smith, Tokkie 99
Snyders, Hendrik 154–5
social capital 26, 29–30; generated by
rugby 30
South African African Rugby Football
Board (SAARFB) 155
South African rugby: anti-Apartheid protest
and 164; black and 'coloured' 156; Choet
Visser Rugby Museum 152; corporate
rugby museum, establishment of 150–4;
heritage and museums in motion 147,
148–50; Mandela's involvement in 1995
Rugby World Cup 153; memorabilia
relating to rugby players 152; museum
tour, rhythm of 153; 'New Museology'
149; in post-apartheid South Africa 148;
professionalization of 148, 150–4; Rugby
World Cup victories 153; Springbok
brand as national heritage 150; Springbok
Experience rugby museum *see* Springbok
Experience rugby museum (South
Africa); victory over the All Blacks 175;
white national identity 148
South African Rugby Board (SARB) 147,
151, 155–6
South African Rugby Football Federation
(SARFF) 155, 157; establishment of
156; friction with SARU and 157
South African Rugby Union (SARU) 147,
155–6, 176; friction between SARFF
and 157; Heritage Day 150; marketing
campaign 148, 150; 'Our Honour, Our
Heritage' campaign 150; rugby archives
152; 'sell-outs' and 'tokens' 156
'Southern Man/Pride of the South'
Speights beer advertisements 27
sponsoring relationships, in rugby 63–4
sport museums: Choet Visser Rugby
Museum (South Africa) 152; sporting
exhibitions 154; Springbok Experience
see Springbok Experience rugby
museum (South Africa)
sport organisations, culture of 53–4

sport participation, legacy of 114
sporting entertainment 100
sport–media–business alliance 108
Springbok Experience rugby museum
(South Africa) 147–50, 158; contested
heritage at 154–8; establishment of
150–4; as national heritage 150; opening
of 153; Springbok Trials Rugby Skills
Zone 153
Stade Français club (France) 41, 45–7
Stade Toulousain club (France) 43–4
'Stadium of Four Million' report 114
'Stop the Stadium' campaign 113
Studie in Stemme ('Study in Voices') 167
Sullivan, Jim 134
Sutherland, Manu 58

Teivovo Rugby magazine 85
television audiences 183; FIFA World Cup
110; in France 42; in Ireland 9, 19; in
New Zealand 27
terrorist attacks: *Charlie Hebdo* shootings
49; in Paris 49
Tew, Steve 30, 64, 83
Third Republic (1870–1940) 41
Thomas, Gareth 127, 138
Thomas, Paul 30
Thornley, Gerry 12
tikanga Māori (Māori culture) 65
Timatanga haka, performance of 65
Toa Saracens Rugby Academy 86
Tobias, Errol 157–8
Tom Brown's Schooldays 94
tourism, impact of sport mega-event on
110, 114
toyi-toyi protest dance 164
Treviranus, Ofisa 78

UEFA European Championship 108, 144

Union Française de Rugby Amateur
(UFRA) 42

Vagana, Nigel 54
Vincent, Joris 38
violence in game 42
vocational planning, for Pacific players 58

Waitangi, Treaty of 74
Wakefield, William Wavell 97
Warburton, Sam 143
Weber, Eugen 41
Welsh nationalism 136
Welsh Rugby Union (WRU) 112, 137–8,
141; Regional and Professional Game
Board 143
Welsh rugby union players 134; migration
of 142–3; nationalities of 142
Western Sydney University (WSU) 52, 55
Wigan Pier: coaches 141–2; opening the
road from 137–9; River Severn, road
across 139–40; road to 133–6; Six
Nations tournament (1999) 136; Wales
and England 136
Williams, Gareth 134, 140
Williams, Raymond 27, 135–6
Wilson, Harold 9
Wolfgramm, Feleti 82
Woosnam, Ian 140
'World in Union: Rugby, Past, Present and
Future' conference (2015) 1
World Rugby 43, 78–9, 93, 101, 109;
broadcast rights, monopolization of 113;
governance of 104; U-20 Championship
86
World War I 97
Wyllie, Alex 28

Zuma, Jacob 161